EDGAR
ALLAN
POE

A Study of the Short Fiction

Also available in Twayne's Studies in Short Fiction Series

Twayne's Studies in Short Fiction

Gordon Weaver, General Editor
Oklahoma State University

EDGAR ALLAN POE
Photograph reproduced from the collections of the Library of Congress, from an 1848 daguerreotype made by W. S. Hartshorn and now held in the collection of the American Antiquarian Society.

EDGAR
ALLAN
POE

—————— *A Study of the Short Fiction* ——

Charles E. May

California State University,
Long Beach

TWAYNE PUBLISHERS
An Imprint of Simon & Schuster Macmillan
NEW YORK

Prentice Hall International
LONDON · MEXICO CITY · NEW DELHI · SINGAPORE · SYDNEY · TORONTO

Twayne's Studies in Short Fiction Series, No. 28

Copyright © 1991 by Simon & Schuster Macmillan
All rights reserved.
Twayne Publishers
An Imprint of Simon & Schuster Macmillan
1633 Broadway
New York, NY 10019-6785

Copyediting supervised by Barbara Sutton.
Book production and design by Janet Z. Reynolds.
Typeset by Compset, Inc., Beverly, Massachusetts.

10 9 8 7 6 5 4

The paper used in this publication meets the minimum requirements
of American National Standard for Information Sciences—Permanence
of Paper for Printed Library Materials, ANSI Z39.48-1984.

Printed and bound in the United States of America.

Library of Congress Cataloging-in-Publication Data

May, Charles E. (Charles Edward), 1941–
    Edgar Allan Poe : a study of the short fiction / Charles E. May.
        p.   cm.—(Twayne's studies in short fiction ; no. 28)
    Includes bibliographical references and index.
    ISBN 0-8057-8337-7
    1. Poe, Edgar Allan, 1809–1849—Fictional works. 2. Short story.
I. Title. II. Series.
PS2642.F43M39   1991
813'.3—dc20   91-12225
                                                         CIP

For Patricia Ruth and Jordan Elizabeth,
with love

Contents

Contents

PART 3. THE CRITICS

Preface

Edgar Allan Poe has always been a paradox in American literary history. Although he is probably the most widely read of all American writers, he is commonly believed to have been no more than an alcoholic and a drug addict who wrote weird horror stories. Moreover, although Poe has probably influenced more artists than any other writer in American literature, academic critics and university professors have never been comfortable with him, often convinced that he was at best an entertainer of adolescents and at worst a third-rate hack.

However, recent studies by phenomenological, structuralist, and poststructuralist critics have begun to justify what loyal Poe readers have always intuitively felt: that he was a tortured genius, who, perhaps more than any other writer of fiction in nineteenth-century America, understood the nature of narrative. His stories, once dismissed as mere gothic thrillers, are now being analyzed for their self-conscious manipulation of narrative devices and their darkly existential view of reality, and Poe is beginning to be recognized as a master of fictional technique and a precursor of the modernist vision.

Books and articles have been written about Poe from various modernist and postmodernist critical points of view, but no one has yet tried to account for the most common and most generally agreed-upon critical assertion about Poe: that in some way he was responsible for the birth of the short story as a literary form. It is the purpose of this study to try to compensate for this critical lack by examining Poe's contribution to what has always been recognized as America's major literary genre. Consequently, although most of the following chapters consist of separate analyses of Poe's most important stories, both the structure of the overall study and the focus of the individual discussions are meant to show how Poe's stories reflect his contribution to the short story as a generic form. All Poe's short fictions are either analyzed in some detail or commented on in relation to their generic subtype or their use of short story generic conventions. Only Poe's long fiction, *The Narrative of Arthur Gordon Pym*, is not discussed; a novella, it poses generic problems beyond the scope of this study.

The first two chapters attempt to establish both a historical and a critical context for understanding Poe's contribution to the form, first by surveying the development of short fiction up to Poe's time and second by summarizing the aesthetic theories that most influenced his work in the form. Chapter 3 takes a fairly close look at Poe's first two short stories—"Metzengerstein" and "MS. Found in a Bottle"—as important indicators of the direction Poe's fiction was to take. The remainder of the book looks at Poe's stories from the perspective of several significant generic and theoretical categories explored by Poe (parody, hoax, cosmic fantasy, psychological obsession, detective fiction) and a number of metaphysical and aesthetic dichotomies that dominate his fiction (truth and fiction, body and spirit, dream and reality). The focus throughout is on Poe's contribution to the development of the short story as a form.

I wish to thank the Scholarly Research Committee of California State University, Long Beach, for giving me a grant during the summer of 1989 to do the major research on this study. I also wish to thank the Sabbatical Leave Committee of the School of Humanities at California State University, Long Beach, for giving me the time during the spring 1990 semester to complete the writing. Thanks also to the editor of this series, Gordon Weaver, and Liz Fowler, editor at Twayne, for their many helpful suggestions. As always I owe more than mere acknowledgments can express to Pat, Jordan, Hillary, and Alex for their love, encouragement, and faith.

Part 1

THE SHORT FICTION

Historical Context

No one questions the fact that short fiction genres existed before Edgar Allan Poe began writing. Short narratives in the form of folktales, legends, parables, and myths actually predate long narratives in the history of human expression, constituting the original fictional form. But most students of literature agree that during the nineteenth century in Russia, France, Germany, and especially in America, something new happened to short fiction that changed it forever. It is a commonplace of American literary history that this something "new" was largely attributable to Edgar Allan Poe. However, with the exception of a few indeterminate remarks about Poe's concept of the "single effect" and a number of general suggestions that Poe's stories were somehow different from previous short prose narratives, no one has really examined the nature of Poe's contributions to the short story.

One of the basic reasons for this failure is that to explain Poe's fundamental contribution to the short story genre requires an acceptance of the concept of genre itself, especially as a means by which to understand literary history. However, until the late 1950s, when Northrop Frye's *Anatomy of Criticism* and Austin Warren and Rene Wellek's *Theory of Literature* introduced American critics to Russian formalism and began to weaken New Criticism's dominance—with its emphasis on explication of the individual story—of American criticism, systematic study of genre was not pursued. Not until the late 1960s, with the rise of the French structuralists, did American critics begin to seriously consider these theoretical concepts and to apply them to the study of specific literary works.

This study of Poe's contributions to the short story as a genre is founded on four basically formalist assumptions: (1) that the study of any literary work should include examination of those conventional artistic devices that constitute the difference between the work and whatever human reality it takes as its subject matter; (2) that a genre is made up of a generative cluster of conventional devices that distinguish it from other literary forms; (3) that the concept of genre constitutes a set of tacitly held structural expectations that makes it possible

3

for one to read a literary work meaningfully; and (4) that the notion of genre is essential for our understanding of how literary works develop and evolve historically.

According to the Russian formalists of the 1920s, a genre consists of a hierarchical relationship of the devices of which it is made; a genre develops or evolves historically because of shifts in that relationship. Roman Jakobson has described this process as follows: "Within a given complex of poetic norms in general, or especially within the set of poetic norms valid for a given poetic genre, elements which were originally secondary become essential and primary. On the other hand, the elements which were originally the dominant ones become subsidiary and optional."[1]

One of the basic methods by which the hierarchy shifts and genres evolve, according to another Russian formalist, B. M. Éjxenbaum, is satire—a particularly important process for understanding the generic contributions of Poe, who began his own narrative experiments by parodying the German *novelle* and the gothic romance. Stages in the evolution of a genre occur, says Éjxenbaum, when a genre, once taken seriously, is parodied or satirized: "An initially serious treatment of the *fable*, with its painstaking and detailed motivation, gives way to irony, joke, parody; motivational connections grow slack or are laid bare as conventions, and the author himself steps to the forefront, time and again destroying the illusion of genuineness and seriousness."[2]

This is obviously not the place to present a detailed history of the evolution of short fiction; however, a brief outline of the major shifts in the form before Poe is necessary before we can understand his own significant contribution. I have argued in other places that the short narrative originally derives from those episodic encounters of primitive consciousness with what anthropologists call the "sacred," those moments set apart from the profane flow of everyday life by a "feeling" of the solidarity of life.[3] The recording of this eruption of the sacred in the midst of the profane was the predominant use of short narrative until a major shift was signaled in the fourteenth century by Boccaccio in *The Decameron*. As pointed out by the nineteenth-century literary historian Francesco De Sanctis, with Boccaccio, "the world of the spirit disappeared and was replaced by the world of nature." And with this departure of God and providence as the determinants of action and events, De Sanctis argued, "a new form of the marvelous was born, not from the intrusion into life of certain ultranatural forces, such as visions or miracles, but from the extraordinary confluence of events which could not be foreseen or controlled."[4]

Although *The Decameron* represents a movement from the spiritual or sacred world governed by the marvelous to the everyday or profane world governed by irony, the "realism" of Boccaccio's short fiction should not be confused with the realism of the eighteenth-century novel as pioneered by Daniel Defoe. The focus of *The Decameron* is not on character presented in a verisimilitude of everyday life, but on the world of traditional story, in which characters primarily serve as "functions" of the tale. One simply cannot describe characters in *The Decameron* without telling their stories, for they *are* the roles they play in the story and little else.

The next major generic transformation in short fiction occurs when Cervantes radically alters the form in the early seventeenth century with his *Exemplary Tales*. The first difference results from the fact that Cervantes does not present himself as a collector of traditional tales as Boccaccio did, but rather as an inventor of original stories. A second difference—which follows from the first—is that Cervantes becomes an observer and recorder of more concrete details in the external world than Boccaccio, as well as a student of the psychology of individual characters. Thus, although plot is still important for Cervantes, character becomes more developed than it was in *The Decameron* and psychological motivation rather than the plot motivation of traditional story seems to propel the action. Characters do not exist solely for the roles they play; they also exist for their own sake, "as if" they were real.

This progressive "displacement" of short fiction from the supernatural toward the natural is carried to further extremes in the seventeenth century in developments that move the form closer to what has since been called "eighteenth-century realism." Charles Mish claims that two basic modernizing trends take place in short fiction in England from 1660 to 1700: interest in psychological analysis and interest in *vraisemblance* or verisimilitude.[5] As these trends drive fiction to the more extensive development of the novel form, the short tale is practically displaced out of existence; it is retained solely for the purposes of edification in exemplary or illustrative forms, albeit in the service of social rather than religious values. As Benjamin Boyce notes, eighteenth-century authors seem to have no real or clear conception of short fiction as a genre except perhaps as a *Tatler-Spectator* genre whose primary virtue is instruction in social values.[6]

However, two important works of short fiction in the eighteenth century deviate from these social uses of the form: Defoe's "A True Relation of the Apparition of One Mrs. Veal" (1706) and Horace Walpole's *The Castle of Otranto* (1765). It is precisely these two deviations that had the most significant influence on Poe and thus on the development of the short story. In different ways these two works serve as paradigmatic examples of the interrelationship between the sacred or mythic source of short fiction and its realistic displacement to everyday life.

"A True Relation of the Apparition of One Mrs. Veal" clearly indicates the separation between two basic forms of fiction, narratives that are presented "as if" the events actually took place and narratives that are presented as inventions or mental projections. The story has most often been discussed as an early example employing the kind of realistic conventions Defoe used to help establish the novel as a viable narrative form. For example, Edward Wagenknecht, in his *Cavalcade of the English Novel*, says that with its use of "testimony skillfully adduced, verisimilitude, corroborative and irrelevant detail, minute particularity," the piece "offers in miniature virtually all Defoe's salient qualities, thus affording an excellent introduction to the study of his technique."[7]

In addition to being cited as an early example of the new narrative technique of verisimilitude, the piece has also been called an example of the gothic mode that began to dominate English short fiction later in the century. However, because it presents a ghostly apparition in a period in which belief in ghosts was no longer accepted as an article of faith, the story must validate what did not need to be validated before. In fact, the modes of validation, which include the common eighteenth-century convention of presenting an eyewitness account, dominate the story. "A True Relation" looks both backward to the most traditional form of short narrative, the fable presented to teach a moral lesson, and forward to the realistic story presented as an account of an actual event. Since it has the content of the old romance story (the manifestation of the supernatural to illustrate a moral purpose) and the technique of the new realism (verisimilitude), it anticipates the kind of experiment with both modes that marks the beginning of the eighteenth-century gothic romance. To see it as old romance is to see it as motivated primarily by metaphoric significance to convince the reader of a spiritual truth. To see it as new realism is to see it motivated by realistic detail for the purpose of convincing the reader of its truth to physical reality.

The next work of English short fiction to have a marked effect on the development of the short story form, Walpole's *The Castle of Otranto*, is an even more self-conscious experiment in combining the conventions of the old romance and the new realism. In the famous "Preface" to the second edition of the work, Walpole says his work is an attempt to blend two kinds of romance, the ancient and the modern: "In the former, all was imagination and improbability; in the latter, nature is intended to be, and sometimes has been, copied with success." Noting that fancy had been dammed up by an adherence to common life in the new novel form, whereas in the ancient romance nature or reality was excluded, Walpole characterized his task as one of reconciliation. Wishing to leave "the powers of fancy at liberty to expatiate through the boundless realms of invention, and thence of creating more interesting situations," Walpole wanted simultaneously to construct "the mortal agents in his drama according to the rules of probability: in short, to make them think, speak, and act, as it might be supposed mere men and women do in extraordinary positions."[8]

However, precisely because Walpole's "ordinary" people are placed in "extraordinary" situations, they do not remain ordinary, that is, "as if real"; instead they become transformed into psychological embodiments of basic human fears and desires. Thus, it is not simply the gloomy trappings and decorations of the gothic castle that constitute the genre of gothic fiction, but rather the fact that "as-if-real" people are placed in "traditional" romance stories and are thus transformed into archetypes of the traditional story. This transformation of "real" people into symbolic figures by the latent thrust of the traditional romance story, an early characteristic of the short fiction form, is effected by means of psychological and aesthetic *displacement*. Psychologically, for Freud, the term "displacement" suggests that taboo desires are displaced to permissible objects and that we can only uncover the taboo desire by correctly interpreting the overdetermination of symbols and corresponding motifs. Aesthetically, for Northrop Frye, "displacement" refers to the writer's efforts to create a sense of verisimilitude for the actions of characters in what is essentially a code-bound metaphoric story.[9] Both forms of displacement are at work in *The Castle of Otranto:* the latent story of the family romance and the competition to be "head of the house" is displaced to as-if-real characters, but is actually embodied in the story by the overdetermination of corresponding repeated motifs rather than by means of the purely two-dimensional allegorical figures of the old romance form or by means of the social or psychological realism of the new novel form.

With the nineteenth-century romantics, the shift from the sacred to the profane reverses in a significant way. German and English writers took the normalized and agglomerative experiences of common life represented in realistic fiction and, by charging them with the subjective imagination of the perceiver, presented ordinary things to the mind in extraordinary ways. In the *Lyrical Ballads,* derived from the prerealistic narrative ballad form, Coleridge's task was to take pure feeling states, those moments when one feels under the influence of the supernatural, and objectify them, as the famous "Preface" states, "so as to transfer from our inward nature a human interest and semblance of truth sufficient to procure for these shadows of the imagination that willing suspension of disbelief for the moment which constitutes poetic faith." Wordsworth's task was similar; only the direction of transfer was different. He was to deal with everyday situations and events, but by means of the imagination give them such an unfamiliar look that they would "excite a feeling analogous to the supernatural, by awakening the mind's attention from the lethargy of custom, and directing it to the loveliness and the wonders of the world before us." In other words, Coleridge was to objectify the internal and present it "as if" it were external, while Wordsworth was to treat the external "as if" it were internal. As a result, the sacred or spiritual base of the old prerealistic ballad or romance form was reborn, but in a new, more experiential and psychologically realistic way.

While English writers were experimenting with narrative genres in the eighteenth and nineteenth centuries, German romantic writers were discussing the theoretical implications of short fiction. Friedrich Schlegel, in his 1801 study of Boccaccio, was the first critic to suggest the importance of the style of the short tale. Although the anecdote itself may be trivial and its matter slight, argued Schlegel, its manner or way of telling must be appealing—an emphasis that throws more light on the narrator of the tale than previously. With later romantic writers, the narrator becomes still more important because he becomes more directly involved in the tale that he tells. Schlegel says: "To what narrator of individual stories without inner connection, either historical or mythical, should we listen for long, if we did not begin to take an interest in the story-teller himself?"[10] This is a more important point than it first appears, for, as Schlegel notes, the modern retelling of already-known traditional stories necessarily shifts attention away from mythic authority and toward the authority of the subjective point of view of the teller as he remodels the tale. An inevitable result of this shift is a gradual movement away from strictly formulaic structures toward techniques of verisimilitude to create credibility and thus authority.

The "return to romance" in the nineteenth century is thus a return with a difference; thematically, the formulaic stories remain much the same, but they are now given a new basis of authority: the subjectivity of the teller, combined with the new verisimilitude with which action is presented as if it were made up of objective events in the phenomenal world. Schlegel explains the particular relevance of this combination of objectivity and subjectivity by arguing that short fiction is particularly suited to present a subjective mood and point of view, indirectly and symbolically, because the story tends greatly to the objective. However, the symbolism Schlegel refers to here is not that of the old allegorical mode of the Middle Ages, but rather a new contextual symbolism: objects are metaphorically meaningful not because they refer to some eternal realm of value outside the story, but because of their patterned contextual position within the story itself.

It is usually agreed that the most important German romantic theorist of the short fiction form is Ludwig Tieck who, like Schlegel, argued that the short story should be strange and unique, but should, in spite of that strangeness, seem commonplace and be presented as objectively taking place. The most controversial concept in Tieck's theory is his notion of a *Wendepunkt*, a "twist in the story" or a turning point "from which it takes unexpectedly a completely different direction, and develops consequences which are nevertheless natural and entirely in keeping with characters and circumstances."[11] It is this "extraordinary and striking turning point," urges Tieck, that distinguishes short fiction from other narrative forms. Tieck's idea has usually been understood by modern critics to be equivalent to the classical notion of peripeteia, or a change in fortune. However, given Tieck's awareness of short fiction's combination of the old supernatural romance with the new narrative realism, it is more likely that he was referring to that point in a story when its ontological status veers from one mode to the other, thus creating an ambiguity about whether events are to be understood naturalistically or supernaturalistically.

Whether we begin with the magical world of the old romance only to reach a point at which we start accounting for the events in terms of psychological realism, or whether we begin in a realistic mode only to have the story turn at some point to a form in which the laws of nature or psychology do not apply—in either case we have a new generic combination of realism and the romance that is typically romantic. Before Boccaccio, the world of story was the sacred world; after Boccaccio it was the world of everyday reality. With the romantics, these two separate worlds become united in such a way that the sacred is secularized and the profane is elevated to the divine. The romantics demythologize the old tales and ballads and remythologize them by internalizing them. They preserve the old religious values without the religious dogma and mythological trappings by perceiving them as basic psychic processes. Value existed in the world outside only because, as the romantics never forgot, it first existed within the imagination of the perceiver.

It is this complex of generic characteristics that forms the historical context for Poe's own generic experiments with short fiction. However, in order to fully understand Poe's innovations, it is also necessary to look briefly at the critical context within which he began writing and how he extended that context not only to cover the short tale form but also to constitute a unified aesthetic/metaphysical philosophy.

Critical Context

The single unifying factor in all of Poe's works is the concept of unity itself. Derived primarily from Poe's familiarity with Augustus William Schlegel's *Course of Lectures on Dramatic Art and Literature* and Samuel Taylor Coleridge's *Biographia Literaria,* Poe's theory is relatively simple and straightforward. This theory so dominated his writing that it can not only be observed throughout his fiction and poetry, but its development can be traced from his early journeyman reviews to his last and most ambitious philosophic prose poem, *Eureka.* As Gerhard Hoffmann has pointed out in the most thought-provoking discussion of Poe's debt to German literature and thought, Coleridge and Schlegel combined to convince Poe that the concept of unity is the fundamental principle of existence.[12] R. D. Gooder, in a recent article, is even more emphatic. The heart of Poe's theory about the validity of literature, says Gooder, is neither the accuracy of the description or the justice of an action, but the "skill in the collocation of words and their effect upon the mind of the reader." Poe's preoccupation with style, continues Gooder, "emerges from an almost preternatural self-consciousness which, having lost touch with external reality, has language as its only resource."[13] And the function of language is not to mirror external reality but to create a self-contained realm of reality that corresponds only to the basic human desire for total unity.

Since Poe's most significant theoretical statements are collected in part 2 of this volume, and since the sources and nature of his theories have been discussed many times in books and articles listed in the bibliography, here I will only offer a brief survey of the main line of Poe's literary theories, focusing particularly on those ideas relevant to his theory of the short story as a genre.[14]

It can be argued that a literary genre does not really exist so long as it is merely practiced. Because a genre concept is just that—a concept—it truly comes into being only when the rules and conventions that constitute it are articulated within the larger conceptual context of literature as a whole. Poe's rigor as a literary critic and genre theorist is thus as important for understanding his contribution to the short story form as is his skill as a short story writer. As early as the 1836 Drake-Halleck review, Poe was insisting that a theoretical understanding of literature was necessary before one might legitimately discuss individual works.[15] The first task he felt necessary was to identify a basic human faculty, a primal human desire instilled in the human mind by God, that the literary work attempted to fulfill. Terming this faculty "Ideality" or, somewhat more narrowly, the "Poetic Sentiment," Poe argued that literary art both arises from and serves to satisfy the Poetic Sentiment. The poet who is highly calculating and logical while patterning language, the poet with the greatest control of technique and literary conventions, is more likely to create a poem that will fulfill the Poetic Sentiment than one who is merely filled with the general quality known as Ideality.

In the 1842 Longfellow review and later in more detail in his essay "The Poetic Principle," Poe named this basic human desire the quest for "supernal BEAUTY" and insisted that such a desire was not to be satisfied by any existing combination of forms in human experience. Furthermore, he suggested that although it was the task of the poet to try to satisfy this desire by combining existent forms of beauty or by combining combinations already created by previous poets, he insisted that achieving that perfect unity that would arouse the sense of ultimate Supernal Beauty was not humanly possible.

The first time Poe refers to A. W. Schlegel's notion of the importance of "totality of interest" seems to be the 1836 Sigourney review. Poe argues that whereas in long works one may be pleased with particular passages, in short pieces the pleasure results from the perception of the oneness, the uniqueness, the overall unity of the piece—on the adaptation of all the constituent parts, which constitutes a totality of interest. In the same year, in a review of Dickens's *Watkins Tottle*, he uses the phrase "unity of effect" rather than "unity of interest"—a shift of emphasis from the source of the Poetic Sentiment in the artist to its arousal in the reader. As in the Sigourney review, Poe emphasized the importance of the overall design of the work as a means of achieving a sense of Supernal Beauty.

Poe uses the word "plot" in his 1842 Bulwer review as synonymous with what he means by the "unity" essential to arouse the Poetic Sentiment. He is careful here to distinguish between the usual notion of plot as merely those events that occur one after another and arouse suspense and his own definition of plot as an overall pattern, design, or unity. The 1842 review of Dickens's *Barnaby Rudge* presents the case for plot being synonymous with overall design even more emphatically. Poe makes a distinction here between story (the events as they might have happened) and plot (the events as the reader receives them) that is similar to the discrimination made by the Russian formalists in the 1920s.[16] Again, Poe emphasizes that by "plot" he means pattern and design, not simply the temporal progression of events. Only pattern can make the separate elements of the work meaningful, not mere realistic cause-and-effect. Moreover, Poe insists that only when the reader has an awareness of the "end" of the work, that is, the overall pattern, will seemingly trivial elements become relevant and therefore meaningful.

Related to the concept of unity, and important for understanding Poe's theory of how short fiction embodies theme, is his distinction between the way "meaning" is communicated by the techniques of allegory and the way meaning is communicated by the techniques of poetry. In the 1839 review of *Undine*, Poe refers to another concept he borrowed from Schlegel, the notion of a "mystic undercurrent" in the literary work, and suggests, without explaining why or how, that it is preferable to the way allegory is meaningful. Given Poe's theory of unity, one might suggest that Poe objected to allegory because it is built on a preestablished set of external ideas to which the various elements of the work refer; the notion of a mystic undercurrent is more like an atmosphere, a self-contained aesthetic realm of reality, created by the unity of the work. Poe objects to allegory more fully in the 1847 Hawthorne review, where he argues that the allegorist endangers both unity and verisimilitude in the work. Because allegory is so dependent on the structure of the external ideas it is meant to communicate, unity must be sacrificed and verisimilitude must be violated to preserve the integrity of those ideas. As Poe says, "if allegory ever establishes a fact, it is by dint of overturning a fiction."

There is little doubt that Poe was, if nothing else, a thoroughgoing formalist, always more interested in the work's pattern, structure, conventions, and techniques than its reference to the external world or its social or psychological theme. The meaning of the work for Poe *was* its technique, so much so that in many of his stories he thematizes aesthetic and literary theory issues, making the creation and explication of unity the central thematic "truth" of the work. Although Poe's formalism and his emphasis on the work's effect on the reader once alienated him from critics, recent structuralist and poststructuralist interest in form has made Poe's theories more acceptable. R. E. Foust has argued that Poe was America's first New Critic and that "Philosophy of Composition" can be read as a "proto-structuralist" analysis of the art work "conceived of as an objective aggregate of literary 'functions.'"[17] Three recent books on Poe have focused on the "life of writing," "the world of words," and the "fables of the mind" embodied in Poe's fiction.[18] Deconstructionist critics in particular have taken a new interest in Poe; in addition to the studies of "The Purloined Letter" by Jacques Lacan, Jacques Derrida, and Barbara Johnson, discussions by John T. Irwin, Joseph N. Riddel, and John Carlos Rowe have probed the ways that Poe's texts focus on their own means of signification.[19] Critics who once complained that "The Philosophy of Composition" was cold-blooded in its manipulation of the reader toward a preexistent effect are beginning to realize that for Poe the overall design was not a preestablished intention, totally in the mind of the writer before the work's composition, but rather that the pattern of the work was achieved in the actual working out of the intentions. The form of the work is the end of the work, not prior to it.[20]

Since no theory of the short prose tale had been developed when Poe was writing, he borrowed theoretical ideas from those genres that did possess a critical history, such as drama and poetry, and applied them to the gothic tale form that was popular during his time. The following generic elements are the most important ones Poe made use of: (1) the conventionalized and ritualized structure of the drama; (2) the metaphoric and self-contained unity of the lyric poem; (3) the technique of verisimilitude of the eighteenth-century novel; (4) the point of view and unifying tone of the eighteenth-century essay; and (5) the spiritual undercurrent and projective technique of the old romance and the gothic story. When you add to these the notion of prose assuming the spatial form of painting, which Poe suggested in the 1842 Hawthorne review, you have the basis for a new generic form. Poe's notion of short fiction as a picture is particularly important, as Robert Jacobs reminds us, for to see narrative as a painting is to see it as a design in space rather than a movement in time. Although the consequent implication of considering characters as static groupings in a composition means a loss of dramatic effect, this loss is compensated by a gain in emphasis on overall pattern, which is equivalent to thematic design.[21]

The 1842 Hawthorne review is the central document for understanding Poe's contribution to the theory of the short story, for it derives from his earlier discussions of the relationship between aesthetic unity and the concept of plot and looks forward to the ultimate implications of pattern and design presented in *Eureka*. The logic of the argument in the Hawthorne review is quite clear: what is most important in the literary work is unity; however, unity can only be achieved in a work that the reader can hold in the mind all at once. After the poem, traditionally the highest form of high literary art, Poe says that the short tale has the most potential for being unified in the way the poem is. The effect of the tale is synonymous with its overall pattern or design, which is also synonymous with its theme or idea. Form and meaning emerge from the unity of the motifs of the story.

Poe carries his concern with unity of effect even further in "The Philosophy of Composition," for here he asserts the importance of considering the work backward, that is, beginning with its end. Obviously, the possibility of beginning with the end is what distinguishes fiction from reality, what transforms reality into narrative discourse. A narrative, by its very nature, cannot be told until the events that it takes as its subject matter have already occurred. Therefore the "end" of the events, both in terms of their actual termination and in terms of the purpose to which the narrator binds them, is the beginning of the discourse. It is hardly necessary to say that the only narrative that the reader ever gets is that which is already discourse, already ended as an event, so there is nothing left for it but to move toward its end in an aesthetic, eventless way, that is, via tone, metaphor, and all the other purely artificial conventions of fictional discourse. Consequently, it is inevitable that events in the narrative will be motivated or determined by demands of the discourse, demands that do not necessarily have anything to do with psychological or phenomenological motivation of the narrated events in the real world.[22]

The full extent to which the concept of unity dominated Poe's work can be seen in *Eureka*, in which he attempted to create a cosmic theory based on his aesthetic principles. Reasoning backward from the fact that the basic desire for Supernal Beauty could only be partially fulfilled by the unity of poetry, Poe argued that the only One capable of achieving absolute unity was God; it therefore followed that the universe itself was a great poem, that is, a fully developed plan or plot (these are convertible terms for Poe) of God. Poe's presentation of *Eureka* as a poem is an inevitable implication of his theory that truth can only be tested by its coherence, not by its correspondence to anything external. Poe's theory is thus a paradigm in the sense that Thomas A.

Kuhn uses that term in *The Structure of Scientific Revolutions.*[23] Its claim to truth lies in its explanatory power, its unity, and thus its intellectual beauty. To claim that the plots of God are perfect and that the universe is a plot of God is to make the artist who strives after the perfect plot one who attempts to fulfill the ultimate human desire: the creation of a freestanding unity dependent on nothing outside of itself. For Poe, the mind longs for symmetry and consistency; what is true is that which is consistent, unified. Thus, a perfect consistency is an absolute truth. This becomes Poe's central theme and the primary technical justification for his fiction.

Beginnings

The fact that Poe's first published short story, "Metzengerstein," was originally subtitled "A Tale in Imitation of the German" does not necessarily mean, as many critics believe, that it is a comic or satiric imitation. Even G. R. Thompson, whose discussion has been the most influential in convincing readers that the story is a satire of the gothic rather than an extension and deepening of the genre, notes that its quality of "near seriousness" is the principle problem in reading it as a satire.[24] What is important for my purpose here is not to argue the story's worthlessness as a "failed gothic," nor its worth as a comic satire, but rather to try to account for those elements of the gothic genre Poe made use of in "Metzengerstein" because he found them to be most conducive to his own theories about the nature of the short prose tale.

The most obvious characteristic of the story is the unifying force demanded by the prophecy that opens the work, for once a prophecy has been announced there is nowhere else for a story to go except toward its fulfillment. As Frank Kermode has suggested in *The Sense of an Ending,* "All plots have something in common with prophecy, for they must appear to educe from the prime matter of the situation the forms of a future."[25] To begin a story with a prophecy is to embed the story's ending in its beginning, as in *Oedipus,* for the prophecy story begins with the language of promise and then moves inevitably toward the fulfillment of that promise in narrative. The prophecy is the sole motivation for "Metzengerstein"—that which propels it forward. However, one of the conventions of gothic romance (a residue from the mythic notion that prophecies must have an authority from some otherworldly source) is that the prophecy must be expressed too ambiguously for ordinary human beings to understand. Finally, a powerful convention of the prophecy story is that the prophecy must create a kind of irony that we usually associate with poetic justice, so called because it is so appropriate, so perfectly balanced and "just," that it seems the result of purposeful or "poetic" pattern rather than natural accident.

As in the story's famous gothic predecessor, *The Castle of Otranto*, the prophecy in "Metzengerstein" is cryptic and paradoxical: "A lofty name shall have a fearful fall when, as the rider over his horse, the mortality of Metzengerstein shall triumph over the immortality of Berlifitzing" (2:19).[26] However, unlike Walpole's story, and typical of Poe, as soon as the prophecy is announced and thus suggested as the conventional cause of the action to follow, it is called into question as a cause of the action—a process effected by the creation of a narrator who not only suggests that the words themselves have little or no meaning, but who also argues for more realistic causes by informing the reader that the two families had long been rivals in local government and noting platitudinously that near neighbors are seldom friends. But even though the narrator calls the prophecy "silly words" and wonders if it implies anything at all, the plot of the story itself suggests that it is the motivational force of this gothic convention that unifies the story rather than the narrator's own generalized suggestions of plausible external causes.

Since the conflict underlying the story is a family rivalry that dates back to antiquity, Poe must incorporate this past in the story in some way, for one of the implications of a prophecy story is that the past inescapably impinges on the present. By making use of the gothic convention of a tapestry image to insert the past into the present, Poe introduces a device that will become central to his later fiction: an art object that interacts with external reality. The tapestries that hang from Metzengerstein's walls and swing slightly give the illusion of movement; images of "dames of days gone by floated away in the mazes of an unreal dance to the strains of imaginary melody" (2:22). The static dance that moves and the unheard melody that is imagined are typical Poe motifs of the illusion of life being created in aesthetic unreality. Furthermore, Poe's typical device of presenting characters caught somewhere between dream and reality is also introduced here, for the baron has unconsciously fixed on, and cannot move his attention away from, the picture of a giant horse filling the foreground of the tapestry, while in the background a Berlifitzing is killed by a Metzengerstein: "It was with difficulty that he reconciled his dreamy and incoherent feelings with the certainty of being awake" (2:22).

This mesmerized state, in which the Baron is enrapt with the image of the past conflict between the two families, is counterpoised against the external action of the present conflict resulting from the baron's having set the Berlifitzing house on fire. After his attention has been drawn momentarily to the outside by the tumult, he looks again at the image to find that the head of the horse has changed its position; its eyes, which were not visible before, have a human expression and the mouth is distended to reveal the horse's "sepulchral and disgusting teeth." When in terror the baron throws open the door, light from the fire casts his shadow against the tapestry in the exact contour and size as the murderer of the Berlifitzing. This superimposition of Baron Metzengerstein over his ancestor in the tapestry begins the story's movement toward the fulfillment of the prophecy (that is, the movement of the plot toward its dénouement) in a way that becomes typical for Poe. To resolve the conflict of the story within the representation of the tapestry itself is to create an aesthetic rather than a realistic or moralistic resolution. If the present Metzengerstein is superimposed over the past, the reverse of this action—the activation of the past in the present—is effected when the baron goes outside and sees his men trying to restrain a gigantic mysterious horse with the letters W. V. B. branded on its forehead.

What makes this use of gothic convention typically Poe's own is the fact that Metzengerstein is not only aware of these aesthetic transferences and their relationship to the fulfillment of the prophecy, but he consciously decides to try to circumvent them. When his page tells him that a portion of the tapestry has disappeared, an expression of "determined malignancy" settles on his face, and he locks up the tapestry room. On hearing that Berlifitzing is dead, he seems impressed "with the truth of some exciting idea." Aware that the aesthetic image of the horse has "come alive" to fulfill the plot or prophecy, the baron's "exciting idea" is to escape the ultimate end that the prophecy had laid out for him; that is, to evade his function as a code-bound character in the story created by the prophecy.

Once these plot/prophecy code elements have been set in place, all that is left is the working out of the promise, the inevitable movement toward the dénouement. The climax occurs when the story repeats itself, as prophecy stories must; this time it is the house of Metzengerstein that catches fire mysteriously, and this time, instead of the horse leaving the painting on the tapestry, poetic justice demands that it return to it and thus fulfill the prophecy simultaneously in the past and in the present. The horse bounds up the staircase of the burning castle and disappears into the room with the tapestry, reappearing in a cloud of smoke in the "distinct colossal figure of—*a horse*" (2:29).

However, the way in which these aesthetic actions fulfill the prophecy still demands explication of its language: "A lofty name shall have a fearful fall when, as the rider over his horse, the mortality of Metzengerstein shall triumph over the immortality of Berlifitzing" (2:19). The "fall" is the fall of the name of Metzengerstein rather than the fall of an individual, and similarly the "triumph" is not the triumph of one person over another but rather the triumph of mortality over immortality. The puzzle of the prophecy centers on the meaning of the simile "as the rider over his horse" and the ambiguity of the phrase "triumph over." If the rider triumphs over his horse by controlling it, how does mortality control immortality in the story in a similar way? As Poe's later stories show, the only immortality there is lies in the idealized pattern of the art work. However, since the death of Metzengerstein is simultaneous with the eradication of the tapestry horse in which the immortality of Berlifitzing is embodied (dissolving the image in an evanescent cloud of smoke), the fulfillment of the prophecy is simultaneous with the resolution of the conflict in the story, both of which are purely aesthetic.

"Metzengerstein" is important in the Poe canon, for as his first story it reflects his initial use of gothic conventions and his early awareness that in the highly conventionalized gothic short tale characters are primarily functions of the pattern of the story and exist solely within a highly unified aesthetic world. Poe knew from very early in his artistic career that a tightly controlled artistic form created a realm of reality as an alternate to the external world. In such a realm, motivation of the plot was not necessarily cultural, social, or even psychological, but rather aesthetic. Moreover, Poe was self-consciously aware that this distinction between the short tale form and the external world was maintained by the use of various artistic conventions that constituted the unity and consequently the effect of the story. And it is this self-consciousness that constantly compels him to focus on characters who are not only caught in alternate worlds—the obsessively unified world of dream, trance, hallucination, hysteria, madness—but who are also self-consciously aware of the aesthetic nature of their alternate states.

In all of Poe's stories the issue of genre is crucial. Beyond the problem of whether a particular story is to be taken as gothic, burlesque, satire, or hoax, a further problem often arises—especially in Poe's first-person stories—of whether the events that make up the narrative are to be seen as taking place in the phenomenal world, in a supernatural realm, or in the imagination of the narrator. Moreover, many stories raise the additional question of whether only some parts of the story as reported by the narrator take place in the real world while other parts project a numinous or a psychological reality. "MS. Found in a Bottle" (October 1833), the prize-winning story that actually started Poe on his writing career, embodies these problems in an explicit way.

One way Poe creates this ontological ambiguity is to present narrators who use the eighteenth-century verisimilitude convention of assuring us that what they tell us actually happened, that they are not mad or drugged. But there is always something about their natures—that they are visionaries, that there is some tarnlike influence, or that they suffer from an hereditary disease—that makes the reader accept the reality of their stories only provisionally, as it occurs within the general unreality of their suspicious point of view. And "MS. Found in a Bottle" offers special problems for the reader's determination of the actuality of what has taken place. First, the narrator tells us at the beginning that he is certainly not visionary; quite the contrary, he is a follower of physical science and not given to reveries of fancy. Second, there seems to be no clue that the event described is the result of any outside influence, such as a poisonous atmosphere, opium, or madness, that could have caused the narrator to dream, hallucinate, or otherwise imagine the events he describes. The problem is: if we take the narrator's words strictly, that he wishes us to read the story as a "positive experience of mind," do we necessarily have to understand it as a positive experience of his body as well? Furthermore, if we do take the story as an experience of the mind only, what event in the story motivates the mind-story to take over from the body-story? There is no act, like the killing of the albatross in "The Rime of the Ancient Mariner" (with which Poe's story has been compared), to set the fantastic story events mythically or moralistically in motion.

The issue here is the one that Tzvetan Todorov raises in his study of the "Fantastic." Todorov says that when we are in a world that is indeed our world and yet an event occurs that cannot be explained by the laws of our world, there are only two possible solutions: either the one experiencing the event is the victim of an illusion or an hallucination, or else the event has taken place and reality is controlled by laws alien to our world. If the reader decides the former is the case, he is in the genre of the uncanny; if he decides on the latter, then he is in the realm of the marvelous. Todorov says that the fantastic occupies only the duration of uncertainty about which choice to make[27]

Previous critics have either read "MS. Found in a Bottle" as an example of the "marvelous" (even though Poe seldom depicts events that cannot be accounted for naturalistically or psychologically) or else they have explicated the story allegorically (even though Poe more than once expressed his abhorrence of the allegorical). The story has never been read as an example of the "uncanny" primarily because no one has found a clue to its hallucinatory nature resulting from madness, drugs, mesmerism, dreams, or any of the other devices Poe usually uses to supply naturalistic motivation for a seemingly supernatural occurrence. Both Daniel Hoffman, in his impressionistic study of Poe, and David Ketterer, in his more traditional critique, see the story as allegorical. Hoffman says it is the journey of the soul back to its beginnings in the vortex of birth;[28] Ketterer says it is the journey through life and into death.[29] Donald Stauffer and David Halliburton are less certain about the generic status of the story, but seem to agree that genre is the central problem. Stauffer argues that the story is Poe's earliest attempt to use techniques of eighteenth-century realism to bridge the gap between verisimilitude and the marvelous,[30] while Halliburton dissolves the events of the story into a phenomenological fantasy of man being cut off both from the past and the future and thus doomed to exist forever in a "kind of indefinite present, an eternal moment of terror."[31]

These various attempts to understand the story's generic, and thus ontological, status indicate that the genre issue is precisely the problem that needs to be addressed directly. Perhaps the best place to begin is with Donald Stauffer's analysis, for he is surely right to suggest that after the whirlpool, which only the narrator and the old Swede survive, "the story moves from a believable, realistic plane to the realm of the supernatural and irrational."[32] Moreover, Stauffer's analysis of the two styles of the story provides ample evidence for his argument that after this crucial event the story must be read in a figurative or imaginative sense. The problem is that neither Stauffer nor anyone else has ever suggested either why the narrator shifts from the realistic to the imaginative plane or what this radical transformation from the real world to a world of imagination means in terms of Poe's art and thought.

Rather than being a romantic or a visionary, as many of Poe's other narrators are, the central character here is a rationalist and a skeptic. He delights in the "eloquent madness" of the German romantics only because of the ease with which his "rigid thought" enables him to point out their falsities. In fact, his deficiency of imagination has been called a "crime" by others, and he admits at the outset that he always refers experience to the principles of physical science for validation.

Such a preface he feels necessary to belie the belief that his incredible tale is the "ravings of a crude imagination, rather than the positive experience of a mind to which the reveries of fancy have been a dead letter and a nullity (2:135). Given the nature of the incredible experience the narrator recounts, this preface is not simply an example of Poe's use of the eighteenth-century stylistic convention of establishing credibility, but rather his use of the nineteenth-century thematic convention of presenting a rationalist point of view as a crime that must be expiated by an assault of the imagination itself. The theme is a popular one for both Ludwig Tieck and E. T. A. Hoffmann, with whose stories Poe was familiar. Because "MS." begins in a realistic style, we read the narrator's description of the ship and its cargo as nothing more than bits of objective detail and evidence of his practical point of view. After noting that the ship primarily carried cotton-wool and oil, he adds: "We had also on board coir, jaggeree, ghee, cocoa-nuts, and a few cases of opium. The stowage was clumsily done, and the vessel consequently crank" (2:136). Even though we may recall Poe's insistence in the *Twice-Told Tales* review on the relevance of all details of a story to its overall unity of effect, we still attribute this cargo detail to mere verisimilitude. Moreover, the Simoom that assaults the ship, although terrible in its fury, is a purely natural event. It is not until the fifth day after the storm, when the sun rises with a sickly yellow luster only to sink into the sea, as if "hurriedly extinguished by some unaccountable power," that events become "unnatural," for, as the narrator says, "we waited in vain for the arrival of the sixth day— that day to me has not arrived—to the Swede, never did arrive" (2:138).

There is only one detail in the narrator's account of those five days that could possibly explain the transition from the credible to the incredible: the fact that the only food he has eaten during this period is a "small quantity of jaggeree, procured with great difficulty from the forecastle" (2:138). If we take this also to be mere verisimilitude in the manner of Daniel Defoe, we might legitimately ask why it is the jaggeree, a coarse sugar, the narrator is able to salvage rather than the other foodstuffs in the hold, for example the ghee or the coconuts, both of which are more apt to survive the storm than sugar.

For the answer, we must go back to the previous bit of seemingly irrelevant detail about the ship's cargo, that is, that a few cases of opium were also in the hold, and that the stowage was clumsily done. Since it is obvious that the sugar and the carelessly stowed opium could have been mixed during the chaos of the Simoom, we perhaps have the immediate answer as to why the narrator's perception and his description of his experience change radically after consuming small quantities of such a diet. The fact that a "Simoom," which derives from an Arabic word meaning "to poison," is the cause of this mistaken ingesting of the drug is additional evidence of Poe's "little joke" here. It is also evidence of two primary devices that Poe takes from the eighteenth-century gothic novel and eighteenth-century realism and transforms by his romantic insistence on aesthetic unity: the meaningful use of a seemingly irrelevant detail and the elevation of a naturalistic device to symbolic meaning, both of which are important short story conventions.

This bit of typical Poe deception is, however, not sufficient evidence with which to make a case for the essentially "uncanny" rather than the "marvelous" nature of the narrator's experience. The more important question is: if this is a purely imaginative experience, what kind of imaginative experience is it? If the narrator's extravagant fancy is an example of a kind of "poetic" justice to compensate for the fact that to him fancy has been "a dead letter and a nullity," then how "poetic" is that justice? In other words, how can we account for these particular experiences as having their source in the imagination of the narrator, and what do they tell us about the nature of Poe's own conception of the imagination? At the setting of the sun, when it is extinguished as if by some unaccountable power, the narrator enters into a realm of opium-induced fantasy. External reality is enshrouded in "eternal night," and although the storm continues, it loses its particularity of surf and foam to be transformed into "horror, and thick gloom, and a black sweltering desert of ebony" (2:139).

As the giant ship seems to come down upon the protagonist, he alone, with a sudden "self-possession," detaches himself from his secure position at the stump of the mizzenmast and waits "fearlessly the ruin that was to overwhelm." Thus, fully accepting his fantasy as reality, when the shock of impact takes place, he is thrown upon the rigging of the strange ship. The Swede is simply referred to no more; not even his death or disappearance is described. At this point begins the narrator's fully developed creation of the fantasy ship and its crew. In effect, the narrator, for whom fancy has been "a dead letter," begins to live solely within his manuscript-created fancy. The very "MS. Found in a Bottle" that the narrator creates and that we read is not "a dead letter," but a living "letter" that testifies to the vitality and life of the imagination that the narrator has previously denied.

The particular characteristics of the ship and its crew suggest their source in the mind of the narrator. He says the crew members are imbued with the spirit of Eld—that it is their "thrilling evidence of old age, so utter, so extreme" that excites in his own spirit a "sentiment ineffable." He notes in detail the antiquity of the ship and its equipment—"strange iron-clasped folios, and moldering instruments of science, and obsolete long-forgotten charts"—all of which are to be expected of the imagination of a man who has been all his life a "dealer in antiquities" and has "imbibed the shadows of fallen columns at Balbec, and Tadmor, and Persepolis, until my very soul has become a ruin" (2:144–45). Moreover, in examining the ship's strangeness, the narrator says, "there will occasionally flash across my mind a sensation of familiar things, and there is always mixed up with such indistinct shadows of recollection, an unaccountable memory of old foreign chronicles and ages long ago" (2:142). Indeed, the ship is projected outward from the narrator's imagination; it represents a transformation of his own previous reading and experience.

The basic thematic thrust of the story is that the writer of the manuscript found in the bottle (and by extension all writers) is one who not only projects his fiction for others to take as reality, but one who takes it to be reality himself, and who lives within his own manuscript creation as if it were reality. What seems strange to the narrator can be easily explained when it is understood as the result of fictional projection. For example, because he does not exist in the same realm of reality as that of his fictional projections, the crew members, they of course do not acknowledge his existence. Moreover, the fact that the ship is constantly threatened by waves like demons of the deep, but "demons confined to simple threats and forbidden to destroy" (2:144), is explained by the narrator's realistic conviction that the ship must be within the influence of some strong current. But the only current influencing the ship is the creative current created by the writer himself; the waves are confined to simple threats and are forbidden to destroy, for if they did destroy, the manuscript would abruptly end.

The fact that the wood of the ship is so extremely porous that it is "singularly unfit for the purpose to which it has been applied" (2:142) the narrator cannot explain, but it reminds him of the saying of an old Dutch navigator who used it whenever someone doubted whether he was telling the truth: "It is as sure . . . as there is a sea where the ship itself will grow in bulk like the living body of a seaman" (2:143). The ship is porous because it is not solid matter at all, but rather matterless fantasy. The truth of the narrator's story is the truth of the old Dutchman's saying; that is, it is as true as the truth of a sea where a ship will grow in bulk like that of a living body. However, the truth of this cryptic simile is like the truth of the prophecy in "Metzengerstein"; it is the truth only of the sea of fable, legend, myth, story. The "world of ocean" that has thrown the narrator into "silent wonder" is indeed the "ocean of story" itself. The ship, the old sailors, the narrator's experiences are not allegorical abstractions; they are the projections of the narrator's imagination, springing from his reading, dreams, and past involvements. What the narrator observes, an experience in which he is both involved and detached, is the art work itself, in which the action always hovers eternally on the brink and thus seems to be stasis in motion.

This reading gives some specific foundation to David Halliburton's generalized remarks about the oxymoronic sense we get in the story of motion shot through with stasis—an oxymoron that Halliburton says is typical of ekphrastic poetry where the "spatial object seems about to free itself into the flow of time."[33] It seems appropriate that "MS. Found in a Bottle," a story about a writer's illusion of being lost in the eternally moving stasis of the art work, should manifest the sense of static-motion that Halliburton suggests. It is even more appropriate that this first successful Poe story, the one that began him on his career as a writer of fiction, focuses on a man who discovers the eternal mystery of fantasy and story itself.

As the narrator notes, a feeling for which he has no name takes possession of his soul: "a sensation which will admit of no analysis, to which the lessons of by-gone times are inadequate, and for which I fear futurity itself will offer me no key" (2:141). Such feelings are the sense of being "captured by the incredible" that is both the very essence of dreams, as Conrad's Marlowe insists in *The Heart of Darkness*, and the essence of story itself; for, as Marlowe says, no "relation of a dream can convey the dream-sensation, that commingling of absurdity, surprise, and bewilderment in a tremor of struggling revolt, that notion of being captured by the incredible which is the very essence of dreams." This realization is what Poe's narrator refers to when he says a "new sense—a new entity is added to my soul" (2:141). Moreover, this is what constitutes the unintelligible letters he unwittingly daubs on the sail, which, when the sail is put in use, spell out the word DISCOV-ERY. For the discovery the narrator makes is the discovery that dominates Poe's art and thought throughout his career: it is the discovery of the power of the imagination and thus the power of story.

Like the narrator, Poe himself felt impelled by a "curiosity to penetrate the mysteries of those awful regions. . . . It is evident that we are hurrying on to some exciting knowledge—some never-to-be imparted secret, whose attainment is destruction" (2:145). As Poe's masterworks "The Fall of the House of Usher" and *Eureka* make clear, the end of the imaginative journey is both the source and the end of life itself, for it is ultimate nonbeing. We imagine the narrator of "MS. Found in a Bottle" lost in his fantasy, penning the last words—"going down"—and tossing his letter into the sea, from whence, eternally detached from its author, it is taken up by countless readers as "a dead letter" only to be made to live again continuously.

Parody and Play

Although Poe is best known for his creation of gothic horror stories, one of the largest single groupings of his short prose is the category of satire, parody, burlesque, and play. Although this category is made up of stories that are, perhaps rightfully, perceived as less significant than his more "serious" psychological stories, a number of studies have been written in recent years on Poe's satiric mode, many of which are collected in *The Naid Voice*, edited by Dennis W. Eddings.[34] Moreover, as several critics have shown, it is often difficult to tell when Poe is being serious and when he is playing; thus, as G. R. Thompson has convincingly suggested, romantic irony is the most significant perspective from which to consider much of his fiction.[35] Although Poe's detailed comic or satiric intentions may be difficult to determine in specific stories, Stephen Mooney has suggested some criteria by which to make general determinations, the most important of which is Poe's purposeful avoidance of proportion. However, Mooney's description of Poe's typical comic structure—"a progression from *disguise* to *action* in disguise, the action based upon a fundamental error in the perception of the real, which leads to the comic *revelation* of truth as a stripping away of appearances"[36]—does not seem to differ radically from the structure Poe used for his more important fictional forays into serious epistemological and ontological issues.

Creating a literary work as a trick or a joke, either as a hoax that purposely mixes reality and fiction or else as a parody that purposely confuses a primary object of attack with its satiric overlay, is not so adolescent an activity as such readers of Poe as Henry James and T. S. Eliot have suggested. Seriousness, Poe might say, is often the result of the mistaken security that one knows exactly where one is at any given time. And, perhaps more than anything else, Poe is concerned with the ambiguity of ontological or epistemological states and dedicated to the proposition that reality is much more mysterious than our usual serious assumptions and commonsense perspective suggest. In short, Poe believes that if we do not allow ourselves to be tricked, we will not learn.

Poe's satires and parodies also have significance because of the evidence they provide concerning the nature of how genres develop. As the Russian formalists have suggested, one important way to transform a genre is to parody a formerly serious form by laying bare its conventions. Consequently, we can come to some conclusions about Poe's contribution to the short story genre by showing how he self-consciously manipulated and laid bare some of the basic conventions of the German romantic tale and the English gothic romance so popular at the time.

"How to Write a *Blackwood* Article" (November 1838) is particularly interesting, not only because it is an explicit satire on the popular *Blackwood* genre, but also because in the companion piece, "A Predicament," Poe creates an artist manqué identified as Signora Psyche Zenobia who takes the advice given to her in the first story and writes an article in the *Blackwood* manner. Although the examples Mr. Blackwood gives Zenobia of the so-called intensities typical of *Blackwood* magazine are absurd parodies, when he lays out the basic rules or conventions of the form they are recognizable as important constituents of the German *novelle* that forms the basis of Poe's own serious short fiction. First of all, the *Blackwood* story requires that the focus be on an extreme situation, something that breaks up the reality of the routinized everyday. Second, the story requires a careful attention to detail to convince the reader of the truth of the matter, for, as Mr. Blackwood says, "'Truth is strange,' you know, 'stranger than fiction'—besides being more to the purpose" (2:340)—that is, more to the purpose of authenticating the event with verisimilitude in spite of the extremity of the situation. Since the short story usually focuses on some breakup of ordinary everyday activity, and since the application of eighteenth-century verisimilitude to such spiritual or ironic breakups constitutes much of Poe's contribution to its development, these are more serious matters than Poe's satiric tone suggests.

And indeed, it is the tone of the narration that is the third important aspect of the *Blackwood* tale suggested to Zenobia. Again, as has been noted earlier, the focus on tone, that is, the introduction of the narrator's attitude or involvement in the story, is an important element in the creation of the short story as a romantic genre. Finally, after having established incident and tone as the two most important elements in a *Blackwood* story (and in a Poe story as well), Blackwood mentions what is called "*the filling up*," that is, giving the article an air of erudition. Although what Poe is making fun of here is the spurious effort of authors to make their articles sound more important than they are by throwing in references to little-known facts and using quotations from other languages, wide-ranging knowledge has an important role in many serious Poe tales, particularly the ratiocinative stories. The man of great erudition perceives that seemingly meaningless bits of information are actually significant clues, that what appears mysterious makes sense if one has a context for it and can see its analogies. The erudite detective/reader created by Poe is an image of the modern superreader who can read a text significantly because he or she reads it intertextually.

I see no need to discuss all the elements of parody in the story "A Predicament." I will simply note those elements that, in more serious gothic stories, contribute to Poe's development of the short story: making much ado about what seems to be nothing, being absolutely particular about seemingly irrelevant details, and creating metaphors out of everyday activities. The central metaphoric predicament of the story—being caught by the inevitable progression of time—is a theme that Poe treats seriously in other stories such as "The Pit and the Pendulum," "The Masque of the Red Death," and "The Tell-Tale Heart." Poe's comic device here, as it is in other satiric stories, is to make the metaphor absurdly literal. Moreover, Poe also makes use here of another typical motif treated more seriously in such stories as "A Descent into the Maelstrom" and "The Pit and the Pendulum"—the device of a character being caught in an extreme situation, yet having the presence of mind to contemplate his predicament in a calm and interested way. The absurdity of the story reaches its climax when Zenobia's head is detached from her body and she contemplates the philosophical problem of whether the head or the body is the real Psyche Zenobia—a mind/body split that Poe uses in a number of more serious stories.

Poe's satire of another common literary convention of the day is indicated by his decision to give his story "Never Bet the Devil Your Head" (September 1841) the subtitle "A Tale with a Moral." For his target here is what he calls in "The Poetic Principle" the "Didactic heresy," perpetuated either by those writers who deliberately create stories for a moral or didactic purpose or by those readers and critics who are determined to find a moral or meaning in every story they read. The narrator ironically notes that "every fiction *should* have a moral; and, what is more to the purposes the critics have discovered that every fiction *has*" (2:621). He then satirizes those critics who find a "hidden meaning" in all works, such as discovering transcendentalism in the fairy tale "Hop of My Thumb." Since critics can find a hidden meaning in every work of fiction, the narrator says, an author need take no care to put one there: "When the proper time arrives, all that the gentleman intended, and all that he did not intend, will be brought to light, in the *Dial* or the *Down-Easter*, together with all that he ought to have intended, and the rest that he clearly meant to intend:—so that it will all come very straight in the end" (2:622). Claiming that there is no just ground for accusing him of writing stories without morals, for critics will always bring a moral meaning out regardless, he offers "Never Bet the Devil Your Head" as a story with an explicit moral just to be sure. Furthermore, he notes that those who do not have the time to read his story carefully may find the moral in the capital letters of the title at the beginning—a better arrangement, he argues, than the fables of La Fontaine and others who "reserve the impression to be conveyed until the last moment, and thus sneak it in at the fag end of their fables" (2:622). This is an important statement of artistic intention by Poe, for it reflects his insistence that the meaning of the short prose tale must be found within its overall design, and not be tagged on at the end as a detachable moral statement.

As a magazine writer and reviewer involved in the literary world of his day, Poe wrote a number of stories designed as parodies of specific authors, works, or the literature industry in general. For example, "The Duc De L'Omelette" (3 March 1832) satirizes the foibles of the author Nathaniel Parker Willis; "A Tale of Jerusalem" (9 June 1832) parodies a novel entitled *Zillah* by Horace Smith; "The Literary Life of Thingum Bob, ESQ" (December 1844) makes fun of the custom of authors and editors who praise each other profusely in order to receive similar treatment; "Lionizing" (May 1835) satirizes the general phenomenon of literary lionizing; "Why the Little Frenchman Wears His Hand in a Sling" (1840) parodies an Irish dialect tale of Lady Morgan: and "X-ing a Paragrab" (12 May 1849) makes play with the results of an error in the printing process. That these works depend on a knowledge of the stories and authors they parody for their effectiveness is indicated by the fact that in annotated editions of Poe's works the notes that gloss the tales are longer than the texts themselves. Source hunting for the targets of the satires in these works was once a minor industry in Poe criticism.

However, four stories in this group of satires with specific targets—"King Pest," "Bon Bon," "The Devil in the Belfry," and "The System of Dr. Tarr and Prof. Fether"—deserve more attention, primarily because they make use of a number of paradoxes that reflect Poe's general philosophic and aesthetic concerns: for example, the presentation of the horrible in the midst of the absurd, the parallel between the physical and the metaphysical, the demonic breakup of the ordinary and the everyday, and the ambiguity of the states of madness and sanity.

"King Pest" (September 1835) has been identified as a literary satire of a chapter of Disraeli's *Vivian Gray* (1826) and a political satire on the administration of Andrew Jackson. What makes it worth notice in terms of Poe's generic experiments is the means by which it successfully combines slapstick satire on the one hand and true horror on the other. Even as the allegorical characters—King Pest, Queen Pest, Duke Pest-Iferous, Duke Pest-Ilential, Duke Tem-Pest, and Arch-Duchess Ana-Pest—are so extreme as to be impossible to take seriously, Poe's description of the stronghold of the plague with its falling houses, fetid smells, vapory and pestilential atmosphere, and corpses rotting in the alleys includes a truly powerful series of images. Constance Rourke says that the story "is one of the most brilliant pure burlesques in the language, transforming terror into gross comedy."[37] And indeed the combination of horror and satiric play embodied in this story reflects Poe's generic combination of gothic seriousness and gothic parody, a combination that contributes much to the creation of the nineteenth-century short story.

The relation between the physical and the metaphysical underlies the game Poe plays in "Bon-Bon" (August 1835), for Pierre Bon-Bon is a restauranteur and a metaphysician, thus one who is an expert concerning both the body and the soul. In Bon-Bon's cafe, Poe says, the "properties of the kitchen and the *bibliothèque*" are in such communion that one can talk about "a dish of polemics," "an ovenfull of the latest ethics," Plato in the frying pan, and volumes of German morality "hand in glove with the gridiron" (2:101). The introduction of Satan advances the theme of the relationship between the physical and the metaphysical by revealing that the devil eats the souls of men, thus giving the lie to those metaphysicians who argue that the soul is a shadow. But, even though Bon-Bon, under the influence of food and drink, offers to give his own soul to Satan, the devil refuses to take advantage of his "disgusting and ungentlemanly situation" and leaves. Although the main barb of the satire is that the devil will not take the bodily soul of Bon-Bon, what the story reflects about Poe's more serious aesthetic position is the combination of materialism and idealism that characterizes all of his work that is manifested by his uniting the verisimilitude of the realists with the disembodied mysticism of the romantics.

In "The Devil in the Belfry" (18 May 1839) the satiric treatment of the appearance of Satan in the real world of man is even more pronounced and emphatic. After some ironically serious consideration of the origins and the name of the town of Vondervotteimittiss, the narrator describes the houses and the people there as being so precisely alike that they could not be distinguished from each other. The prosaic nature of the town is further emphasized by the two most common items around which everything else revolves—cabbages and clocks—and the three resolutions on which the town depends: "That it is wrong to alter the good old course of things—That there is nothing tolerable out of Vondervotteimittiss—That we will stick by our clocks and our cabbages" (2:369). Of course, the only reason for a Poe story to paint a state of being in which everything is regulated like clockworks and everything is as ordinary as cabbage is to break it up; and in folklore and gothic romance the most conventional means to effect such a breakup is the appearance of the devil, who indeed, one day at five minutes till noon, comes into the town, bounds into the clock tower that stands at its center, and resets the clock so that it strikes 13, forever destroying the order that characterized the town's existence. "The Devil in the Belfry" is Poe's most obvious thematic treatment of the short story's basic convention of breaking up the ordinary and the everyday by an eruption of the demonic.

In "The System of Dr. Tarr and Prof. Fether" (November 1845), another satire on the supposed "sanity" of everyday life, instead of merely disrupting the everyday, Poe creates a situation in which everything is reversed, and what "seems" to be the sanity of ordinary reality is actually only a similitude or charade masking madness. Poe's technique in the story, typical of his major work, is to set up the protagonist and the reader with an action that is actually a charade and then to strip away the false appearance in a comic revelation of the ironic state of things. The protagonist enters the madhouse, assuming that its policy is to make use of the so-called soothing system in which the mad are allowed to mingle with the keepers. As a result of this expectation, he cannot know if those he meets are mad or sane. Although the first woman he encounters talks in a perfectly rational manner, he says that "a long acquaintance with the metaphysics of *mania*, had taught me to put no faith in such evidence of sanity" (3:1005). His expectations change when he is told by the head of the institution that the woman he suspects of madness is the head's own niece and that they no longer use the soothing method at this institution.

However, at dinner, the protagonist senses something odd about the manner and dress of the guests and thus once again begins to suspect that the soothing system is being used and that some of the dinner guests are lunatics. Once again, he is reassured that such oddities are mere eccentricities, not madness. The central statement that directly reflects the theme of the story is the description of madness provided by Tarr and Fether; that is, that madness is an imitation of sanity, for "the dexterity with which [the madman] counterfeits sanity, presents to the metaphysician, one of the most singular problems in the study of mind. When a madman appears *thoroughly* sane, indeed, it is high time to put him in a straight-jacket" (3:1018). This technique of using one state as a fictional similitude of another is a common Poe device that is thematized in many of his more serious works.

The climax of the story occurs simultaneously with a self-reflexive reference to the story's own duplicitous nature. The head of the mad-house narrates a story about a madman who devised a better system of "lunatic government," overthrew the keepers, and established the in-sane in charge of the madhouse. He explains that the inverted system has been successfully maintained by allowing no visitors except one stupid-looking fellow who he allowed in one day, having no fear of his revealing the reversal. Of course, what is narrated here is a miniature version of the overall story, which, like Hamlet's play within a play, reflects the external narrative itself. Poe further emphasizes the self-reflexive nature of the charade by describing the scene when the lunatics manifest their true mania in terms of theater, presenting the "climax of the drama" with the bursting in on the scene of the tarred and feathered original keepers of the madhouse. At this point the narrator finally understands the "dénouement of this tragedy" to be con-current with the dénouement of the inner story told by the head of the madhouse, who has turned mad himself.

Some of Poe's satires were written merely to meet the demands of his daily quota of writing for the newspapers and magazines and thus are not particularly helpful in understanding his unique contribution to the short story genre. "Four Beasts in One/The Homo-Cameleopard," earlier entitled "Epiphanes" (March 1836), is of interest only because of its narrative technique of presenting a second-person point of view in which the teller engages the reader in a dialogue. "The Man that Was Used Up" (August 1839) is interesting primarily because of its use of the basic Poe device of literalizing a metaphor and presenting a narrator to whom the "slightest appearance of mystery" puts him into a "pitiable state of agitation." "The Business Man" (February 1840) and "Three Sundays in a Week" (27 November 1841) are anecdotal trifles, and the only reason that "Diddling" (14 October 1843) is of any concern to this analysis is because it provides a significant Poe definition of man as one who is above all a trickster or a con artist. The artist, who for Poe is man par excellence, as trickster is a central Poe concept, for the con artist is one who undermines his victim's secure sense of what is truth and reality by displacing it with an autonomous alternate reality.

"The Angel of the Odd" (October 1844) is worthy of more attention because of its emphasis on those odd "accidents," which, even as he satirizes the writers who use them, Poe makes use of himself in major stories that focus on events that disrupt the everyday, expected sense of reality. The narrator calls such things lies and hoaxes, the work of "penny-a-liner" hacks who, "knowing the extravagant gullibility of the age, set their wits to work in the imagination of improbable possibilities—of odd accidents, as they term them" (3:1101). But just when the narrator insists that he believes nothing that has anything of the "singular" about it, the Falstaffian figure of the Angel of the Odd appears—a grotesque physical embodiment who presides over the "*contretemps* of mankind, and whose business it was to bring about the *odd accidents* which are continually astonishing the skeptic" (3:1104). Of course, as is usual in Poe, someone who claims not to believe in the odd must inevitably be made to confront the odd. The story plays with Poe's awareness of the paradox of accident in fiction, since in a short fiction, by its very pattern or design, there can be no accidents or coincidence, only the similitude of coincidences set in place by the artist or by the conventions of the genre to create dramatic irony.

"Loss of Breath" (September 1835), subtitled "A Tale Neither in Nor out of *Blackwood*," literalizes the metaphorical meaning of such phrases as "I am out of breath" or "I have lost my breath." The effect of the narrator's loss of breath while he is scolding and cursing his wife on the morning after their wedding is that even though he is alive he has the qualities of the dead—"an anomaly on the face of the earth."

Poe plays with this paradox of a character who is both living and dead in other stories—most notably in such hoaxes as "Mesmeric Revelation." The story is similar to the nineteenth-century German *novelle* convention used by E. T. A. Hoffman in "A New Year's Eve Adventure" (1814) and by Adalbert von Chamisso in *Peter Schemihl* (1813) of characters who have lost their shadows, for the protagonist goes in search for his lost breath in closets, corners, and drawers.

Mr. Lackobreath's lack of breath motivates the picaresque plot until he meets Mr. Widenough in a tomb, placed there after having caught the protagonist's breath while walking under his window. The remainder of the narrative nonsense involves the protagonist getting his breath back and the two men being released from the tomb. Although Daniel Hoffman has suggested that Poe is having fun with a bawdy joke here, arguing that the protagonist is a victim of sexual impotence, it seems more likely that the kind of power of which he is deprived is the "power of words" and that Mr. Widenough satirizes the double-winded idiot who spews out words with no power at all. The story is a comic treatment of themes treated more seriously in "The Power of Words" and "Silence," for to steal one's breath is to steal one's power of words and thus to deprive one of what provides life and identity.

"The Spectacles" (27 March 1844) is another example of Poe's literalizing a metaphor; this time, the play is on the expressions "love at first sight," "love is blind," and "making a spectacle of oneself." Moreover, the story depends on the theatrical conventions of stage comedy, for it is structured solely around ironic reversals resulting from the protagonist's falling in love with his great-great-grandmother, primarily because of his near blindness—an oedipal error indicated comically by his vanity of not wanting to wear glasses. The reader's discovery of the story's ironic pattern accounts for the "magnetic" sympathy the protagonist feels for his great-great-grandmother, as well as his fascination with her Madonna-like and matronly air; although he senses some mystery in her expression that disturbs him, her familial familiarity heightens his interest. The protagonist's insistence that she is his first love is ironically appropriate since the great-great-grandmother figure is a displaced image of the mother. This oedipal foolishness reaches its comic climax on the wedding night when, after a bit of verbal nonsense about names, the protagonist discovers the truth. In the dénouement the plot of the story is revealed to be dependent on the literal plot of the great-great-grandmother to teach the protagonist a lesson about his absurd vanity. It reflects Poe's frequent use of the plot-within-a-plot convention as a means to create a deceptive similitude that corresponds to nothing in the real world.

Poe's self-conscious play with conventions, in which he thematizes his own inextricable combination of seriousness and satire, is embodied in his story "Mystification," originally entitled "Von Jung" (June 1837). The story falls into a three-part structure similar to the ratiocinative tales featuring Poe's detective Dupin: the introduction of the Baron Ritzner Von Jung and his penchant for mystification, the central event of mystification, and the resolution of the mystification. The narrator says he is perhaps the only one at the school who knows that the baron has made "the science of *mystification*" his sole study, although no one else would suspect him to be capable of a joke either verbal or practical. The beauty of the baron's *art mystique,* says the narrator, lies in his ability (resulting from his knowledge of human nature) to make it appear that his drolleries result from his efforts to prevent them. Moreover, it is the nature of his art to shift "the sense of the grotesque from the creator to the created—from his own person to the absurdities to which he had given rise" (2:295). Although the baron is constantly "enveloped in an atmosphere of whim," he appears to live only "for the severities of society."

The central event of mystification in the story results from the discussion of several young men on the art of dueling—an art bound strictly by codes, rituals, conventions, and specific methods of proceeding. The baron takes part in the discussion and expresses a great deal of enthusiasm for dueling, even though the narrator knows that at heart he ridicules all the points he seems to support and that he holds dueling etiquette in contempt. The baron is another Poe artist manqué, for one of Poe's most predominant techniques is the serious presentation of those elements of modern life and gothic conventions that he holds to be ridiculous and the comic presentation of those habits that he takes quite seriously.

The mystification begins when Hermann, the victim of the baron's satiric attack, challenges the baron in a hairsplitting way, declaring that his opinions are not those of a gentleman. At this point the baron, acting with the utmost seriousness and severity, although the narrator sees that his face is radiant with a quizzical expression, throws a decanter of wine in the mirror, claiming that by so doing he fulfills the spirit, if not the letter, of resentment at Hermann's insult and thus obviates the need for physical violence. The resolution of the mystification is effected when the victim goes back to his room and tries to find the rules of dueling etiquette governing the baron's strange behavior. When he sends a note asking that the baron give him an explanation of the occurrences of the evening, the baron writes back that he will find it in a book entitled *The Law Written on Duelling, and Not, and Otherwise*. Although after reading the relevant passages Hermann says he is satisfied, declaring it the fullest and most relevant explanation he could ask for, the narrator says he could not understand a word of it.

The explanation for the mystification, presented much the way Poe's detective Dupin presents his resolutions, turns out to be a joke. The chapter of the volume to which the baron refers is about a duel between two baboons, made nonsense by language framed in such a way as to "present to the ear all the outward signs of intelligibility, and even of profundity, while in fact not a shadow of meaning existed" (2:303). However, the baron knows that his victim will never admit his inability to understand everything that has ever been written about dueling and thus will "make sense" even of that which has no sense at all. Poe is poking fun at pomposity here, but the story is more important for its representation of Poe's own posture as a mystifier—one who seems serious when he is being whimsical and whimsical when he seems to be serious.

"Hop-Frog" (17 March 1849) is a generically problematical story in the Poe canon because, uncharacteristically, it is told in the third person, much the way a parable or a folktale is told. Consequently, it is worth looking at as an indicator of Poe's nineteenth-century transformation of the traditional folktale form for his own ironic purpose. The story revolves around two kinds of jokes: the kind the king likes and the kind that Hop-Frog devises. The king has a special "admiration for *breadth* in a jest, and would often put up with *length*, for the sake of it. Over-niceties wearied him. He would have preferred Rabelais's 'Gargantua' to the 'Zadig' of Voltaire: and upon the whole, practical jokes suited his taste far better than verbal ones" (3:1345). The court jester, Hop-Frog, a professional at joke making, inclines more to ironic verbal joke. An imaginative artist, he is the only one in the story capable of being inventive; he is particularly good at arranging costumes and creating characters for masked balls. Indeed, what the king demands from Hop-Frog is "characters—*characters*, man—something novel—out of the way. We are wearied with this everlasting sameness" (3:1347). When he berates Hop-Frog and says "we are in need of characters—all of us," he and his seven ministers laugh, for the narrator says this was "seriously meant for a joke." But it is not until the king throws wine into the face of the female dwarf Tripetta, who is described as small but of "exquisite proportions," that Hop-Frog decides on a masquerade, declaring that the beauty of the game lies in the fact that the other masqueraders will take the king and his ministers for the reality they depict.

This, of course, is the joke on which the story rests. For what Hop-Frog plans is a plot of "poetic justice" in which the bestial nature of the king and his ministers will be externalized. This ironic fulfillment is further emphasized when the king, on hearing the plan, says, "Hop-Frog! I will make a man of you" (3:1350). The verbal irony is that whereas Hop-Frog is taken to be a repulsive creature, he is actually already a man; while the king, taken to be a man, is really a repulsive beast. Once this is established, the rest of the story is a working out of Hop-Frog's plot. The joke carries a final twist of vicious verbal irony when Hop-Frog destroys the king and his ministers by fire, for at the end, the reader is thrown back to the irony of the first lines of the story: "I never knew any one so keenly alive to a joke as the king was. He seemed to live only for joking. To tell a good story of the joke kind, and to tell it well, was the surest road to his favor" (3:1345). Of course, at the end, the king dies for a joke, as Hop-Frog not only has the last joke, but has made the king and his ministers characters in that joke (the king did, after all, ask for characters).

Poe's frequent use of parody is an important element in his transformation of the gothic romance into the modern short story, for by laying bare the conventions that underlie the gothic he self-consciously becomes able to manipulate those conventions for his own purposes. But perhaps more importantly, Poe's inveterate joking, trickery, punning, parody, and play suggest that he embodies Friedrich von Schiller's theory of play as the expression of surplus energy that forms the primal origin of art.[38] More specifically, Poe saw play as an analogue for the art work itself, especially the short prose tale, for as an interruption of the everyday continuity of life, it establishes a self-contained entity with its own playlike rules and conventions.[39] Moreover, as a result of Poe's playing, the reader is not only never really sure when to take him seriously, he is also never really sure when Poe is presenting fact or fiction. Consequently, closely related to Poe's satiric stories are his hoaxes, in which the truth/fiction issue is more emphatically thematized and laid bare.

Truth and Fiction

Poe's central concern with the relationship between truth and fiction is reflected in the several short pieces he wrote in which he tries to pass off a fiction as scientific truth or in which he uses a fictional frame to enclose actual scientific truths. Poe frequently focused on the relationship between science and art, for he knew that scientific theories or hypotheses are indeed but poetic paradigms—models with no claims to truth because of a correspondence to external reality, but whose truth value lies in their coherence.

Although this concept underlies Poe's own "scientific-poetic" theory in *Eureka,* he presents it most explicitly in the story "Melonta Tauta" (February 1849). After criticizing Aristotle's deductive method and Bacon's inductive method for arriving at truth, his futuristic narrator Pundita claims that previous thinkers missed what now is seen as the great highway to truth, consistency. Pundita says that since it has been discovered that a perfect consistency must be an absolute truth, investigation has been given over to the only true thinkers: the men of imagination who theorize. "These men, I say *theorize;* and their theories are simply corrected, reduced, systematized—cleared, little by little, of their dross of inconsistency—until, finally, a perfect consistency stands apparent which even the most stolid admit, because it *is* a consistency, to be an absolute and an unquestionable *truth*" (3:1298). The concept is made even more emphatic in *Eureka:* "A thing is consistent in the ratio of its truth—true in the ratio of its consistency. *A perfect consistency, I repeat, can be nothing but an absolute truth*" (*Works*, 16:302).[40]

Poe knew that the best way to destroy his audience's comfortable assumption that they knew the difference between truth and fiction, science and art, or reality and fantasy was to make truth look like fiction and fiction look like truth. In a number of stories he self-consciously plays with this confusion, thus following the more general romantic tradition by which the unusual is made to seem strange and the strange is made to seem usual. These stories constitute a bridge between the eighteenth-century German and English gothic tales, which still clung to the supernatural assumptions of the old romance form, and the modern realistic story pioneered by Defoe that denied such supernaturalism; in them Poe either makes use of the techniques of verisimilitude to make believable events that cannot be true, or else to put a fictional frame around real events in such a way as to accentuate their seemingly fantastic nature. The stories range from the relatively simplistic fictional framing of real events, such as "The Thousand-and-Second Tale of Scheherazade," to the more complex cosmic concerns of "The Facts in the Case of M. Valdemar." They also run the gamut from actual hoaxes in which nonexistent but plausible events are presented as actually having taken place, such as "The Balloon-Hoax," to the metaphysical hoaxes in which implausible events are presented for their philosophic implications, such as "Mesmeric Revelation."

Poe's use of *The Thousand and One Nights* in "The Thousand-and-Second Tale of Scheherazade" (February 1845) as a fictional frame for presenting truths stranger than fiction is not surprising considering his primary concern with the nature of narrative. After all, Scheherazade enjoys mythical status as the fountainhead of all storytelling—a status that such latter-day storytellers as John Barth and Jorge Luis Borges have more explicitly exploited. The fictional frame Poe creates for the story is a quadruple one: the unnamed narrator (1) *tells* of looking into an oriental book entitled *Tellmenow Isitsoörnot* (a self-conscious reference to the fiction/truth motif) to discover (2) the *tale* of Scheherazade (3) *telling* (4) the unfinished *tale* of Sinbad. The story's effect thus depends on a known storyteller, in fact, the best-known storyteller in all literature, telling truths within the context of fiction. The structure of the story Scheherazade tells is a simple one, for throughout its picaresque plot Sinbad relates seeing many strange sights, ranging from natural wonders such as the Mammoth Caves of Kentucky and the petrified forest of Texas to such scientific wonders as the effects of electricity and the use of the calculating machine. These separate descriptions are punctuated by ejaculations of disbelief from the king, until at the end he declares Scheherazade has given him a dreadful headache with all her "lies"; therefore, he has her killed.

Poe's irony, of course, is that whereas Scheherazade's stories or "lies" saved her life in the original *Thousand and One Nights* tales, her truths now lead to her death; thus, one might say, for Poe, whereas the lie, or fiction, preserves, the truth, or fact, kills. Ironically, the only event in the story that the king says he believes is Sinbad's description of entering a continent resting on the back of a sky-blue cow with 400 horns—a bit of Middle-Eastern mythology that the king accepts as truth because he read it in a book somewhere. What is interesting about the story is not simply that it is concerned with the relationship between truth and fiction, but that the truth/fiction motif is thematized as its central focus.

"Some Words with a Mummy" (April 1845), published a couple of months after the Scheherazade piece, uses a similar device of presenting wonders of the modern world from within an elaborate fictional context. In its focus on a revived mummy from ancient Egypt who is not impressed with such advances as electricity, modern architecture, and railroads, the story is ostensibly a satire on the supposed superiority of nineteenth-century technology; however, the basic premise—"there is nothing new under the sun"—has a more pervasive relevance to Poe's thought, for he always argued in his criticism that creation of the "new" is actually the combination of the old.

Like the art work itself, the mummy is not a dead artifact but rather a living text contained inside a mysterious oblong box made of papyrus and inscribed all over with hieroglyphics. As the story proceeds predictably enough, with modern men posing questions to the mummy about his own civilization, the most extensive discussion, and the only one initiated by the narrator of the story himself, deals with the fact that embalming made it possible for men of ancient Egypt to live their lives in installments. A historian would write a book and then get himself embalmed, leaving instructions that he should be revived in 500 years. However, when he resumed life, he would invariably find his book made into a "kind of literary arena for the conflicting guesses, riddles, and personal squabbles of whole herds of exasperated commentators" who so overwhelmed and distorted his original text that he had to rewrite it (3:1189). The mummy concludes by saying that "this process of re-scription and personal rectification, pursued by various individual sages, from time to time, had the effect of preventing our history from degenerating into absolute fable" (3:1189). The discussion suggests that for Poe truth and reality are textual determinations—that although reality derives from written history, it can be altered by annotation of the text, which may then be rewritten to create still another reality. For Poe, reality derives from whatever text is made to be authoritative by purely textual devices of discourse.

The difference between Poe's hoaxes that depend on verisimilitude and his satires that depend on a satiric tone and the intention of parody can be seen quite clearly in the difference between "The Balloon-

Hoax" (13 April 1844) and "Hans Pfaal" (June 1835). "The Balloon-Hoax" was originally published in a newspaper as a true journalistic account, carrying the conviction of its truth solely by the technique of verisimilitude, or the inclusion of "minutest particulars" respecting the "extraordinary voyage." The story is divided into two parts: a description of the balloon itself, which is said to be "authentic and accurate in every respect" because it is copied verbatim from the diaries of the two balloonists, and direct quotations from the journal of the two balloonists as transcribed by the reporter. What is significant about the second part is the contrast between the report of the man of science, the balloonist Monck Mason, and the postscripts by the author of novels, Harrison Ainsworth. The fictional "truth," that is, the factual story supposedly told by the scientist, is more compelling than the flowery and metaphoric language written by the novelist. However, since the entire report is fictional, what we really have is the presentation of two different styles of fictional storytelling—the one posing as fact and the other presented as feeling, for whereas the scientist deals with the immediacy of the situation, the novelist generalizes subjective reactions.

"Hans Pfaal" announces its satiric intention immediately by poking fun at some of the same devices of verisimilitude that make the scientist's report in "The Balloon Hoax" so convincing. First, in the tradition of the nineteenth-century German *novelle*, the events are said to be novel but true, and second, they are said to have taken place on the "——day of ——," for the narrator says he is not positive about the date. To use the verisimilitude convention of naming the exact date of an event, only to leave the date blank, is to expose the convention itself and to announce the story as parody. Furthermore, when the balloon descends, instead of being described in minute and believable particulars as it is in "The Balloon-Hoax," it is metaphorically made of what indeed the balloon in "The Balloon-Hoax" was made of literally—that is, newspapers. Instead of having the aerodynamic shape it has in "The Balloon Hoax," it has the satiric shape of a huge fool's cap turned upside down.

Although the bulk of the story, which purports to be from a manuscript dropped from the balloon by a strange little man, presents Hans Pfaal's journey to the moon in a strictly verisimilar style, at the end Poe suggests the fictionality of the story by pointing out that many people have called it a hoax. Then, as if to undercut what he has exposed, he claims that for such people the word "hoax" is a "general term for all matters above their comprehension." In other words, for

Poe, "hoax" is simply a word for a fiction presented as if it were a reality.

In a note appended to a later edition of the tale, Poe makes additional comments about the nature of hoaxes by referring to the famous "moon story" hoax of *New York Sun* editor Richard Adams Locke, which appeared soon after this own story was published. Although Poe admits that his own story has the tone of banter, whereas the Locke hoax is presented in earnest, he notes that both attempt "to give plausibility by scientific detail." He then proceeds to expose the "fictionality" of Locke's hoax and to review other "voyage to the moon" stories, most of which are satirical in aim, but none of which makes any effort at plausibility. He claims that his own design in "Hans Pfaal" is original, inasmuch as it combines a whimsical tone and satiric intention with scientific principles and verisimilitude. The importance of this combination for Poe is that whereas in satire the tone makes it obvious that the work is fictional, in verisimilitude (which is synonymous with hoax) the technique is to convince the reader of the reality of the event. To combine satiric tone with the presentation of "as if" reality is to present a subjective and an objective narrative simultaneously, in which one is to serve the aims of fiction and the other is to serve the aims of truth.

"Von Kempelen and His Discovery" (April 1849) is another Poe story that hovers between satire (i.e., dominated by subjective authorial intention and tone) and hoax (i.e., dominated by the objective technique of verisimilitude). In a letter to publisher Evert A. Duyckinck, on 8 March 1949, Poe declared it to be an exercise in the "plausible or verisimilar style" which, although without a word of truth in it, will create a sense of belief in nine out of ten who read it (*Letters* 2:433).[41] Poe dismisses a paragraph appearing in newspapers that claims the invention of Von Kempelen for someone else, for although he notes that there is nothing implausible or improbable in the paragraph, his belief that it is fictional is based on its "manner"; he argues that it does not look true: "Persons who are narrating *facts*, are seldom so particular as Mr. Kissam seems to be, about day and date and precise location" (3:1358). For Poe, truth is determined by manner, not by matter—by coherence rather than by correspondence. The irony is that the more the fictional work tries to convince the reader by precise detail that it is true the more the reader should be aware that its verisimilitude is a pure convention and that it is fictional.

Two stories that make use of verisimilitude to convince the reader they are true rather than fictional and, like the balloon hoaxes, make use of science (in this case mesmerism) are "Mesmeric Revelation" and "The Facts in the Case of M. Valdemar." Poe uses mesmerism as a means of exploring his own metaphysical views about the nature of reality, for, like a hoax, mesmerism is a fiction posing as a reality; in its similitude of death it can be mistaken for the real state. In "Mesmeric Revelation" (August 1844), the assumption is that at least some of the speaker's revelations come from the realm of death, whereas in "The Case of M. Valdemar" mesmerism is a fictional similitude of death that mocks death by preserving the body.

Under a hypnotic trance, Vankirk in "Mesmeric Revelation" responds to questions from the hypnotist about the nature of God, thought, and material reality with theories that Poe develops later in *Eureka*. The primary points of his position are as follows: there is no radical difference in kind between matter and spirit, for there is only matter in various states of gradation, from that level we usually understand as matter to a rarefied level of ultimate unparticled matter—what Poe understands as the indivisible One, or what man calls God. However, to call Poe a materialist because of this description of reality is to play semantic games, for, as Vankirk says, the ultimate unparticled matter of which he speaks is the "mind" or "spirit" described by the idealists. God is actually the ultimate perfection of matter. To rise up through the gradations of matter is to aspire toward ultimate unparticled matter, or spirit, that is, complete unity.

However, in spite of the fact that such a complete unity is the object of ultimate desire, achieving it is not humanly possible. Man divested of body would be God, says Vankirk, but that can never be. Man is made up of two bodies: the rudimentary body, by which we designate ordinary physicality, and the ultimate body, which is not physical at all, but rather what we might call form. Although man aspires to complete unity, that is, pure form, he can never achieve this ultimate goal. This is an important passage for understanding Poe, for it once again points to his insistence that ultimate reality is design, pattern, and form, rather than mere materiality.

The story ends with the death of Vankirk and with an ambiguity about whether the latter part of his discourse has been addressed from the realm of death. The story could be called Poe's ultimate hoax, for it presents metaphysical theories with the authority of having been spoken from the realm of death, although the "truth" of Vankirk's death is actually the "fiction" of his mesmeric state. Earlier in the story Vankirk provides a rationale for this fiction/fact combination by noting that if man is to be convinced of his immortality, he will not be convinced by abstractions, that is, by the generalized discourse of philosophy or religion, but rather by concrete experience. However, such "concrete experience," as it always is in Poe, can only be presented in a fictional similitude, in this case the similitude of death known as mesmerism. "Abstractions," says Vankirk, "may amuse and exercise, but take no hold on the mind. Here upon earth, at least, philosophy, I am persuaded, will always in vain call upon us to look upon qualities as things. The will may assent—the soul—the intellect, never" (3:1031). As Poe well knew, the advantage of art over philosophy is that it presents the abstract by means of the concrete in an "as if" situation, that is, in a fiction parading as a fact—in short, in a hoax.

The way Vankirk describes mesmerism—as a halfway point between sleep and waking, that is, a halfway point between primary and secondary process—makes it sound very similar to what Gregory Bateson has described as the realm of play and thus the realm of art. The play frame, like the art work, implies a special combination of primary and secondary processes, says Bateson: "In primary process, map and territory are equated; in secondary process, they can be discriminated. In play, they are both equated and discriminated."[42] Vankirk says that while he is in the mesmeric trance, what he calls "sleep-waking," his reasoning and its effect exist simultaneously, whereas in his natural state the cause vanishes and the effect only remains. A realm neither sleep nor waking in which both cause and effect are simultaneous, a realm in which both abstraction and concreteness are one—this best describes the realm of the art work for Poe.

Whereas "Mesmeric Revelation" is primarily an exploration of mesmerism as a similitude of death and thus an opportunity for abstractions to be presented as if they were concrete experiences, "The Facts in the Case of M. Valdemar" (December 1845) is a less metaphysical and more physically shocking experiment in the use of verisimilitude to present an impossibility as if it were real. The story is described by Elizabeth Barrett as one which threw readers of her circle into dreadful doubts as to whether it was true: "The certain thing in the tale in question," she says, "is the power of the writer, and the faculty he has of making horrible improbabilities seem near and familiar."[43] P. Pendleton Cooke elaborates on this judgment by noting that Poe has

Defoe's "peculiar talent for filling up his pictures with minute life-like touches—for giving an air of remarkable naturalness and truth to whatever he paints."[44] But at least one recent critic has questioned the seriousness of the work, suggesting that the story represents Poe's common technique of transforming a theme he has originally treated philosophically (in "Mesmeric Revelation") into "a graphic mockery whose powers derive from its impossible literalness."[45]

The central assertion in the story, as has been pointed out by Roland Barthes, is Valdemar's paradoxical statement, "I am dead," when he is actually in a mesmeric trance. As Barthes says, the phrase asserts two contraries at the same time: "the signifier expresses a signified (Death) which contradicts its utterance." The phrase, Barthes says, means both "I am dead and I am not dead" simultaneously.[46] Although Barthes takes the implications of this statement deep into Lacanian psychoanalytical reflections, it will suffice to point out here that it is precisely the kind of statement that can only be uttered within the play/art similitude that Gregory Bateson describes as presenting both the map and the territory simultaneously, that is, both primary and secondary process at once. Valdemar is both actually dead and simultaneously within a similitude of death, that is, mesmerism. One can only make the statement "I am dead" and mean it both literally and metaphorically at once from within a fiction, for to speak from within the mesmeric trance, itself a similitude of death, is to speak metaphorically. It is only when Valdemar is taken out of his trance, that is, when he leaves the metaphoric realm of mesmerism and reenters actuality, that he is actually dead; and, of course, in this state he cannot utter the statement, "I am dead." Thus, the rapid decomposition of the corpse of Valdemar at the end is inevitable, for his body has only been sustained by the persistence of the mesmeric similitude of death itself. Once the similitude has been disrupted, that is, once the map has been destroyed, the territory that has been sustained by the mesmeric metaphor is also destroyed.

Poe's ability to unsettle one's sense of what reality really is through the metaphor of mesmerism can also be seen in "A Tale of the Ragged Mountains" (April 1844), a story that Arthur Quinn has called Poe's best realistic treatment of the supernatural.[47] The story embodies many typical Poe motifs: it pretends to be the truth, even though it is fiction; it makes use of the theme of metempsychosis as does "Metzengerstein" and "Ligeia"; and it presents the same cosmic notions of the dividing line between life and death embodied in "Mesmeric Revelation" and "The Case of M. Valdemar." The protagonist Augustus Bedloe is, like many of Poe's protagonists, of mysterious origin, of an indeterminate age, melancholic, and with a vigorous and creative imagination. Frequently stricken with attacks of neuralgia, he must be attended by a physician, Dr. Templeton, with whom he has a very marked "*rapport*, or magnet relation," partially due to the doctor's ability to mesmerize Bedloe to ease his pain.

The story centers on an account Bedloe himself relates after a long walk in the hills on an Indian summer day. The strangeness of the journey is emphasized by the dense fog surrounding the path and by the intensity of his morphine-induced impressions of the world around him. He enters into a realm of palm trees, hyenas, and finally an Eastern-looking city, such as might be described in an *Arabian Nights* tale. However, Bedloe declares that his experience is not a dream, for all is "rigorously self-consistent," with none of the idiosyncrasies of a dream. Furthermore, he says he noted the onset of the dream state while it was occurring, and he insists that if "the vision had occurred to him without his suspecting it was a dream, then it may have been a dream, but having suspected it as a dream, he is convinced it was not" (3:946).

The ultimate problem about the ontological nature of the experience arises when Bedloe enters the city and is struck on the head and dies. The narrator now insists the event must have been a dream, because the very fact that Bedloe is telling the story obviously means he is not dead. The piece comes to a climax when Templeton shows Bedloe a watercolor drawing of a dead friend of his, a Mr. Oldeb, to whom Bedloe bears a striking physical resemblance. Templeton then relates a tale from the past that replicates Bedloe's dreamlike episode and says that at the very period that Bedloe was having his experience in the hills Templeton was at home writing the past experience down in his notebook. Thus, we have a typical Poe device of presenting a transcribed past event as a present real one, similar to the interface between life and art in "Metzengerstein" and "The Oval Portrait."

The postscript of the story resolves the issue in the only way it can be resolved: aesthetically. After Bedloe dies because Templeton accidentally puts a poisonous leech on him to bleed him, a newspaper clipping is introduced detailing the death and spelling Bedloe's name as *Bedlo*. When the narrator asks the editor of the paper what "authority" he has for this spelling, the editor attributes it to a typographical error. Pointing out that "Bedlo" is "Oldeb" spelled backwards, the narrator says it has come to pass "that one truth is stranger than any fiction" (3:950). Indeed, the fact that the spelling that makes possible the reversal of the names—an example of the word play known as a palindrome—is attributed to a typographical error is further evidence that Bedloe's fantasy journey is motivated by the writing process rather than by supernatural or psychological processes.

The idea of reality being something created by the mind rather than merely perceived "out there" in the world is also the focus of "The Sphinx" (January 1846). The story is a parody treatment of the religious conviction that things in the external world are symbolic reflections or omens; Poe asserts that only within the contextual world of the art work can such an intrinsic relationship between signifier and signified be true. The story starts with the convention used by Boccaccio in *The Decameron* of a retreat to the country to escape the plague, here cholera. The relative the narrator visits is a familiar Poe character, with a "richly philosophic intellect" unaffected, he says, by "unrealities." He is conscious of the physical "substance" of terror, such as the cholera, but of its "shadows" he is not afraid.

The thematic center of the story focuses on the narrator's belief in omens based on a particular perceptual experience he describes. The event, in which the narrator perceives a "living monster" out of the window of the house, is attended by, as is usual in Poe, several possibly extenuating circumstances. First, the narrator is reading a book, a "certain volume" from the host's library, of a "character to force into germination whatever seeds of hereditary superstition which lay latent in my bosom" (3:1247); and second, his thoughts have wandered from the book to the "gloom and desolation of the neighboring city." When he sees the monster, he at first doubts his sanity or the evidence of his own eyes, but then convinces himself that he is neither mad nor in a dream—the two usual alterations of ordinary reality we encounter in Poe.

The narrator does not tell the host about the experience until three or four days later when he sees the monster again. Because the host cannot see the creature, the narrator feels it is a spiritual vision—something that exists in his mind only, and thus an omen of death or madness. However, after the host questions the narrator about the physical appearance of the monster, he begins to discuss those points of speculative philosophy that they have discussed earlier—particularly the host's idea that "the principal source of error in all human investigations, lay in the liability of the understanding to under-rate or to over-value the importance of an object through pure misadmeasurement of its propinquity" (3:1249–50). After taking down a book and changing seats with the narrator, he says it was the narrator's "exceeding minuteness" that made him recognize the monster; he then reads a description of a butterfly of the genus *Sphinx*, which has terrified folk in the past because of its melancholy cry and the insignia of death on its breast. The host notes that he can indeed see the creature, but it is only about a sixteenth of an inch in length and only about a sixteenth of an inch from the pupil of his eye.

Although it is obvious that a moth could not be a sixteenth of an inch from one's eye and fail to be detected as such, Poe is less concerned with verisimilitude here than he is with the problem of determining the difference between a psychic occurrence and an occurrence in the external world. Although in such stories as "The Tell-Tale Heart" the narrator mistakes inner stuff for outer stuff, in "The Sphinx" a narrator mistakes outer stuff for inner stuff. He does not believe that the monster is actually "out there," but that he is seeing a psychic omen, an unreality—a radical contrast to Bedloe in "A Tale of the Ragged Mountains," who experiences a psychic phenomenon with such specificity of detail that he thinks it is real.

Two final stories to be discussed in terms of fiction and reality are "The Oval Portrait," originally entitled "Life in Death" (April 1842) but shortened and given its present title three years later (26 April 1845), and "The Assignation" (January 1834). In "The Oval Portrait," the perception problem again springs from several possibly external circumstances. In the first version of the story the narrator has taken an overdose of opium; even in the final shortened version he is in a delirium after being attacked by bandits. Moreover, the fictional context of the story is announced by the narrator when he describes the chalet to which his valet has brought him as a pile of "commingled gloom and grandeur which have so long frowned among the Apennines, not less in fact than in the fancy of Mrs. Radcliffe" (2:662). Moreover, the immediate context and cause of the central perceptual experience in the story is the fact that the narrator is engaged in two activities often presented by Poe as capable of throwing one outside of ordinary reality: he is looking at pictures and reading a book that describes them.

By moving the candles in a certain way to throw more light on his book, the narrator instead throws light on a painting of a young girl he had not seen before. At this point, struck by something unusual about the picture, he closes his eyes to make sure that his vision has not deceived him. When he opens them again, he confirms his first reaction to the painting, for he feels the flashing of the light on the canvas has dissipated "the dreamy stupor" that was stealing over his senses and startled him into "waking life." In the next two paragraphs the narrator describes his own reaction to the painting and then cites a quotation from the book he is reading, which gives the story of its background. Thus, we have two responses to the painting, one from seeing and one from reading. The thematic difference arising from the two responses is the key to the motivation and the effect of the story.

The crux of the matter has to do with the distinction between "living" and "lifelike." The painting has had a definite effect on the narrator and he looks at it for an hour to determine why. He dismisses the notion that he could have at first taken the painting for a living person, for the vignette nature of the painting (that is, the arms, bosom, and hair seem to melt into the background) and the frame (which is oval, richly gilded, and filigreed) must have not only dispelled such an idea, but have prevented the idea being entertained even momentarily. Furthermore, he says that neither the execution of the work nor the immortal beauty of the face could have caused such an effect. After an hour of looking at the painting, he comes to the conclusion that the "true secret of its effect" lay in its "absolute *life-likeness*" of expression, which at first startled him and then finally "confounded, subdued, and appalled" him (2:664).

The story he reads about the painting does not deal with an art work being "like life," but rather with a painting that is in competition with life itself. Although the painter marries a young girl, he already has a bride in his work. When he paints her, he is so involved in his art that he does not see that she begins to wither and fade. As the painting proceeds, his ardor grows and those who see it say it is so "life-like" that it speaks of the power of his deep love for her. Of course, it is not love for the girl that motivates the painter but love for the idealized image of her in the painting: "And he *would* not see that the tints which he spread on the canvas were drawn from the cheeks of her who sat beside him" (2:665). At the climax of the story the painter finishes his work and looks upon his painting, declaring "This is indeed *Life* itself," only to turn to his beloved to find that "*She was dead!*" (2:666).

The thematic thrust of the story centers on the distinction between "Life" that is organic and therefore mortal in everyday reality, and "life" that is idealized and therefore immortal in the art work. In his cosmic dialogues and *Eureka* Poe notes that the ultimate aim of life was originally immortality, but that actual life falls short of God's plan. Thus, man constantly aims in the art work for the perfection of ultimate form that is denied him in reality. "The Oval Portrait" is not a moral parable of a man's overweening pride in his creative abilities, such as Hawthorne's "The Birthmark," with which it is often compared; it is rather a story of Poe's secret of "effect," the secret of "lifelikeness," which is not the same as life itself. The artist is dedicated to the ideal bride, the bride who is the only possible manifestation of Supernal Beauty for Poe, that is, the art work itself. The only way that there can be life in death is in the lifelikeness of the art work—which is more "alive" than physical life because it is a similitude of the original plan of oneness and form.

Life in the organic world versus life lived as if in an art work is also the subject of "The Assignation," originally entitled "The Visionary." The story opens with an invocation to the protagonist (generally taken to be an image of Byron) by calling him to mind, not as he is, in the cold valley and shadow of death, but as he "*shouldst be*" in magnificent meditation in Venice, the city of visions. The narrator then begins the narrative itself, which starts at midnight in a time past when the "Genius of Romance" stalked the narrow Venetian canal. Indeed, both the events and the language of the story suggest not reality but romance. The story begins as the narrator is going down the canal and a woman's scream makes his gondolier drop his oar so they drift down toward the Bridge of Sighs "like some huge and sable-feathered condor" (2:152). The scene is described in a static and conventional way, with the major figures placed in paintinglike poses. First there is the Marchesa Aphrodite standing alone, "no motion in the statue-like form" as she looks not at the dark abyss of the canal where her child has disappeared, but rather across to the prison. Also in the scene, standing several steps above the Marchesa, strumming a guitar, the picture of *ennuyé*, is the "Satyr-like figure of Mentoni himself," the husband of the Marchesa.

With the disappearance of the child into the dark water, the picture abruptly becomes an operatic stage play, as out of the wings comes a figure muffled in a cloak who springs into the water, rescues the child, and takes it to the Marchesa, thus making the "statue" she has become spring to life. "The pallor of the marble countenance, the swelling of the marble bosom, the very purity of the marble feet, we behold suddenly flushed over with a tide of ungovernable crimson" (2:154).

The last section of the story takes place at the apartment of the Byronic stranger, who the narrator describes as having classical regular features he has never seen before except in a statue of the Emperor Commodus. When the narrator is astonished at the nature of the apartment, which lacks *decora* or *keeping* of the kind that Poe describes in "The Philosophy of Furniture," the stranger laughs at the narrator's astonishment at the "originality of conception of architecture and upholstery" and tells him, "to dream has been the business of my life" (2:165); thus he has built a bower of dreams to separate himself from ordinary reality, much as the narrator in "Ligeia" does after the death of his ideal. He says the grotesques and arabesques that surround him prepare him for the wilder visions of the land of "real dreams" to which he is going. The story ends when a servant of Mentoni comes in and says that his mistress has been poisoned. The narrator, seeing that the stranger's limbs are rigid and his eyes riveted in death, looks at the blackened goblet, and the "consciousness of the entire and terrible truth flashed suddenly over my soul" (2:166).

The truth here is that the stranger and the Marchesa have transformed themselves into an art work, a frozen static reality much like the tableau the audience sees just before the final curtain comes down on Shakespeare's *Romeo and Juliet*. The ultimate end of the ultimate love is precisely the immortality that results from the two dying as one and thus living forever in the art work. As in "The Oval Portrait," to say "This is life indeed" is to say "This is art." For only in the art work is there the fulfillment of the original intention of unity, order, and pattern that Poe says is God's plan. The story thus ends in perhaps the most explicit example in Poe's fiction of his ultimate epiphany: the transformation of the temporal into the unchanging spatial unity of the art work.

Body and Spirit

At least since Edward Davidson's important study of Poe and the influential essays by W. H. Auden, Richard Wilbur, and Allan Tate in the 1950s, Poe has been understood as a religious writer, in spite of the fact that he had no formal religious faith.[48] Poe understood ultimate reality to be an absolute aesthetic pattern. Thus, any set of materials that can be unified can arouse the Poetic Principle or Supernal Beauty, even the external world itself. In keeping with this idea, Poe wrote several stories in which the physical world is manipulated in such a way as to transform it from physical reality to spiritual reality. Poe's notion of the spiritual is that it is matter so perfectly organized that its materiality becomes matterless; only its pattern or form remains.

Perhaps the most complex and developed of these stories is "The Domain of Arnheim" (March 1847), an expansion of a piece published in 1842 entitled "The Landscape Garden." A typical Poe combination of the essay form and the tale, it can be seen as a narrative embodiment of Poe's claim in "The Poetic Principle" that landscape gardening was one of the modes by which the Poetic Sentiment might be manifested. The central character in the story is not a typical Poe protagonist, for he is described as a happy man. He is handsome and intelligent, has a beautiful bride, and had inherited $450 million when he turned 21. It seems clear that Poe wishes him to represent the acme of the fulfillment of human desire: he has everything and is everything one could ask for.

What does make him a typical Poe protagonist is that he is an artist who understands that the sole proper satisfaction of the Poetic Sentiment lies in the creation "of novel forms of beauty." Moreover, since he is, like Poe himself, a materialist, he believes that the sole legitimate field of the poetic exercise "lies in the creation of novel moods of purely *physical* loveliness (3:1271). Consequently, Ellison is not a musician nor a poet, but rather holds that the landscape offers the most magnificent of opportunities for the artist: "Here, indeed, was the fairest field for the display of imagination in the endless combining of forms of novel beauty; the elements to enter into combination being,

54

by a vast superiority, the most glorious which the earth could afford" (3:1272). Ellison feels that although nature makes an effort at creating physical loveliness, no combination of scenery can match what a great painter can produce. "In the most enchanting of natural landscapes, there will always be found a defect or an excess—many excesses and defects" (3:1272). Especially, he notes that while the component parts may defy the skill of the greatest artist, the "arrangement" of the parts will always need improvement. In details, we cannot compete with nature, says Ellison, but in "composition" nature is deficient.

The metaphor of manipulating landscape as a means of compensating for nature's defects reflects Poe's concern with pure organization of parts as the only "creation" possible. In the natural world all the separate parts are already given; all that can be done in landscape gardening is to "compose" the preexistent parts into a new pattern—a process that reflects Poe's idea that man should constantly strive toward a return to the primal perfect purpose of God. Ellison believes that the primitive first intention of nature was immortality, but that it must have been disturbed by geological disturbances. In a metaphor for the transformation of matter into spirit, striking even for Poe, Ellison affirms that an artist with enough money might imbue his landscape designs with enough beauty to convey the sentiment of spiritual interference by means of pure design. He suggests finding a landscape that expresses the art of the Almighty and then bringing that in harmony or consistency with the sense of human art; the result would be the air of a secondary art that, like the handiwork of the angels, seems to hover between man and God.

At this point, where the original "Landscape Garden" story ends, the narrator says he despairs of trying to give a conception of what Ellison accomplished. He hesitates "between detail and generality," finally deciding that perhaps the better course will be to unite the two in their extremes. This relationship between detail and generality, emphasized in other Poe stories, is one of the key elements in Poe's transformation of eighteenth-century essay conventions into nineteenth-century short fiction, for it emphasizes the paradoxical nature of fiction's ability to communicate thematic generality by means of specific detail.

As the narrator moves up the winding river toward Ellison's aesthetic creation, however, he is "enrapt in an exquisite sense of the strange." Although the scene still suggests nature, "her character seemed to have undergone modification; there was a weird symmetry, a thrilling uniformity, a wizard propriety in these her works" (3:1279). To use such adjectives as "weird," "thrilling," and "wizard" to describe the unity and symmetry of nature suggests that artistic composition inevitably alters the natural into an alternate aesthetic reality. The remainder of the story describes the approach to Ellison's art world, but not the actual Paradise itself; when it is reached, the narrator hears a melody, smells a sweet odor, and sees a dreamlike scene, but the picture has no real detail. And indeed, given Poe's notion that a perfect physical unity creates a nonphysical spiritual experience, no real detail is possible.

"Landor's Cottage," subtitled "A Pendant to 'The Domain of Arnheim'" (9 June 1849), continues to explore the process of spiritualizing the physical by means of the aesthetic patterning of concrete details. It is less interesting than "The Domain of Arnheim" because it begins approximately where the earlier story leaves off—that is, with the arrival of a traveler to an area that has already been transformed by aesthetic pattern—thus the setting is no longer mere matter but rather a spiritual or aesthetic reality. Moreover, since the journey has been completed, there is no way the observer can describe the perfect pattern itself except by means of unsatisfactory generalities. He can say that an artist with a scrupulous eye for form must have superintended all the arrangements, that "it was a piece of 'composition,' in which the most fastidiously critical taste could scarcely have suggested an emendation" (3:1330), but he cannot detail the pattern in such a way as to communicate its perfection. He can only describe the nature of the pattern by means of analogies to what we usually take to be aesthetic creations. For example, the house strikes him with the "keenest sense of combined novelty and propriety—in a word, of *poetry*" and he can attribute its "marvelous *effect*" to its artistic arrangement *as a picture*" which some eminent landscape painter had "built" with his brush (3:1335). But to claim that the house is like a poem made of words or like a picture built with a brush instead of with wood and nails is as close to a description of its aesthetic reality as the narrator finds possible.

Richard Wilbur has suggested that "Island of the Fay" (June 1841) is typical of Poe's fiction in that it depicts the process by which reverie transforms "a landscape into a mirror of the psyche" and thus an "interiorization of nature."[49] This is just another way of saying that physical nature is perceived as spiritually alive because of the organizing and unifying imagination of the perceiver/creator. The narrator says of mountains that he loves to regard them as but the "colossal members of one vast animate and sentient whole—a whole whose form (that of the sphere) is the most perfect and most inclusive of all" (2:600). This is a notion of mind as immanent, not only in the body, but also in the world outside, which Gregory Bateson has called indicative of a modern cybernetic epistemology.[50] (This conviction, that there is a larger mind of which the individual is only a subsystem, is one that Poe develops to its ultimate extreme in *Eureka*.)

The narrator says that since we see that the endowment of matter with vitality is the leading principle in the operation of the Deity, we are "madly erring" in thinking that we are more important than a valley. Similarly, Gregory Bateson warns that as long as one arrogates all mind to the self alone and sees the world around as mindless, one is involved in a dangerous split between thought and emotion. As Poe recognized, it is the artist who is concerned with building bridges between different kinds of thought and different levels of the mind to make, as Bateson says, "a statement of their combination" rather than an expression of a single level. What makes "Island of the Fay" typical of Poe is the fact that although the story is about the spiritualizing of the physical it is simultaneously about the perceptual creation of the aesthetic nature of reality, for what the narrator is describing here is not an actual physical scene, but rather an engraving that appeared in the magazine with Poe's sketch. Thus, what motivates the appearance of the fay is its unified nature as picture, not its real nature as exterior scene.

"Morning on the Wissahiccon" (1844) also deals with the aesthetic transformation of reality, but in a radically different way. The sketch is somewhat like "The Island of the Fay" in that it was written to accompany an etching and because it combines the conventions of the objective essay with the subjective involvement of the writer. Whereas the essay portion of the sketch generalizes about natural scenery in America—"real Edens" that no fiction has ever approached—the narrative portion begins when the writer recounts a visit to a brook called the Wissahiccon. There he sees on a cliff "an object of very extraordinary nature" identical with the images about which he has been fantasizing as existing in the same place in a more primitive era. However, in a typical Poe device of undercutting fantasy with mundane reality, his illusion is broken when a servant comes out to feed the elk and the writer realizes that it is a pet that belongs to an English family who occupy a villa in the area. The story is like a satire on "The Island of the Fay," for it reverses the direction of the fantasy process, obliterating it with irony rather than elevating it to the status of reality.

On the opposite end of the spectrum from Poe's fantasies about spiritualizing the physical are his cosmic fantasies in which the spiritual is objectified. This technique is, of course, a more conventional artistic device, since it primarily involves the allegorical method of allegorically objectifying abstract ideas. Nina Baym has argued that the setting of a Poe story is never the external world at all, "but the world of the imagination made substantial for the purpose of coming to know it better. The drama of the setting is the drama of the spectator because he has created, or imagined, that setting."[51]

"The Conversation of Eiros and Charmion" (December 1839), the first of Poe's colloquies that take the pure world of the imagination as their setting, uses the device of having an aged spirit, Charmion, induct a new spirit, Eiros, into the realm of spirit itself, which is here called Aidenn, or Eden. A fulfillment of the romantic ideal, it is a realm in which there is no separation between primary and secondary processes, no separation between map and territory. When Eiros says, "This is indeed no dream," Charmion intones, "Dreams are no more." Indeed, there is no distinction here between dreams and reality. "The Colloquy of Monos and Una" (August 1841) also emphasizes the realization of the ultimate romantic aspiration to return to a prefall state of complete unity. Most of the dialogue is spoken by Monos, who describes the fall of man in the typical romantic way as a fall in perception, as the fall from concrete life into the life of science and abstraction. However, also significant in the piece is the process Monos describes of his own transition from life to death and the concomitant development of a sixth sense that enables him to experience time as pure duration, rather than as the succession of separate events. "The sense of being had at length utterly departed, and there reigned in its stead—instead of all things—dominant and perpetual—the autocrats *Place* and *Time*" (2:617). "Place and Time" here do not refer to a specific location in space nor to a specific point in time, but rather to the abstract concepts of Time as pure duration and Place as ultimate Unity and Oneness. As in *Eureka*, this marks the final dissolution of the physical into the spiritual.

Perhaps the most significant of these so-called cosmic fantasies for an understanding of Poe's basic epistemology is "The Power of Words" (June 1845). Again, the convention used is a colloquy between a new spirit, Oinos, and an older spirit, Agathos. The dialogue begins with the epistemological center of Poe's thought: the quest for ultimate knowledge. When Oinos complains that he thought in his spiritual existence he would have all knowledge and thus be happy, Agathos says that happiness lies not in having knowledge, but in the process of acquiring knowledge, a notion that fits in well with Poe's related romantic idea that although man must continually strive for perfection and Supernal Beauty, he will never achieve it.

Furthermore, Agathos here expounds Poe's idea, derived largely from Coleridge, about the nature of imaginative creation. He argues that creation, or the Primary Imagination, occurred only at the beginning when God spoke everything into existence with the first word; since then, the only creation possible has been that of combination. Furthermore, Agathos expresses the idea Poe develops more fully in *Eureka*—that every act, every impulse on the air affects every individual thing that exists in the universe. If one could trace the undulations of a single impulse one would discover that all so-called new forms are the modifications of old forms. But only the Godhead is able, if given a specific phenomenon, to trace it back to its origin, for only God can refer to all epochs, all effects, and all causes. This is an important element in Poe's notion of the aesthetic nature of reality, for it suggests a cosmological "intertextuality," a thoroughgoing phenomenology in which all "new" forms and perceptions are but the result of schemata created by previous forms and perceptions.

Finally, Agathos presents the argument that gives the piece its title. Since all motions, or impulses on the air, create, and since the source of all motion is thought, words, which spring from thought, are literally impulses on the air. Thus, words have the physical power to create, to call things into being. At this penultimate point in the sketch, as if to indicate that the previous discursive analysis has been but preparatory to the final speaker involvement, Oinos asks Agathos why he weeps over a fair star whose flowers look like a fairy dream and whose volcanoes look like the passions of a turbulent heart. Oinos replies—in what is perhaps Poe's ultimate expression of the romantic ideal of the return to that unified state before the fall into separation between the word and the act, the signifier and the signified—that they are not "like" dreams or a turbulent heart: "They *are!*—they *are!*" He says he "spoke" this star into existence three centuries ago: "Its brilliant flowers *are* the dearest of all unfulfilled dreams, and its raging volcanoes *are* the passions of the most turbulent and unhallowed of hearts" (3:1215).

Two final pieces that share these characteristics of presenting the spiritual as the physical are "Shadow: A Parable" (September 1835) and "Silence: A Fable" (1838), whose subtitles indicate their more traditional method of giving abstractions the status of entities. The two are often considered as a pair, for they share the same elliptical, prose-poem style; moreover, since both seem to be based on the works of other authors, both have also been considered as satires or parodies. As is often typical of Poe, the pieces are simultaneously satiric and serious. "Shadow" is a parable about death, imaged as "vague, and formless, and indefinite—the shadow neither of man, nor God" (2:190). When the shadow speaks, its tones are not those of one being but of a multitude, for it has the accents of thousands of dead friends. The concept is one in which Death is an abstraction, formless and vague, but composed of the actual concrete deaths of all those who have died. The image is tautological, for it suggests that if no one ever died, there would be no Death, for death is an embodiment of all deaths. The parable thus supports Poe's notion of an abstraction being the unified transformation of specific realities.

"Silence," originally named "Siope," is primarily spoken by a demon who describes a dreary desert region where there is a huge gray rock on the shore of a river. Engraved on the rock is the word DESOLATION. A man, whose face shows sorrow, weariness, and disgust with mankind, stands on the summit of the rock as a demon tries to move him. The demon first tries the curse of tumult and brings a tempest, but the man is unmoved; then he tries the curse of silence, and indeed the characters on the rock change to SILENCE. When the man listens but hears nothing, he is terrified and runs away. Like "Shadow," the story reflects the fear of nonbeing, the terror of the loss of individuality. Whereas the Shadow is a nonentity made up of entities, Silence is but a word that does not speak. And indeed, as Poe's more developed fictions show, it is nothingness that terrifies; it is that which cannot be spoken that constitutes the ultimate horror. If words have power, then that which cannot be spoken leaves man powerless.

According to Taylor Stoehr, Poe and many of his narrators are "practitioners of word-magic. They believe that there is a natural (or supernatural) connection between the word and what it names—not merely a conventional semantic relationship."[52] Since for Poe such word magic exists only in the realm of art where things exist only by virtue of words, silence is the ultimate horror because it suggests ultimate nonbeing.

Poe's so-called Beautiful Woman stories are all concerned with the body/spirit dichotomy, for they all deal with the transformation of the female character into a metaphoric function—usually as an embodiment of the bodiless Idea. However, they all differ in terms of their generic status. "Morella" is actually a double story; "Bernice" is a grotesque horror story; "Ligeia" is an allegory; and "Eleanora" is a parable.

"Morella" (April 1835) is primarily about Poe's notion of whether identity is lost at death. Like most women characters in Poe, Morella is not real, but rather idealized, made into a metaphor by the needs of the central male character. The narrator makes it clear from the beginning that what he feels for Morella is not the fires of Eros, but a burning of the soul, a desire whose meaning he can in no way define. Although his fascination for Morella seems to have something to do with her erudition, which is derived primarily from "mystical writings which are usually considered the mere dross of the early German literature," he denies that his desire is related to conscious thought: "In all this, if I err not, my reason had little to do. My convictions, or I forget myself, were in no manner acted upon by the ideal, nor was any tincture of the mysticism which I read, to be discovered, unless I am greatly mistaken in my deeds or my thoughts" (2:230). He seems most concerned with the doctrines of "identity" borrowed from Schelling: that which we call "ourselves," that which distinguishes us from others, is not our physical selves but our consciousness. Once he realizes this, the narrator longs for the physical death of Morella so that her true identity or consciousness, delivered from the dross of the body, might live.

Morella is self-consciously aware of the narrator's obsession with her, for when she is dying, she makes the central assertion in the story about the narrator's need to make woman into metaphor: "The days have never been when thou couldst love me—but her whom in life thou didst abhor, in death thou shalt adore" (2:232). Morella's consciousness or identity does indeed survive in the only way that it can be embodied, that is, in the child, born simultaneously with her death. Because the child has no physical presence for the narrator, he loves her with a "love more fervent than I had believed it possible to feel for any denizen on earth" (2:233). However, at her baptism, when he names her Morella, he identifies her as an individual embodied self and thus "causes" her death.

That body means life and thus death is a central Poe theme that reaches its most famous development in "Ligeia" (September 1838). This is one of Poe's most discussed stories for it provides a particularly clear case of the problem of determining the ontological status of the central character, as well as the epistemological status of the narrator's perception of that character. The ongoing debate need not be rehearsed in any detail here, but, briefly, it began with an essay by Roy Basler in 1944, which argued that the narrator hallucinates Ligeia's return—a position that was vigorously refuted in an article in 1961 by James Schroeter.[53] Other critics see the story as an allegory, in which Ligeia represents either German idealism, the Platonic ideal, or the Jungian anima.[54]

Again, as in "Morella," we have a woman who is noted for her erudition, "buried in studies of a nature more than all else adapted to deaden impressions of the outward world" (2:310). But Poe pushes the metaphoric nature of Ligeia to further extremes than in "Morella." Ligeia seems to have no source in the real world. The narrator cannot remember when he first met her, nor does he know her paternal name; she is less a physical reality than a metaphoric vehicle for that which has no name or presence. What most characterizes Ligeia is what the narrator calls her "expression," a physiognomic pattern that the narrator finds it impossible to describe, for "expression" is a unified combination of individual features, an overall pattern that exceeds the sum of its parts. About "expression," the narrator says: "Ah, word of no meaning! behind whose vast latitude of mere sound we intrench our ignorance of so much of the spiritual" (2:313). This is a central passage in Poe, for whatever is thought to be spiritual is a result of expression, the pattern of the human face.

The problem of expression or pattern, a pattern for which one finds no concrete correlative, is best expressed by the narrator when he talks about just being on the verge of "full knowledge" of Ligeia's expression, feeling that knowledge approaching and yet not being able to fully possess it. The closest he can come is what he calls the strangest mystery of all, for he finds in the commonest objects of nature "a circle of analogies to that expression. . . .I derived, from many existences in the material world, a sentiment such as I felt always aroused, within me, by her large and luminous orbs" (2:314). He recognizes it in a rapidly growing vine, in a moth, a butterfly, a chrysalis, a stream of running water, certain sounds from stringed instruments, and from some passages in books—all of which suggest that Ligeia is a metaphoric embodiment of intangible and inchoate experience in a much more extreme way than Morella is.

The story also deals more explicitly than "Morella" with the idea that true identity is consciousness, not body, and that the ultimate human desire is to "live" truly, that is, not physically, but as consciousness, or "Will." The repeated passage from Glanville emphasizes the notion: "And the will therein lieth, which dieth not. Who knoweth the mysteries of the will, with its vigor? For God is but a great will pervading all things by nature of its intentness. Man doth not yield him to the angels, nor unto death utterly, save only through the weakness of his feeble will" (2:310). Will and consciousness are synonymous in the story, for Ligeia represents the desire for sustaining life as consciousness, as form, as aesthetic reality—a "desire for life,—for life—*but* for life" (2:317). The ultimate human desire is for life as consciousness, which would be possible if it were not for life as physical reality.

After the death of Ligeia, the story becomes merely the narrative working out of the theme of sustaining life as consciousness; but it seems quite clear that it is not the consciousness or will of Ligeia that sustains her, for she signifies a nonconscious ideality, but the consciousness or will of the one who desires her. The fact that Ligeia is but a pattern that can be imposed metaphorically on inchoate experiences is further indicated by what the narrator calls his perversity in setting up a surrounding that is all pattern. The importance of the room in which he lives after Ligeia's death is indicated by Poe's decision to spend almost a thousand words describing it. And what characterizes it is not that it has any central theme or motif, not that it has any "system" or what in "The Philosophy of Furniture" he calls "keeping," but rather that it is a chamber of dreams, like the room of his Byronic hero in "The Assignation." The carpets have bedlam patterns; the ceiling has semigothic, semi-Druidical devices and a censer of a Saracenic pattern, and the walls are hung with tapestries with arabesque patterns that are changeable in aspect when viewed from different points of view and that have on a phantasmagoric effect when the breeze animates them. What we see here is a context that is pure pattern, with no correspondent reality in the external world and with no external world to interfere with it, a world of romance.

And within this world, since it is the world of art that is also the world of desire, the consciousness of Ligeia can be reanimated in the mere shell of a body that is Rowena. The last part of the story depicts the battle of the narrator's own will to bring Ligeia into being in the art-world chamber in which Rowena lies dead. The waves of animation alternating with death reflect his own desire, for each time that he has memories or visions of Ligeia, Rowena stirs. All night he participates in what he calls a "hideous drama of revivication" that repeats and relapses. "Let me hurry to a conclusion," he says, and indeed moves to the climax in which Rowena, as if in a dream, moves across the room toward him, until he recognizes in her, as the narrator did in "Morella," the features of the one who was lost.

Of course, the fact that the story ends at just this point, with no explanation of what follows the seeming reanimation of Ligeia, indicates that no such supernatural phenomenon occurred. Instead, what the narrator has observed is the projection of his own desire to see the similitude of life within death, to see metaphoric vitality in dead matter, to see true identity of consciousness in which physicality is merely a carrier. And in Poe, the most intense kind of consciousness is that which perceives the reality of expression, that ineffable sense of identity that is constituted by pattern alone. In this sense, the narrator is the romantic artist who, to use Coleridge's terms, projects the "I AM" on to things in the world and makes them live.

"Berenice" (March 1835) is either a purposeful parody of this same metaphoric theme or else a serious version of the theme which Poe, like many critics, recognizes as a failure. It is one thing to use the expression of the eyes in "Ligeia" as the metaphoric carrier of meaning; it is somewhat more difficult to make the white teeth of Berenice such a vehicle, although it must have seemed plausible enough to Poe in concept. After all, what Poe wanted was some physical manifestation of identity that was both expressive of the self and suggestive of permanence. And the one last remnant of expression that remains after death and decay of the body would be the teeth. As Jules Zanger, who sees the story as a case of Poe's failure to achieve the transformation of the sensational gothic of the day into a "genuine fantasy of ideas," points out, the teeth "represent the external aspect of the skull beneath the skin, that which will be left when all the living changes have come to an end."[55]

Perhaps the strange and seemingly overgeneralized first paragraph of the story indicates Poe's realization that his metaphor did not work, for it seems a case of special pleading. He focuses on the manifold misery and wretchedness of the earth that derives from the fact that beauty results from unloveliness, that evil results from good, and that joy is born out of sorrow: "Either the memory of past bliss is the anguish of to-day, or the agonies which *are* have their origin in the ecstasies which *might have been*" (2:209). Again, as in "Ligeia," the narrator focuses on a chamber, this time filled with books rather than arabesque images—"a palace of imagination . . . the wild dominions of monastic thought and erudition" (2:210). Spending his childhood with books and in reverie results in what he calls an inversion in his thoughts: "The realities of the world affected me as visions, and as visions only, while the wild ideas of the land of dreams became, in turn,—not the material of my everyday existence—but in very deed that existence utterly and solely in itself" (2:210). This is the most resounding statement in Poe's fiction of the central thrust of his vision, for it reflects the basic romantic mode of presenting the everyday world as strange and unusual and the fantastic world of dream and imagination as the only reality.

Moreover, this is Poe's most emphatic statement of his idea of the intensity of interest. Although the disease that falls on Berenice is the disease of epilepsy (therefore another metaphor, like mesmerism, for death), the narrator's disease, what he calls a "monomania," consists of a "morbid irritability of those properties of the mind in metaphysical science termed the *attentive*" (2:211). He describes an "*intensity of interest*" for "even the most ordinary objects of the universe." The objects with which he becomes absorbed are not objects as such, for he singles out such things as a frivolous device in the typography of a book, a shadow falling aslant a tapestry, the steady flame of a lamp, the perfume of a flower, and the monotonous repetition of some common word, "until the sound, by dint of frequent repetition, ceased to convey any idea whatever to the mind" (2:212).

This condition, like the condition of the perverse, defies analysis or explanation. Furthermore, he insists that his "undue, earnest, and morbid attention thus excited by objects in their own nature frivolous" (2:212) is not to be confused with mere rumination. It is not, he argues, even an exaggeration of such rumination, but something quite different. Whereas the dreamer gradually loses sight of the object of his attention in deductions and suggestions deriving from it, in his own case, the primary object of his attention assumes an unreal importance and at the termination of the reverie, instead of disappearing, attains that "supernaturally exaggerated interest which was the prevailing feature of the disease. In a word, the powers of mind more particularly exercised were with me, as I have said before, the *attentive*, and are, with the day-dreamer, the *speculative*" (2:212).

The narrator is fully aware of his obsession, for he notes that he never loved Berenice as a living and breathing individual, but as the embodiment of a dream: "not as a being of the earth, earthly, but as the abstraction of such a being; not as a thing to admire, but to analyze—not as an object of love, but as the theme of the most abstruse although desultory speculation" (2:214). As Berenice becomes more and more emaciated, that is, as the body wastes away and the face becomes more skull-like, the teeth become more predominant. Consequently, it is the teeth that become the focus of his monomania; "they alone were present to the mental eye," for he transforms them into a metaphoric embodiment of pure "idea" and thus the ultimate metaphor of his desire. The only twist in the story, a grotesque twist that contributes to its ghastly nature, is the fact that Berenice is not dead but only in a epileptic coma when the narrator pulls out her teeth as she lies in her tomb. This "turn of the screw" suggests the theme of "The Oval Portrait"—that the body must be drained off so that the spirit, which can only exist as art or pure consciousness, can survive.

"Eleanora" (4 September 1841) is Poe's parable version of this body/spirit theme. In this version the protagonist recalls a visionary female from his youth who represents the idea of pure consciousness. Like Poe's many other male protagonists, he is a man of vigorous fancy whom men have called mad; however, he says, in an explicit statement of Poe's own epistemological preferences, the question is not yet settled: "whether madness is or is not the loftiest intelligence—whether much that is glorious—whether all that is profound—does not spring from disease of thought—from *moods* of mind exalted at the expense of the general intellect. They who dream by day are cognizant of many things which escape those who dream only by night. In their gray visions they obtain glimpses of eternity and thrill, in awakening, to find that they have been upon the verge of the great secret," (2:638). Curiously, of the two different conditions the narrator recognizes, the lucid side is aligned with the memory of events of the first part of his life (which is idealized and parablelike in style) whereas the shadow and doubt relate to the present (which is ordinary and physically real). At the beginning of his story, he says that what he will tell of the first period we should believe, but what he tells of the present period we may doubt. This is a puzzling reversal, for the fable part of the story is the most cryptic, whereas the second part is self-evident.

The early life has all the earmarks of the fairy tale, for the protagonist and his cousin Eleanora live an idyllic isolated life in the Valley of the Many-Colored Grass, knowing nothing of the world outside at all. The valley is characterized as a world of dreams and fantasy, penetrated only by the River of Silence, until Love enters their hearts and a change falls over all things in the valley: "Strange brilliant flowers, star-shaped, burst out upon the trees where no flowers had been known before. The tints of the green carpet deepened, and when, one by one, the white daisies shrank away, there sprang up, in place of them, ten by ten of the ruby-red asphodel" (2:640). It does not require a Freudian to recognize that this imagery suggests the intrusion of physicality into the fairy-tale world of the children of the valley. The result is a cloud that covers all things, shutting them up within "a magic prison house of grandeur and of glory." Inevitably, Eleanora feels the "finger of Death was upon her bosom—that, like the ephemeron, she had been made perfect in loveliness only to die" (2:642). She makes the narrator promise that he will not transfer their love to some woman in the outer, everyday world, a vow he willingly makes, involving "a penalty the exceeding great horror of which" will not allow him to reveal (2:642). As we know from other Poe stories, the fact that the penalty cannot be named means that it is the ultimate horror: the disintegration of the self. It means the fall into the pit, the fall into nothingness.

In the final portion of the story we learn little of the protagonist's present life, except that he finds himself in a city where all things "might have served to blot from recollection the sweet dreams I had dreamed so long in the Valley of the Many-Colored Grass" (2:644). Indeed, he does forget and falls in love with the ethereal Ermengarde, whom he marries without dreading the curse he has invoked; in the silence of the night he hears the familiar voice of Eleanora: "Sleep in peace!—for the Spirit of Love reigneth and ruleth, and, in taking to thy passionate heart her who is Ermengarde thou art absolved, for reasons which shall be made known to thee in Heaven, of thy vows unto Eleanora" (2:645). This story is so problematical because there is no basis from within the story itself by which to explain Eleanora's forgiveness of the protagonist. Nothing in the conventions of the parable nor in its ostensible body/spirit theme can account for the fact that the protagonist does not have to suffer the unspeakable punishment for the violation of his promise. The most plausible explanation—one that seems consistent with Poe's other stories of the Beautiful Woman—is that Eleanora's whispered exoneration of his transgression suggests that the "Spirit of Love" transcends any individual manifestation of love—an idealization that indeed can only be made known to the narrator in Heaven, as it was made known to Eleanora herself after her death.

Poe's obsession with the ideal and his abhorrence of body is less likely to be a result of his own psychological anxieties and fears, as some readers have assumed, than an inevitable implication of his metaphysical and aesthetic theories that true reality is purely pattern rather than merely physical.

Obsession and Unity of Effect

One of the most significant of Poe's contributions to the development of the tight aesthetic unity of the short story form derives from one of his most typical themes: the theme of psychological obsession embodied in a first-person narrator. Poe transforms the ironically distanced and discursive first-person narrator familiar to readers of *Spectator* essays and the stories of Washington Irving into a narrator who is so obsessed with the subject of his narration that the obsession itself becomes the thematic center of the story and thus creates the story's tight aesthetic unity. When one is obsessed, by definition, one's obsession becomes the center of one's experience and perception. As a result, everything the obsessed person experiences or perceives is transformed into an image of the obsession, and nothing is allowed to enter into the experiential framework of the person except those things that fit in with the obsession. David Karnath has suggested that in a typical Poe story, unity is achieved by means of sustained intense attention: "With the characters this derives from acute logical attention to a single problem, or from madness, grief, or threat. There is no relaxing and the dominant mood washes out all others and gives all events its own coloring."[56]

A story that is unified around a single impression calculated to create a single effect is indeed the artistic equivalent of a psychological obsession. By single effect, Poe does not mean a simple sensational effect, but rather what Aristotle means by *dianoia*, that is, that point when *mythos* or story is transformed into theme or overall pattern.[57] The overall pattern, the almost obsessive center that holds the relevant motifs together, is the single effect. Moreover, as in an obsession, not only are all irrelevant things excluded, but seemingly trivial things are magnified or transformed into meaningful motifs relevant to the central theme.

Such essay/stories as "The Premature Burial" and "The Imp of the Perverse" reflect the transition from a first-person story with a seemingly detached discursive narrator to a first-person story with an obsessed narrator involved in the topic of his discussion; they thus mirror the movement from the ironic, urban eighteenth-century narrator to the obsessed narrator-protagonist developed by Poe. Although "The Black Cat" begins with a discursive exposition on perverseness, its immediate movement toward involved narrative marks an intensification of Poe's development of the complete obsessive narrative. "The Tell-Tale Heart" and "The Cask of Amontillado" go even further; consisting solely of narrative, they no longer need the motivational support of the essay base.

Poe's focus on perversity introduces still another element of the aesthetic unity that results from psychological obsession. In such a highly unified story built around a central effect, the establishment of motivation is an inevitable problem, for when one is motivated by an obsession, there is no way to present the motivation in a realistic fashion in terms of ordinary cause and effect. Events motivated by obsession indeed seem unmotivated. But in a highly unified romantic story, as opposed to a realistic mimetic fiction, the question of why certain events are included rather than others becomes a question of "motivation of the motifs," as the Russian formalists discuss that process, rather than motivation of "as if" real human action. In stories that are highly unified as a result of narrator obsession, motifs are motivated less by similitude or the need to create a correspondence with the external world than by the demands of coherence; that is, by purely aesthetic demands.

Poe's discussion of his composition of "The Raven" in "The Philosophy of Composition," makes it clear that aesthetic motivation, not realistic motivation, is what matters to him—for Poe motivation by demands of coherence rather than by demands of correspondence is crucial for the construction of the short story. Furthermore, in Poe's stories, when characters become self-consciously aware of their own narrative style or the problems of narration, the reader becomes aware that what is truly obsessive in these protagonists is not so much a psychological compulsion as an aesthetic one; the protagonists, like Prince Prospero in "The Masque of the Red Death," create hermetically sealed texts, in which they live.

"The Premature Burial" (31 July 1844) has some elements of the hoax, for it depends on the "truth is stranger than fiction" convention so common to the hoax stories. Indeed, the story begins with the basic problem of the ambiguity of truth and fiction, for the narrator, who at first seems little more than an objective journalistic teller piling up examples of a modern phenomenon, begins by noting that there are certain themes too horrible for fiction. These themes can only be presented with propriety if they have the "severity and majesty of truth [to] sanctify and sustain them" (3:955). He notes that such horrors as earthquakes, plagues, and massacres give us "pleasurable pain" only because their "reality" or "history" excites us. As is usual with Poe, the narrator is not interested in generalities of disaster, which are indeed only diffuse and abstract; he asserts that the ultimate woe is particular: "the ghastly extremes of agony are endured by man the unit, and never by man the mass" (3:955). This very assertion establishes "The Premature Burial" as a fiction rather than an essay or history, for, as Poe often emphasizes, fiction deals with the individual, even though when it does it suggests a universal horror by its representativeness.

Poe is interested here, as he often is, in the ambiguity that distinguishes life and death, for the narrator notes that the boundary line between the two is vague and shadowy. In some of the hoax stories, such as "Mesmeric Revelation" and "The Case of M. Valdemar," it is the actual line between the two that so fascinates Poe; elsewhere he is concerned with states that "mimic" death, such as "madness," "hallucination," or "sleep"—in short, any state that is an alternative to ordinary everyday experience. As he makes clear in the narrator's opening expository remarks, Poe's choice of the premature burial theme is as calculated as his choice of the motifs in his discussion of the composition of "The Raven":

> It may be asserted, without hesitation, that *no* event is so terribly well adapted to inspire the supremeness of bodily and of mental distress, as is burial before death. . . . We know of nothing so agonizing on Earth—we can dream of nothing half so hideous in the realms of the nethermost Hell. And thus all narratives upon this topic have an interest profound; an interest, nevertheless, which, through the sacred awe of the topic itself, very properly and very peculiarly depends upon our conviction of the *truth* of the matter narrated. (3:962–63)

With his discursive introduction completed, the narrator moves from the eighteenth-century technique of verifying the truth by reporting factual events to the nineteenth-century technique of verifying the truth by invoking his own personal experience. As usual, personal experience in Poe is anything but straightforward.

When the narrator begins to relate his own experience, we learn that he is just the opposite of a disinterested journalistic reporter. Because he suffers from catalepsy, he lives in constant fear that he will fall into a trance, be taken for dead, and be buried alive. He is so preoccupied with what he calls this "one spectral and ever-prevalent Idea" that he takes elaborate precautions, such as placing food and water in the family vault, padding the coffin, and providing a bell. This comic treatment of the place of death as a place of life is an ironic reversal calculated to prepare the reader for the comic reversal at the end.

Another Poe motif introduced here is the movement from one state to another and the resultant lack of memory concerning the previous state—a motif most emphatically dealt with in "The Pit and the Pendulum." For when the narrator finds himself emerging from total unconsciousness, two questions are immediate: "Where am I now?"—that is, what is my current physical state or ontological status; and "How did I get here?"—that is, what has motivated my current ontological status? Many Poe characters deal with this problem by asking whether they are awake or asleep, whether they are under the influence of opium, whether they are mad, or whether they are alive or dead. When the narrator faces pitch blackness and feels a hard wood substance only six inches above his face, he confronts what he takes to be the reality of his nightmare: that he has been entombed alive. At this point, he makes the ultimate challenge to the nature of his ontological or psychological state and screams, thereby regaining full possession of his memory and realizing that he is in the quite ordinary situation of being in a closed berth in a ship.

But the reversals here are not so simple as they first appear. The narrator's obsessive belief that he will be buried alive is like a fiction he creates; a psychological obsession is like the short story in that the obsessed character creates a story about his experience that is completely coherent, even though it may have no correspondence with external reality. In "The Premature Burial" the narrator presents two kinds of accounts of premature burial: true-life histories and his own nightmares about the phenomenon. However, the event narrated in the story is neither a real premature burial nor a nightmare, but rather an actual event that so simulates premature burial that it deceives the narrator into thinking that his obsession, that is, his fiction, has come true. But what he discovers is that what seemed so "real" (fulfillment of his obsession) was indeed merely real (a similitude of his obsession). As a result of this experience, the narrator frees himself from his obsession and gives up reading stories about it; no longer will he be a collector of premature burial tales: "I read no 'Night Thoughts'—no fustian about churchyards—no bugaboo tales *such as this*" (3:969). Although there are "bugaboo tales" in "The Premature Burial," it itself is not such a tale, but rather a parody that contains the "bugaboo" and the debunking of the "bugaboo" both at the same time.

"The Imp of the Perverse" (July 1845) is not a debunking parody, but it does embody the transition from the objective narrator of the discursive essay to the involved and obsessed narrator of the subjective tale. The story begins in the essay format with the author (one cannot call him a narrator until a narrative is recounted) describing a human propensity—what he calls a "*prima mobilia* of the human soul"—previously ignored because there seems to be no reason for it, either in a divine or a human plan. The writer argues that if one proceeded a posteriori from observable evidence, rather than a priori from previous assumptions about God's plan, thinkers would have to admit "an innate and primitive principle of human action, a paradoxical something, which we may call *perverseness*, for want of a more characteristic term" (3:1220). He then describes the principle as a "*mobile* without motive, a motive not *motivirit*" (3:1220). However, more than acting without a comprehensible object or motive, the principle involves acting precisely because one should not. This radical impulse fascinates Poe because it cannot be broken down any further; it evades analysis by its very elementary nature. Like the notion of unparticled matter he discusses in *Eureka*, it is a singleness, an irreducible oneness.

After citing two somewhat trivial examples of perverseness—circumlocution by a speaker and procrastination about performing a task—the writer discusses the ultimate implication of the phenomenon in relation to vertigo experienced at the edge of a precipice: "To indulge for a moment, in any attempt at *thought*, is to be inevitably lost; for reflection but urges us to forbear, and *therefore* it is, I say, that we *cannot*" (3:1223). Perverseness is for Poe a fascinating paradox, for it is unreasonable precisely in proportion to the fact that reason urges it. It is an example of pushing the reason to such extremes that it becomes unreasonable.

Having presented the ultimate motiveless obsession and given examples of it, the objective essayist now becomes an obsessed narrator, telling the story that will account for his "wearing these fetters" and "tenanting this cell of the condemned" (3:1224). But the crime he committed was not the result of perverseness, and thus not the reason he is now incarcerated; rather he is where he is because of his confession, which resulted from uttering the phrase, "I am safe." By thinking that he is safe if only he does not confess, he is perversely drawn closer and closer to making a confession. To call his confession the result of "guilt" is to oversimplify the problem, at least unless we accept "guilt" as more than a mere moral fear. The man confesses only because he knows he should not, not because he feels guilty. He is caught only because he says, "I am safe." There is just as much reason to believe he confesses because he is proud of his cleverness in getting away with the crime as there is for believing he feels guilty for committing it. For after all, there is no pleasure in getting away with a crime unless it is known that you got away with it; and then, of course, you cannot get away with it.

"The Black Cat" (14 August 1843) is closely related to "The Imp of the Perverse," for the narrator uses some of the same exposition about the phenomenon of perverseness. But "The Black Cat" is primarily a narrative in which the exposition is embedded rather than separated as a preliminary motivating device as it is in "The Imp of the Perverse." Although no one would mistake this story for a journalistic article about external reality—for it begins with the voice of the obsessed narrator— its predominant motif is the typical short story device of transforming the ordinary into the extraordinary by means of obsession. By beginning with the phrase, "For the most wild, yet most homely narrative which I am about to pen, I neither expect nor solicit belief" (3:849), the teller makes several things quite explicit: that he is writing rather than speaking, that the story is both ordinary and extraordinary at once, and that it is true—even though he does not expect any one to believe it to be true. Furthermore, he makes it clear that what he will describe is not the result of those alternate states of reality known as madness or dream, but an actual event that takes place in the ordinary, everyday world. He claims his purpose is to place before the world without comment "a series of mere household events" (3:849), adding that he hopes that sometime in the future someone more calm and logical than he will perceive in the circumstances that he details "with awe nothing more than an ordinary succession of very natural causes and effects" (3:850).

Once again, as so often with Poe, precisely by suggesting that the events manifest merely naturalistic causes and effects, the narrator suggests that they are the result of obsession, which, by its very nature, is a cause that evades analysis. Although the narrator says he is not so weak as to try to establish a "sequence of cause and effect" between his killing the cat and the mysterious burning of his house on the night of the deed, he then describes the only motivation possible for the burning of the house; that is, the purely aesthetic motivation of imprinting the image of a cat as in bas relief on the one remaining wall of his house. The naturalistic explanation—that someone must have seen the fire and cut the dead cat down and thrown it inside to wake him— only suggests the absurdity of trying to find reasonable explanations for purely aesthetic signifying actions. The "cause" of the image of the cat is the obsessive nature of the narrator that has been translated into the obsessive unity of the story—a unity that demands the plaster image of the cat, just as it demands the reappearance of another cat that reflects the first—a cat that, like the original one, has lost one eye and has the image of a gallows around its neck. Indeed, the creation of such obsessive images is precisely what this story is about.

Because killing a cat is not a sufficient crime to justify the poetic justice demanded by the dénouement, the deflection of the blow meant for the cat must strike the wife. The narrator has no sense of guilt for this act; thus, to claim that his final undoing is the result of simple guilt is to make a claim for the only motive that common sense and ordinary morality can understand. It is not guilt that undoes him, but glee, as he raps on the very wall behind which his wife's body rots upright. That the cat embodies this very image of paradoxical perverseness is suggested by the way the narrator describes the sound it makes when he raps on the wall: "A howl—a wailing shriek, half of horror, half of triumph, such as might have arisen only out of hell, conjointly from the throats of the damned in their agony and of the demons that exult in the damnation" (3:859). To embody both agony and exultation at once is the essence of the paradox that makes up his obsession—his motiveless motive—and thus the obsessive unity of the story itself.

The relationship between obsession and unity is even more obvious in "The Tell-Tale Heart" and "The Cask of Amontillado," for these two stories are narratives of obsessive acts with no exposition to account for their motives at all. In fact, the lack of a clearly explained motive in the two stories indicate that they have moved the farthest away from the eighteenth-century essay voice and the closest to the nineteenth-century obsessive voice. "The Tell-Tale Heart" (January 1843) begins with the establishment of the oral nature of the narrative as a response to a direct accusation of madness: "True—nervous—very, very dreadfully nervous I had been and am; but why *will* you say that I am mad?" (3:792). And since the narrator claims that the only proof of his sanity is the manner of the telling itself ("Hearken! and observe how healthily—how calmly I can tell you the whole story" [3:792]), it is precisely the manner of the telling that the reader must attend to to determine the nature of his madness.

But as soon as the narrator begins, the problems of determining motivation in this story also begin. The first thing the narrator does is to insist that he has no object in killing the old man, no passion; the old man had never wronged him, never insulted him, and the narrator has no desire for his gold. "I think it was its eye!": to try to account for the murder of the old man any other way than in terms of the "eye" is to try to escape Poe's presentation of a motive that is obsessive and metaphoric rather than logical and realistic. To understand motive in terms of metaphor—and this indeed is the connection between unity and obsession that Poe contributes to the development of the short story—one cannot refer to a corresponding external reality outside the story. Instead, the reader must determine the identification of the story's unity and the narrator's obsession by analyzing the manifestations of the obsession within the story; that is, those elements that by their very obsessive recurrence distinguish it. The first element is, of course, the eye itself, but since there is nothing naturalistic, or even supernaturalistic, about the eye to account for the narrator's aversion to it, the reader must find other related motifs that will lead him or her back to this central metaphor and thus to the primary obsessive/metaphoric motivation.[58]

One obvious motif in the story is the theme of time. In opening the door to the old man's room, the narrator says "A watch's minute hand moves more quickly than did mine" (3:793). He also notes the old man sitting up listening to "death watches" (a kind of beetle that makes a ticking sound) in the wall. The primary time reference is the sound he claims he hears of the old man's heart beating as he listens at the door—"a dull, quick sound, such as a watch makes when enveloped in cotton" (3:795). The linking of the notion of time with the beating of the old man's heart connects with two other important motifs in the story: the title "The Tell-Tale Heart," and the narrator's identification with the old man. If we ask what kind of tale the heart "tells" in this story we know that it does not "tell" in the usual metaphoric way; that is, we cannot look into the secret heart of the narrator to ascertain his motive. Instead, the tale the heart tells is linked to the beating of the heart being identified with time; that is, the tale the heart tells is the tale every heart tells: every beat marks an irretrievable moment in time that takes one closer to death.

By looking at obsessive repetitions in the story to determine significant motifs, we can recognize the identification between the narrator and the old man. When the narrator puts his head inside the door, he knows the old man is listening to the death watches in the wall, for he says it is "just as I have done" (3:794). When the old man groans, he says he knew the sound well, for many a night at midnight a similar groan has welled up from his own heart: "I knew what the old man felt, and pitied him" (3:795). Moreover, as he stands with his head just inside the door and hears the sound like a watch in cotton, he says he knows that sound well, for it is the beating of the old man's heart. Excluding the possibility that he can hear the old man's heartbeat from across the room, we can only conclude he mistakes his own heartbeat for that of the old man. Not only does this suggest that the relationship between the narrator and the old man is one of identification, in which the narrator sees himself in the old man, but it also suggests that the motif of overacuteness of hearing has the further function in the story of leading the narrator to mistake inner reality for outer reality.

This identification with the old man—which the narrator metaphorically alludes to when he tells the police that the scream that was reported was his own in a dream—and his mistaking inner reality for outer reality (the basis for metaphor itself) reaches its dénouement when, as the narrator sits with the police he begins to hear a sound in his ears: "a low, dull, quick sound—*much such a sound as a watch makes when enveloped in cotton*" (3:797). Although he insists that the sound is not within his ears but outside in the world, we know that it is inside his mind and being projected outward. The fact that the story deals centrally with this mistaken interpretation of inner reality for outer reality is further indicated by the narrator's claim that he becomes more agitated, foaming and raving, grating the chair across the floor, while the police chat pleasantly—obviously an hallucinatory projection. Finally, when he gives himself away by shrieking, "It is the beating of his hideous heart," the projection and identification are complete.

After having pieced together all these motifs, we can confront the initial problem of motivation: what does the eye have to do with the narrator's killing the old man? The answer lies in determining the relationships between time/heart, identity/eye, and inner reality-versus-outer-reality/overacuteness of hearing. In terms of the overall obsessive unity of the story one would think that if the narrator's hearing were so acute, it would not be the old man's eye, that is, the organ of sight, that would be so important to him. However, by saying that hearing is important, the narrator instructs the reader, "don't look, but listen." When we listen to the word "eye," rather than look at it, we understand that when the narrator says he must destroy the "eye," he means he must destroy the "I"—a hypothesis that ties together all of the motifs except the time/heart theme. Once we know that by killing the old man the narrator fulfills his desire to destroy himself, all that is left to understand is the motivation for this act of self-destruction.

Since every beat of the heart is a tick of time that brings one closer to death, once one becomes obsessively aware of this inevitability, one desires to avoid it. The logic that the narrator follows, a kind of "psycho-logic" of obsession that holds the story together and provides a metaphoric explanation embedded within it, is that since it is one's identity or ego, that is, one's "I," that makes one the inevitable heir to time and thus death, the only way to combat this inevitability is to destroy the ego or self. Since to save the self by destroying the self is an intolerable paradox, the narrator projects the self onto the other. He does not wish to destroy the "I" directly, but only indirectly, by destroying the "eye" of the old man with whom he identifies. Such an explanation is the kind of cause-and-effect analysis that the narrator of "The Black Cat" calls for at the beginning of his story.

The single effect of "The Tell-Tale Heart" is indeed its *dianoia*, the overall pattern embodied in the telling of the story itself. What the narrator describes is what he would call a "flawless plot," that is, a plot to commit a crime and get away with it. But it is precisely the plot or the pattern that gives him away. The central dramatic event underlying "The Tell-Tale Heart" is the narrator's plot to kill the old man; the overall pattern of the fiction is his telling of the plot to the story's embedded listeners. Even as the themes of the murder are those of time, identification, the eye, and inner-versus-outer reality, the themes of the telling are those of methodical calmness, madness, sanity, cleverness, dissimulation, sagacity. The method with which the narrator performs the central dramatic event also characterizes the tone with which he now tells of it. What in effect the teller does is create a plot to catch himself. And every time he tells the story he is caught all over again; its series of "tell-tale" signs "tells the tale" by revealing the pattern of the plot.

"The Cask of Amontillado" (November 1846) is, if possible, even more tightly organized than "The Tell-Tale Heart" around an obsession that is synonymous with the unity of the story itself. Again, obsession and plot and the telling of the story to reveal its overall pattern are the central issues. The reader is cued in the first paragraph about the problems of motivation and the status of the story, for the first sentence seems to establish the motive for the central dramatic event even as it does not: "The thousand injuries of Fortunato I had borne as I best could, but when he ventured upon insult I vowed revenge" (3:1256). The reader has no way of knowing what these "thousand injuries" and the mysterious insult are and thus can make no judgment about whether Montresor's revenge is justifiable. By referring to "you, who so well know the nature of my soul," Montresor also makes it clear that, as in "The Tell-Tale Heart," what we have here is an oral presentation directed at an embodied but silent listener rather than a manuscript intended for reading by absent readers.

The first paragraph establishes not only that this is a story about a successful revenge, but also the criteria for the success: "I must not only punish but punish with impunity. A wrong is unredressed when retribution overtakes its redresser. It is equally unredressed when the avenger fails to make himself felt as such to him who has done the wrong" (3:1256). Once these criteria have been set, it is clear that the unity of the story must derive from the successful completion of the revenge. As in "The Tell-Tale Heart," what the reader needs to do to understand this story is to determine its pattern, its overall plot— remembering that Montresor's plot to revenge himself on Fortunato is only the pattern of the event, not the pattern of the completed discourse, which is not only the event but also the telling of it. Almost immediately the reader determines that the principle of unity is the principle of irony, for the first and most obvious of the many ironies presented is the fact that Montresor has made sure that his servants will all be gone by explicitly ordering them to stay at home.[59]

Irony by its very nature is rhetorical, an element of discourse, not an element of external reality. Although in everyday reality an accident or coincidence may sometimes be taken to be ironic, this is a purely human attribution. In discourse, on the other hand, where there is no such thing as coincidence or accident—since the author controls all the elements of the story—we can legitimately designate certain events or remarks as ironic. There are two kinds of irony in "The Cask of Amontillado": the obvious ironies that Montresor creates and controls—such as urging Fortunato to leave the dangerous catacombs, knowing that the more he urges him to leave the more he will want to stay—and the ironies motivated by the overall pattern of the story—such as the fact that Fortunato, who fancies himself a wine expert, is wearing the cap and bells of a fool.

Among the ironies created and sustained by Montresor are the verbal ironies of telling Fortunato he is "luckily" met, agreeing with him that he will not die of a cough, and drinking a toast to his long life. Such remarks are understood by the reader as ironic, of course, only after the story has ended and one understands its overall pattern; however, because Montresor has already constructed his plot and thus predetermined its end, he can engage in ironies that give pleasure to him both as he utters them in the past and as he tells the story in the present. In contrast, the irony that Fortunato's name suggests he is "fortunate" is an irony created by the overall ironic pattern of the story, as is the most important such irony: Montresor's coat of arms and his family motto. The motto—No one attacks me with impunity—has already been alluded to in the opening revenge criteria, but the image on the coat of arms—"A huge human foot d'or, in a field azure; the foot crushes the serpent rampant whose fangs are embedded in the heel"—is a sign that sets up an ambiguity that will not be resolved at the end of the action, but only at the end of the telling of the action. For it is only when we understand the present storytelling situation of Montresor that the total irony of the discourse becomes clear.

The last paragraph of the story brings us back from the past event of the story to the present telling of it, for after Montresor describes finishing the wall and rebuilding the old rampart of bones, he says, "For the half of a century no mortal has disturbed them" (3:1263). At this point we are concerned not about Montresor's motivation for killing Fortunato, but about his motivation for telling about it. If we go back to the first paragraph and ask who would know the nature of Montresor's soul, we cannot say it is the reader, for at that point in the story the reader knows nothing about Montresor's soul. We can legitimately hypothesize that the listener is a priest and that Montresor is an old man who is dying and making a final confession. If such a hypothesis is plausible, we can refer back to Montresor's criteria for revenge and determine whether it has been fulfilled. And, given the fact that irony has dominated the structure of the story, we might expect that the dénouement has not resolved that question straightforwardly. Indeed, it seems that Fortunato has fulfilled the revenge criteria better than

Montresor has. For whereas Montresor never makes it clear to Fortunato why he is walling him up, Fortunato has for 50 years continued to make his vengeance clear as such to Montresor. Furthermore, if Montresor still feels guilt for the crime, he has not had his revenge with impunity, whereas Fortunato has, for no one can further harm the dead.

With this hypothesis, the relevance of other elements in the story, such as the coat of arms, become clear. If we say that the foot signifies Montresor, then the snake Fortunato who has bitten him still has his fangs embedded. One final irony, however, is that even if our hypothesis that Montresor tells the story as a final confession to cleanse his soul before death is correct, the tone or manner of his telling makes it clear that he has not atoned, for he enjoys himself in the telling too much—as much, in fact, as he did when he committed the crime itself. Thus, Montresor's plot to murder Fortunato so delights him by its perfection that in the very telling of it he undercuts its nature as repentant confession and condemns himself in gleeful boast.

Detective Fiction

The most significant contribution Poe's detective stories make to the development of the short story consists of their basing a story's central theme and structure on the very process by which the reader perceives that unifying structure and pattern. The detective stories are Poe's most explicit example of works in which questions of interpretation are not outside the story but are involved in every stage of the narrative development. As Ann Jefferson has noted in her discussion of the prophetic in fiction, narratives not only depict events and actions, they also depict interpretations of those events and actions: "The characters of narrative are not just agents or actors, but continuously involved in a process of reading and analyzing the events and situations in which they find themselves. What the endings of narrative bring is a final adjudication among the various and uncertain interpretations put forward in the course of the narrative, whether by characters, narrators, or readers."[60] The detective story, as created by Poe, is a paradigm of this aspect of narrative, predating the aesthetics of postmodernism but aligning Poe with such postmodernist writers as Vladimir Nabokov, John Barth, and Jorge Luis Borges, all of whom have noted their debt to Poe. Maurice Bennet makes the case quite specifically in comparing Poe's detective stories to those of Borges: "The man who creates order out of the heterogeneity of casual fact duplicates the divine act of creation; similarly, the individual who reads order into the same heterogeneity indulges in an exegetical exercise which confounds him with the creator."[61]

Poe was self-consciously aware that he was embodying both the creator and the explicitor in his so-called stories of ratiocination, as his remarks in a letter to Philip Pendleton Cooke in 1846 indicate: "These tales of ratiocination owe most of their popularity to being something in a new key. I do not mean to say that they are not ingenious—but people think them more ingenious than they are—on account of their method and *air* of method. In the 'Murders of the Rue Morgue,' for instance, where is the ingenuity of unravelling a web which yourself (the author) have woven for the express purpose of unravelling"

(*Letters*, 2:328). Poe's detective stories are about creating patterns, which, for Poe, means discovering patterns that are already there. It is all a matter of accepting a mystery as a text, a contextual pattern made up of motifs or clues that have meaning precisely because of the role they play within the pattern. According to Shawn Rosenheim, Poe's detectives work with abstract symbols alone, which they obtain by converting the material world into a surface of discrete signs in which nothing is hidden. This method is also related to gothic fiction, says Rosenheim, for it transforms representations of three-dimensional space into binary codings.[62] In this transformation of the world into an intertextual network, the detective, as G. K. Chesterton has one of his own detective characters say, is the critic, while the criminal is the creative artist who creates the plot the detective must perceive as pattern. Chesterton also notes that the detective story expresses a sense of poetry in everyday life, for every stone in the city street and every brick in a wall has a human imprint and thus constitutes a deliberate symbol.[63] Truly, as Chesterton suggests, the detective is the master of the "romance of detail"; and the transformation of ordinary detail, previously mere verisimilitude, into contextually meaningful motifs is a key factor in the creation of not only the detective story but the short story as a genre.

Poe's minor experiments with the ratiocinative story, "The Oblong Box" and "Thou Art the Man," were published only two months apart in 1844, three years after the appearance of the first story in the Dupin series, "The Murders in the Rue Morgue." These experimental tales differ from the "true" detective story in significant ways. First, the solver of the enigma or riddle in each one is also the teller of the story; thus the reader is deprived of the intermediary narrator who has such an important port to play in the Dupin stories and "The Gold Bug." Poe's technique of employing a Watson-like narrator puts the reader in a crucial hermeneutic situation between the narrator and the protagonist in which he knows less than the latter but more than the former.

Second, these works do not present the story as the unraveling of a hermeneutic puzzle in the manner of the Dupin stories. In "The Oblong Box" the narrator is proven to be wrong about his hypothesis, whereas in "Thou Art the Man" the narrator unfairly withholds information from the reader until the end of the tale. As a result, the reader does not become involved in the ingenious means by which the detective or solver of the puzzle creates the dénouement. In "The Oblong Box" there is only a rather sad mystery revealed at the end, and in

"Thou Art the Man" there is the solution of a mystery which the reader did not even know existed until the end.

The narrator of "The Oblong Box" (September 1844) is not a professional or an expert in ratiocinative thinking as Dupin is; his motive for trying to lay bare the mystery is no more than idle curiosity. Although the piece is often placed with Poe's ratiocinative stories, it bears more resemblance to those Poe fictions about the conflict between body and art, for the narrator's mistake is to suspect that the oblong box hides a painting when in fact the box conceals the body of a beautiful young woman. Indeed, at night when he hears the sounds of someone opening the box and then a sobbing or murmuring sound, the narrator imagines Wyatt to "feast his eyes on the pictorial treasure within." The metaphor of "feasting" is grotesquely ironic considering that the narrator believes the painting to be a copy of *The Last Supper.* The fact that Wyatt is borne down to the bottom of the sea by the oblong box suggests the mistake of tying oneself to the physical image of the Beautiful—a theme that Poe deals with in such stories as "Berenice" and "Ligeia."

"Thou Art the Man" (November 1844) also includes an "enigma" to be solved, but the reader does not know what the mystery is until he reaches the end of the story. The narrator, who says he will play Oedipus to the Rattleborough enigma in the first line of the story, is actually the creator of the so-called miracle that forms its dénouement. Furthermore, although the narrator says he would be sorry to discuss the event in a "tone of unsuitable levity" (3:1044), such a light tone actually dominates the story. The plot begins with the disappearance of the character Shuttleworthy, who has been good friends with a man named Goodfellow. The structure of the plot is not built on the explication of a hidden pattern, like the Dupin stories, but rather on the creation of an ironic pattern. Throughout, the reader is led to believe that Goodfellow is indeed a "good fellow," a man concerned with finding out what happened to his dear friend, and that, as various clues seem to indicate, Mr. Pennifeather, the nephew of the missing man, is responsible for his disappearance. The narrator notes that Goodfellow tries to defend Pennifeather, but that he runs into many blunders, mistakes, and errors in speech in his zeal, so that everything he says to defend Pennifeather has "the effect of deepening the suspicion already attached to the individual whose cause he pleaded, and of arousing against him the fury of the mob" (3:1050).

After Pennifeather has been found guilty of his uncle's murder and sentenced to death, Goodfellow receives a letter informing him that he will receive a case of wine promised to him by Shuttleworthy a few months before his disappearance. Of course, at the dénouement, when the case of wine is opened, we are presented with a classic example of Poe's poetic justice; the dead body of Shuttleworthy himself sits upright in the box and cries out the title, "Thou art the man." The narrator now explains that he never really believed in Goodfellow's "good fellowness," for it seemed too extreme; thus he searched for and found the body of the missing Shuttleworthy, wired it to spring up like a grotesque jack-in-the-box, and then used his ventriloquism skills to complete the plot to catch the criminal. What is actually revealed by this dénouement is not so much the criminal plot, but the aesthetic motivation for the light tone maintained throughout the story, for now we know that the narrator has maintained this tone precisely because he was the one who set up the plot to catch Goodfellow. Thus, instead of the crime being solved by the major narrative thrust of the story— the irony arising from Goodfellow's incrimination of Pennifeather by seemingly trying to clear him—it is solved by a narrator who projects his discovery (concealed until the end) through the body and voice of the dead man himself.

A more important experiment with ratiocination as a structural device, although still not a detective story, is "The Gold-Bug" (21, 28 June 1843), the most popular story Poe wrote during his lifetime. There is no detective in this story, nor is there a crime exactly, but it does make use of a narrator-friend of a central character who, like Dupin, is not only somewhat eccentric and without resources, but also an expert in the solution of puzzles. The primary motif in the story is misunderstanding or miscommunication. First, Legrand tells the narrator about finding a type of *scarabaeus*, but then reveals that he has lent it to someone. He says to the narrator, "Stay here to-night, and I will send Jup down for it at sunrise. It is the loveliest thing in creation." To this the narrator responds, "What?—sunrise?" (3:808). This trivial ambiguity about the referent for the pronoun "It" is not justified by anything in the story and exists solely to introduce the motif of ambiguity or cross-communication. Other examples occur when the ex-slave Jupiter misinterprets correct English, transforming the words he thinks he hears into new words in his own dialect. For example, when Legrand comments about the *antennae* of the bug, Jupiter replies, "Dey aint no tin in him. . . . de bug is a goole bug" (3:809). Other examples occur when Jupiter tells the narrator that Legrand has been "syphon" all the time, because he has misheard and misinterpreted "ciphering," and when the narrator asks Jupiter if he brought any messages from Legrand, Jupiter hands him a note, saying "No, massa, I bring dis here pissel" (3:813). Jean Ricardou has argued that these and other examples indicate that Jupiter and the narrator are "bad readers" that is, on "bad terms with language," and Michael Williams in a stimulating essay included in the present volume has further developed the issues of interpretation embodied in the story.[64]

After the narrative events have reached their climax with the discovery of the gold, the real story of explication begins. As in most short stories, the primary interest lies in the analytical interpretation of pattern based on following certain conventions and rules, not on following the temporal narrative line of the story. What first fascinates Legrand is the seeming coincidence that the drawing of the bug he made on one side of the parchment is of the same size and outline as the drawing of the death's head that the heat of the fire brought out on the other side. He admits that the coincidence stupefied him at first: "This is the usual effect of such coincidences. The mind struggles to establish a connexion—a sequence of cause and effect—and, being unable to do so, suffers a species of temporary paralysis" (3:829). According to Daniel Kempton, Legrand reads into these coincidences the image of his own desire, for he looks on the world as if "temporal reality were a kind of cipher, an encoded message, written for the elect by the hand of God."[65] However, as usual in Poe, there is no temporal reality in a story, only the spatial pattern that the author/God has created; the elect for whom it is written are those readers who can perceive the relevance of the details within the contextual pattern of the work.

The bug in the story, if I may be excused for using a mixed metaphor, is actually a red herring, for it has nothing to do with the treasure. As an index of the treasure, its function is solely metaphoric. It is by Legrand's act of laying his own drawing of the bug over the preexistent but hidden death's head drawing, combined with the "rare and happy accident" of the cold day, that what was previously hidden is laid bare. If accepting the bug as an index marks the first step toward the discovery of the treasure, then understanding the picture of a kid as an icon is the second step. The final step, the breaking of the secret code, depends on Legrand's understanding the structural nature of the message. Whereas the relationship between the characters of the code and their meaning may be arbitrary, their contextual position is compelling;

in short, the message can be understood when one develops a grammar to lay it bare.

"The Murders in the Rue Morgue," "The Mystery of Marie Roget," and "The Purloined Letter" are Poe's most famous detective stories, for they introduce that mainstay of mystery fiction—from Sherlock Holmes to Hercule Poiroit—the amateur sleuth who solves crimes from the comfort of his armchair. The story that takes the credit for being the first detective story, "The Murders in the Rue Morgue" (March 1841), begins under the guise of an essay, as many of Poe's other stories do, taking its generic cue from the eighteenth-century essay form characteristic of Addison and Steele. The subject of this opening essay, presented objectively by a writer who has not yet identified or dramatically located himself, is, as it is in "The Imp of the Perverse," a particular mental state. Although analysis is in some ways just the opposite of perverseness (for whereas one creates mysteries, the other resolves them), like perverseness, it is not susceptible of analysis itself. Like the perverse, the analytical faculties reveal themselves in their effects only. There is no way to determine their cause; the process of analysis is simultaneous with its effects. Furthermore, what characterizes the analytical is that even though it is the "soul and essence of method," to the ordinary perception it appears intuitive; even though it is the result of *acumen*, it appears to be "preternatural." These are also key terms for understanding Poe's contribution to the short story, for, as Poe shows, although the form requires careful control and method, it results in a work with a shadow of the "mystic" or the seeming preternatural about it.

The narrator notes that he is not writing a treatise, but rather prefacing a "somewhat peculiar narrative"; however, at the point when the actual narrative begins, he says the narrative to follow "will appear to the reader somewhat in the light of a commentary upon the propositions just advanced" (2:531). If one asks which is primary, the narration or the exposition, the answer, of course, is that neither is, for, as the dénouement shows, when Dupin begins his own exposition and illustration of the analytical method, narrative becomes exposition. The "re-solution" of the mystery is the presentation of the hidden narrative itself, laid bare by the "disentangling" method of the analyst. Indeed, for Poe, who earlier rejected Coleridge's assertion that imagination was constructive, the one who creates is he who discovers the pattern that is already there. The narrator observes in Dupin what he calls the "Bi-

Part Soul," seeing a "double Dupin—the creative and the resolvent" (2:533). And, indeed, for Poe the creative *is* the resolvent, for to create is to re-solve, to engage in a re-solution—the discovery of the hidden pattern that made the mystery a mystery.

The first indication in the story of Dupin's special analytical ability occurs when he seems to read the narrator's mind. But what seems preternatural is only the result of "method," beginning with observation, which presupposes, as the narrator has said earlier, the key element of knowing what to observe. The next step in the method is to forge a series of links in a chain, which Dupin achieves by following a process of association in which one idea suggests another either by some similarity or some previous connection. What Dupin does is to make explicit a tacit chain, what we often feel to be unconscious connections. The next section of "The Murders in the Rue Morgue" is primarily constructed from newspaper accounts of the deaths of the two women—the key elements of which have to do with conflicting reports about the nature of the language overheard at the scene of the crime. Dupin notes that the problem with the French police is that they often hold things up too close, and thus lose sight of the matter as a whole. Dupin's point here is that what must be perceived is the overall pattern—how the objects fit together. Moreover, he notes that to stare too intently at the object directly and straight on is to make it disappear, that one must look at mysteries in a "side-long way," that is, indirectly, the way one must often look at a literary text.

Another element of the crime story that contributes to Poe's development of the short story genre is that what most confounds the police is the fact that the crime, like Poe's notion of the perverse, seems completely unmotivated. Although the lack of a motive is what makes the mystery so seemingly insoluble for the police, for Dupin, it is precisely this lack of a motive, precisely its outré features, that makes it so easy to solve. Dupin says that it is by these very deviations from the ordinary that reason feels its way toward truth. What one should ask, says Dupin, is not "what has occurred?," but rather "what has occurred that has never occurred before?" (2:548). Whereas the police are looking for precedents for the crime in the past and for some realistic or logical motive for its severity, Dupin succeeds precisely by throwing himself out of the ordinary and accepting the extraordinary nature of the event. Dupin's discourse, as he follows step-by-step the objects that must be explained—the closed room, the mode of descent from the upper floor of the house, the ambiguity of the overheard voice—

leads the narrator, as it does the reader, to link what Dupin has described as "unusual activity" with what the newspapers have described as a "very peculiar" voice.

The real thematic problem of the story is what motivates Poe to use what might be called the outré Ourang-Outang as the cause of the crime. The answer is that Poe wishes to illustrate one of the key factors of the detective story: that to try to solve the mystery by postulating the usual is futile, for crime itself is a breakup of the ordinary and the everyday. Moreover, it is another example of Poe's literalizing the metaphoric, for one is often apt to say that a particularly brutal crime is bestial or animalistic. Thus, Poe literalizes this metaphor of crime as the outbreak of the animal in man by actually making the "criminal" an animal. The fact that there is no motive for the crime is a typical Poe device, for it forces one to abandon so-called realistic motivation and concentrate on the purely contextual or aesthetic motivation.

"The Mystery of Marie Roget" (November–December 1842, February 1843) is, most agree, the weakest of the three Dupin stories, primarily because it is so lacking in narrative interest. And indeed it is lacking in narrative interest because it is so bound to an actual murder that Poe, in the Dupin guise, hopes to resolve. As a result, the detective here is so firmly ensconced in his armchair that the readers of the story take little interest in his attempts to lay bare the mystery. But the piece is worth looking at briefly not only for its further illustration of the motifs of the analytical, but also because Poe poses it as a classic example of a fiction being superimposed over a reality. The prefatory note from Novalis suggests the issue that interests Poe here: "There are ideal series of events which run parallel with the real ones. They rarely coincide. Men and circumstances generally modify the ideal train of events, so that it seems imperfect, and its consequences are equally imperfect" (3:723). The narrator then provides a brief exposition on coincidence by which he justifies the paralleling of the ideal (i.e., the fictional events of Marie Roget) with the real (i.e., the actual events of Mary Rogers). The parallel between the names and the exact parallel between the events makes it clear, of course, that there is no coincidence here, at least not as we understand that term in everyday reality. What people call coincidence in everyday reality, Poe wishes to remind us, is in fiction the artistic calculation of putting things together in a unified, parallel fashion.

Dupin's method in "The Mystery of Marie Roget" is similar to that of the Rue Morgue case in that he investigates the crime by studying actual texts, that is, newspaper accounts; thus, he is dealing with events already at a textual remove from actuality. The story differs from "The Murders in the Rue Morgue" in that it has nothing of the outré about it; it is ordinary and is for that reason all the more difficult. However, the main reason it is more difficult than the Rue Morgue case is that there can be no "Bi-Part" Dupin/Poe here, one who both creates and resolves. The event is ordinary precisely because it is real, not fictional, and thus has no aesthetic pattern. What Dupin must do in this case is just the opposite of what he did in the Rue Morgue case. In the first, he had to create an unusual pattern to fit the events of the case; that is, he had to create a fiction. In this case, he has to expose the fictions that the newspapers have created about the events. For example, the idea of one newspaper that Marie Roget is still alive, Dupin attributes to the appeal of both the epigrammatic nature of its "pungent contradiction" and its melodramatic nature, not its plausibility. That is, Poe/Dupin exposes the fictional conventions of the newspapers, although it is precisely fictional conventions that he himself used in "The Murders of the Rue Morgue" to create that story. Thus, what Poe does in "Marie Roget" is to expose the methods he used in "Rue Morgue."

In the postscript to the story, the narrator, who is identified here as Poe himself, returns to the problem with which the story began, for he wishes to remind the reader that he is only dealing with coincidence, that he does not claim that the facts of the Marie Roget case are completely parallel with those of the Mary Rogers case. He says that although he has no faith in the preternatural, he does hold the following: Nature and God are two: God created Nature and can at will modify Nature. However, we insult God in imagining a possible necessity for modification, for God's laws embrace all contingencies. "With God all is *Now*" (3:772). This is an important clue to Poe's own understanding of the spatial pattern of his work, for, according to Poe in *Eureka*, the universe is a plot of God, a perfect plot, and thus a plot the parts of which exist all at once; consequently, even though there may appear to be accidents or coincidences, there can be none since for God, as it is for the artist, all is now (*Works*, 16:292).

"The Purloined Letter" (September 1844) has been, in recent years, the most frequently discussed Poe detective story, first as a pretext for Jacques Lacan's discussion of psychoanalytic subplots and then as a motivation for deconstructionist debate by Jacques Derrida. Ultimately, the story has become a rallying point for numerous critics who have used it to discuss, not Poe, but rather the methods of Lacan and Derrida. It is not surprising that of all Poe's works this story would appeal most to the advocates of poststructuralism, for it is a model of the self-reflexive parable of the act of analysis itself. Although the story has been discussed by numerous critics and certainly needs no further extensive analysis here, I wish to note some of those elements in the work that mark it as one of Poe's most important experiments in the creation of the short story.[66]

That the story centers on a letter—both a means of written communication and, in postmodernist terms, the unit of arbitrary meaning in grammatical structures—has particularly interested contemporary critics, as has the ironic nature of the letter itself. This detective story does not focus on what is unknown but on what is known; the only thing that is unknown is the whereabouts of the letter; nothing else in the mystery story is a mystery at all. Moreover, the French prefect of police makes it clear that the one who took the letter is known and that he still has it. When Dupin asks how this is "known," he replies that it is inferred from the nature of the document and the nonappearance of certain results that would occur if the robber made use of it. Indeed, it is crucial that the owner of the letter knows who has stolen it for the letter to have its blackmailing power. As Dupin says, the power of the robber results from "the robber's knowledge of the loser's knowledge of the robber" (3:976).

The prefect describes in great detail the means by which he has physically tried to find the letter, but his method is defective for the same reason it was in the Rue Morgue case: he is looking too closely, failing to step back and allow the very nature of the case to reveal its pattern. After Dupin gives the letter to the prefect a few months later, the real story begins with Dupin's exposition of the means by which the letter was found. The primary method Dupin uses here is indeed the "Bi-Part" method of the artist and the reader, for it first involves identification and then explication. Dupin gives an example of the schoolboy who is a master at playing the game of "even and odd"—a guessing game in which one holds a number of marbles in his hand and asks someone to guess whether they are even or odd in number. The boy succeeds in guessing by projecting himself into the one holding the marbles, identifying with the opponent's intellect. He says he fashions the expression of his face in accordance with the face of the opponent and then waits to see what thoughts come to him. This is a significant Poe notion, for it is by Poe's romantic projection of himself into a first-person narrator that his stories mark a crucial difference from preromantic short fictions in which the narrator was either objectively removed from, or maintained an ironic stance toward, the experience he described.

By projecting himself into the intellect of the minister, Dupin realizes that he would not use ordinary means of hiding the letter, but rather extraordinary ones, by which Dupin means, at least in this case, ordinary means. To hide the letter by putting it in plain sight is to make the ordinary into the extraordinary. The minister, says Dupin, is a poet and a mathematician—a combination of identification and analysis—that makes his reasoning sound; if he had reasoned as a mathematician only, he would have been at the mercy of the prefect. Because the minister is also a poet, Dupin knows that he would have anticipated all the efforts the police would make to find the letter and would be driven as a matter of course to simplicity as being the most unusual means to hide it. The story's conclusion with the quotation from Crébrillon's "Atrée"—"A plot so deadly, if not worthy of Atreus is worthy of Thyestes" (3:993)—reminds us of Poe's own fascination with plots as patterns in which the unwitting are captured. What so fascinates us about "The Purloined Letter" is Poe's creation of a story that is about its own explication.

Alternate Realms of Reality

Poe was interested in all human experiences that challenged or undermined the easy assumption that everyday reality was the only reality worth attending to. Although some readers may think that this preference for alternate realms of experience was part of his psychological makeup, it is much more likely that it grew out of his acceptance of the German romantic tradition of short fiction as a vehicle for presenting experiences that break up the ordinary.

One of the most common of such "alternate" experiences, of course, one that is accessible to every human being, is the experience of dream. Poe was not only interested in presenting dreams as if they were reality, he was also interested, as was typical of the *Blackwood* fiction of the day, in presenting experiences that were so extreme that they seemed to have the nightmarish quality of dream. To present dream as reality and reality as dream was, for Poe, to blur the lines between the two forms of experience. It was to give the human construct of a dream the hard feel of the external world and to give the seemingly hard contours of the external world a sense of being a human construct.

Two of Poe's best-known stories that blur this dream/reality distinction are "Descent into the Maelstrom" (May 1841) and "The Pit and the Pendulum" (1842). Both present characters placed in an extreme situation; however, the situations differ in a crucial way. In the first the extreme situation is a natural phenomenon, in spite of the fact that its extremity makes it seem unnatural. It is a favorite Poe technique to create the extreme situation by pushing the ordinary situation to extraordinary lengths, to suggest the supernatural by pushing the natural to extremes. In the second story, the ontological status of the situation is ambiguous, for although the character knows physically where he is, he does not know psychically what state he is in. The stories also differ in terms of what motivates the extreme state. In "A Descent into the Maelstrom," Poe devotes most of the story to setting up the situation, normalizing it, locating it in space; once the situation is established the story is almost over. In "The Pit and the Pendulum," how the character got to his present situation is left vague; a great deal of the story is spent considering whether he is in a dream or a waking state. However, the means by which the two characters cope with their situations is similar; both make use of careful and lucid observation to try to escape their fate.

"Descent into the Maelstrom" begins in the typical *Blackwood* magazine manner by presenting a character who has undergone an "event" that has never happened to a human being before and who feels compelled, like Coleridge's Ancient Mariner, to tell about it. Moreover, Poe follows the device common to romantic dramatic lyric poetry of having the narrator tell the story while located at that point where the events of the story took place, informing his wedding guest–like auditor: "I have brought you here that you might have the best possible view of the scene of that event I mentioned—and to tell you the whole story with the spot just under your eye" (2:578). The teller also makes use of the eighteenth-century technique of verisimilitude, using a "particularizing manner" to give precise details of the physical phenomenon he is describing. The listener adds to this particularizing technique of authenticating the event by quoting from written sources such as Rasmus and the *Encyclopedia Britannica*, but asserts that no matter how "circumstantial" or detailed the descriptions are, they fall short of conveying the horror, the magnificence, or the "sense of the *novel*" that the scene of the whirlpool elicits—noting, however, that he is not sure from what "point of view" previous commentators viewed the whirlpool. It is this notion of point of view that motivates the story, for, as the teller has said at the beginning, no one has had the viewpoint he has had—the typical romantic perspective from within rather than from without.

The storyteller presents himself as an inadequate teller, for he often claims the inability of his words to capture the event; he says it is "folly to attempt describing" the hurricane that hit, and when he knows he is close to the whirlpool, he says, "no one will know what my feelings were at that moment" (2:586). But if his feelings of horror are indescribable, his feelings when he loses his sense of horror are calm and logical. Indeed, when he makes up his mind to hope no more, he becomes composed and begins to reflect on how magnificent it would be to die in this manifestation of God's power: "I became possessed with the keenest curiosity about the whirl itself. I positively felt a *wish* to explore its depths, even at the sacrifice I was going to make, and my principle grief was that I should never be able to tell my old companions on shore about the mysteries I should see" (2:588–89).

It is precisely this obsession to observe, an obsession that Dupin experiences also, that saves the narrator. The nearer he comes to the bottom of the whirlpool, the keener grows what he calls his "unnatural curiosity." It is a combination of memory and observation of the geometric shapes that are less apt to be drawn down deeper into the whirlpool that marks the means of his escape. Lashing himself to a barrel, he throws himself off the fishing boat into the whirlpool and hovers half-way between the top and the bottom, between chaos below and salvation above, until the whirlpool—which is, after all, limited in time—subsides. At this point, the teller ends his tale by moving from the past to the present tense, reflecting on the tale itself: "As it is myself who now tell you this tale—as you see that I *did* escape—and as you are already in possession of the mode in which this escape was effected, and must therefore anticipate all that I have farther to say—I will bring my story quickly to conclusion" (2:593). And indeed, he does; however, he has been transformed by the experience from participant to manipulator of his own discourse, for he says his companions on shore "knew me no more than they would have known a traveller from the spirit-land."

"The Pit and the Pendulum" is much more ambiguous about the epistemological or ontological state of the extreme situation than "A Descent into the Maelstrom." Although the entire story takes place inside a prison cell into which the narrator of the story, and indeed the story's only visible character, has been thrown, the story does not indicate what the nameless narrator has done to deserve the tortures he endures in the pit, nor does it deal with any of the religious or social implications of the Inquisition responsible for his imprisonment. It simply recounts, in excruciatingly exact detail, the step-by-step means by which the torturers try to break the protagonist's spirit and his own methodical attempts to escape each new horror that they put in his path.

Although "The Pit and the Pendulum" only focuses on one character, the reader actually discovers very little about him. We do not know his name, what he has done, whether he is guilty, whether he is a criminal, what he misses about life in the everyday world—in short, we know none of those things about the character that we might expect to learn if this were a novel in which a man spends several years in prison. Although such a lack of knowledge would make readers quickly lose interest if they were reading a novel, this lack does not impede the reader's willingness to become involved with Poe's short story. For this is not a realistic story of an individual human character caught in an unjust social system, but rather a nightmarish, symbolic story about every person's worst nightmare and an allegory of the most basic human situation and dilemma. Harry Levine has described the story as such an allegory, and David Hirsch has further argued that the character's situation embodies the modern existential experience: "the surface of Poe's world has broken and cracked, and man stands at the edge of the bottomless abyss."[67]

The story is a Poe paradigm. Focusing on a character under sentence of death and aware of it, it moves the character into a concrete dilemma that seems to "stand for" a metaphysical situation in an ambiguous way that suggests its "dreamy," "indeterminate" nature. In this story we find the most explicit statement in Poe's fiction of his sense of the blurry line between dream and reality. The narrator considers that although when we awake even from the soundest sleep, "we break the gossamer web of some dream" (2:682), the web is so flimsy that a second later we forget we have dreamed at all. But sometimes, perhaps much later, memories of the details of the dream come back and we do not know where they have come from. This sense of having a memory of that which did not in fact occur is central to the story's ambiguity, for as the narrator tries to remember his experience, it is not clear whether the memory is of a real event or a dream event that has been forgotten.

He does not know in what state he is; the only thing he does know is that he is not dead, for he says, "Such a supposition, notwithstanding what we read in fiction, is altogether inconsistent with real existence;—but where and in what state was I?" (2:684). The narrator's task is simply to save himself, but in order to survive he must know where he is; the first crucial task he undertakes is to try to orient himself. However, his efforts are complicated by his moving back and forth between sleep and waking; each time he falls asleep, he must reorient himself all over again. This explains why even after trying to demarcate his position, he awakes and, instead of going on forward, retraces his steps and thus overestimates the size of his cell.

Like the protagonist in "A Descent into the Maelstrom," he is preoccupied with curiosity about the mere physical nature of his surroundings, taking a "wild interest in trifles." Nonetheless, in spite of his deliberative efforts, it is the accident of tripping that saves him from the pit the first time. Waking from another interlude of sleep, he finds himself bound and notes above him a picture of time, synonymous with death, carrying not the image of a scythe, but rather an actual pendulum that sweeps back and forth. In this situation, surrounded by the repulsive rats, with the scythe of time and thus death over his head, he again moves back and forth between the states of sensibility and insensibility. This pattern of moving in and out of consciousness is much like the pattern in "Ligeia" and is typical of Poe, for in such an alternating state consciousness has some of the characteristics of unconsciousness and vice versa; one state is imbued with the qualities of the other state. As a result, Poe's stories are neither solely like the consciousness of realism, nor the projective unconsciousness of romance. Later, when the narrator totters on the brink of the pit, the walls rush back and an outstretched arm catches him as he falls. The ending is not an ending at all, but rather the beginning of waking life, the movement from the gossamer dream or nightmare that constitutes the story itself.

Two stories that seem radically different from the extreme cases presented in "A Descent into the Maelstrom" and "The Pit and the Pendulum" but are also Poe experiments with blurring the line between external reality and psychological projections are, ironically, the two stories that critics have often termed his most straightforward and most socially grounded: "William Wilson" (1839) and "The Man of the Crowd" (December 1840). In fact, "William Wilson" has been called Poe's "cleanest" story, by which critics usually mean the one least cluttered with gothic trappings, a story more like a parable of Hawthorne or a cautionary tale of Dostoyevski, in which the supposed fantastic event is easily explainable as a moral allegory. To see the double of William Wilson as his conscience is to make the story a simple parable that does not create the kind of uneasy epistemological ambiguity of some of Poe's other stories. Even the style of the story seems to differ from other Poe pieces, reflecting a formality and order, with a strong analytical and moral tone.[68] In fact, Ruth Sullivan has used the story's seeming straightforward face value as the very reason to doubt it, creating ambiguity where it seems that ambiguity does not exist, pointing out, without really accounting for it, the central mystery that in spite of the fact that the double is said to be Wilson's conscience, in his description of his motivation for telling the story, nowhere does he mention guilt.[69]

Part 1

The story begins by calling attention to the fictional nature of the character's name. Although we do not know his real name nor his real state at the time of the telling (as a fictional character he has no "real" name), we do know he perceives himself as an "outcast of all outcasts" cut off from the sympathy of his fellow man. He declares that the motivation for his creating this discourse is, as it was for the narrator of "The Black Cat," to determine the logic and meaning of his experience: "I would fain have them believe that I have been, in some measure, the slave of circumstances beyond human control. I would wish them to seek out for me, in the details I am about to give, some little oasis of *fatality* amid a wilderness of error. . . . Have I not indeed been living in a dream? And am I not now dying a victim to the horror and the mystery of the wildest of all sublunary visions?" (2:427). The fact that the story derives from the dreamy state of memory is indicated by Wilson's description of the "large, rambling, Elizabethan house, in a misty-looking village of England" (2:427) that he remembers as a "dream-like" place. The house itself he recalls as a structure incomprehensible in its windings and subdivisions, a place where one could not locate oneself. He says during the five years he was there he was never able to determine exactly where he slept, for the branches of the house were so innumerable and inconceivable that his ideas of it were like those with which he pondered infinity.

It is in the midst of this dreamy memory that he first meets the boy who is his exact double, bearing the same name as he does, having entered school on the same day, having the same birthday. The double differs from the protagonist by his 'intolerable spirit of contradiction," suggesting a split in Wilson like that caused by perverseness. The fact that the double perfects an imitation of Wilson and that his whisper is a echo of his own voice suggests his status as a projective doubling. But the duplicate is not a "caricature," as Wilson recognizes, but rather an "exquisite portraiture," which no one but Wilson can see. That the double is not the conscience of Wilson, but rather a perverse side of his divided self, is indicated by the fact that in the first section of the story he has a sarcastic and sneering smile and chuckles at the success of his imitation.

The most puzzling element of the doubling in the story is Wilson's sense of an air in his double that brings to mind "dim visions of my earliest infancy—wild, confused and thronging memories of a time when memory herself was yet unborn" (2:436). He says he can only express the sense he has by believing he has been acquainted with his double at "some epoch very long ago—some point of the past even infinitely remote" (2:436). This sense of something infinitely remote suggests a split more profound and primal than merely the moralistic split of the self from the conscience.

The story folds in the middle at the scene when Wilson creeps in to look at his double while he sleeps. Awe-stricken by what he sees, he decides to leave the school forever. Although he does not say so, what Wilson sees is precisely his own perverse self, that is, an exact duplicate, Narcissus looking into the distorting mirror of the pond. The balance of the story is not as interesting as this first part, for it documents quite straightforwardly the fact that Wilson becomes unscrupulous and a gambler, but is accosted by his double again when Wilson has cheated a man in a card game.

However, even as he calls him his "arch-enemy and evil genius," Wilson says, "let me hasten to the last eventful scene of the drama." And indeed in the last scene, when Wilson is pursuing the young wife of an aged nobleman, he hears the whisper once again and we have the final encounter in which the self battles with its perverse side. After plunging his sword repeatedly through his double, Wilson is horrified to see what appears to be a large mirror where none has been before; as he steps up to it sees himself with features all dabbed with blood. "Thus it appeared, I say, but was not. It was my antagonist—it was Wilson, who then stood before me in the agonies of his dissolution" (2:448). When the stricken double speaks, Wilson says he could have fancied it was himself speaking: "*You have conquered, and I yield. Yet, henceforward art thou also dead—dead to the World, to Heaven, and to Hope! In me didst thou exist—and, in my death, see by this image, which is thine own, how utterly thou has murdered thyself.*" To live aware of a split in the self, rather than in a deception of the unified self, is the thematic thrust of "William Wilson." It is not conscience that Wilson's double represents, for he seems to have a devious motivation for his imitation. Indeed, the double changes to represent the opposite of whatever Wilson is; he is a reverse/perverse reflection, as all reflections are.

"The Man of the Crowd" is another problematical Poe story. Often characterized as his only socially significant story, or the one most clearly about the everyday social world of his time, it is not as simple as it seems. The story is much like the combination essay/stories "Premature Burial" and "Imp of the Perverse," for the first half of the story presents the narrator's theories about what motivates the mysterious man of the crowd, whereas the second half presents the narrative on which the theories are based. However, the narrator's discovery of what drives the old man is a secret that cannot be told; he is like a certain German book that "does not permit itself to be read" (2:506). The pattern of the story is thus a secret that the story itself cannot reveal.

The most problematic aspect of the first part of the story is the psychic state of the narrator. He has been ill, but now, during convalescence, he is in a mood just the opposite of ennui, a mood "of the keenest appetency, when the film from the mental vision departs" and intellect surpasses its everyday state and he feels a "calm but inquisitive interest in every thing" (2:507). While sitting in a London coffeehouse, watching the scene out the window, the process of his observation mirrors the transformation of the eighteenth-century essayist into the nineteenth-century artist: "At first my observations took an abstract and generalizing turn. I looked at the passengers in masses, and thought of them in their aggregate relations. Soon, however, I descended to details, and regarded with minute interest the innumerable varieties of figure, dress, air, gait, visage, and expression of countenance" (2:507). Even then, he observes not individuals but classes of people—clerks, gamblers, beggars—all those types that make up the crowd. It is only when he notices one old man whose idiosyncrasy of expression catches his attention that the narrative interest begins. For it is with the narrator's assumption of a "wild history" he imagines for the old man that he is drawn out of the coffeehouse to follow him through the streets so that he might "know him."

The image of the narrator following the strange old man all night and all the next day until he is wearied unto death is a haunting one, for it may suggest, as some critics have noted, that this is another Poe double story, in which the narrator sees the secret side of himself—his perverse shadow—in the old man. The last half of the story follows a typical Poe structural pattern of alternating between purposefulness and aimlessness, dynamism and stasis. The old man purposely seeks people, only to mingle with them in a detached way—desiring to be among the crowd but not to be touched by the individual. The narrator's explanation at the end when he stops the old man and faces him directly, much as William Wilson faces his double at the end of that story, does not seem adequate to the complex imagery that leads up to the dénouement: "'This old man,' I said at length, 'is the very type and the genius of deep crime. He refuses to be alone. *He is the man of the crowd*,'" (2:515), concluding that it is perhaps a mercy of God that he does not permit himself to be "read." This resolution that does not really resolve is a typical Poe device of ending a story with a self-reflexive reference; the only resolution possible is an aesthetic one. Thus, the process of the story is from the particular to the general: the narrator plucks the old man out of the crowd and by particularizing, elevates him out of the generalizations and types he has been naming, only then to symbolize him, that is, to create him as a symbolic type, a metaphor of some deep metaphysical mystery of ultimate isolation.

The Retreat into Art

The ultimate implication of Poe's theories of art as the highly unified and patterned creation of a bodiless ideal is the human desire to escape the consequences of being mere body by retreating into the art work itself. And indeed two of Poe's best-known stories make this simultaneously irresistible and horrible desire their central theme.

"The Masque of the Red Death" (30 April, 1842) is one of Poe's most obviously allegorical stories, in spite of the fact that he said he did not like allegories. As a result, it also seems one of his most straightforward stories, for it appears to be a clearly delineated parable about the impossibility of man's attempt to escape from death. But, as is typical in Poe, it is not as straightforward as it first appears. The first problem the reader faces in reading the story allegorically is the fact that the "masque" or mask that represents death is the redness of blood on the face of the victim. However, if we consider the fact that the redness of blood is a "sign" of life, Poe's metaphor becomes more complex,[70] for if red is the sign of life, then life in turn *is* the sign of death.

The next problem an allegorical reading of the story must deal with is Prince Prospero's attempts to escape death by retreating into his abbey, "an extensive and magnificent structure, the creation of the prince's own eccentric yet august taste" (2:670). Once everyone is inside, the gates are welded shut to make sure that there is no means of "ingress or egress," and the prince says that "the external world could take care of itself" (2:671). Furthermore, the prince makes sure that inside he has all the "appliances of pleasure," such as buffoons, improvisatori, ballet dancers, musicians, and wine. "All these and security were within. Without was the Red Death" (2:671). And indeed, what Prince Prospero (named for Shakespeare's imaginative creator of his own world in *The Tempest*) has done is to create a palace of art by which he attempts to lock life, and thus death, outside. Like other Poe protagonists, the prince is thought to be mad, for the masquerade ball he devises simulates a painting, a patterned unreality: "There were delirious fancies such as the madman fashions. There were much of the beautiful, much of the wanton, much of the *bizarre*, something of the terrible, and not a little of that which might have excited disgust. To and fro in the seven chambers there stalked, in fact, a multitude of dreams" (2:673). However, what cannot be locked outside is the notion of time, which is embodied in the palace in the seven rooms ranging from east (sunrise) to west (sunset) and the giant ebony clock at whose chiming the "dreams" become "stiff-frozen." The balance of the story is the ultimate and inevitable working out of the motifs established. The Red Death enters, the prince chases it down the seven rooms toward the black room of death until the masked figure of life/death turns on the prince and he falls down dead. And indeed all those in the revel fall dead and the flames of the tripods go out, "and Darkness and Decay and the Red Death held illimitable dominion over all" (2:677).

The real complexity of the story lies in its combination of the temporal and the spatial. Harry Levine has called the story Poe's "most pictorial composition,"[71] and David Halliburton discusses its pictorialism by noting how the house is set up in such a way as to transform time into space in an attempt to vanquish mutability.[72] The fine essay by Kermit Vanderbilt, included in this volume, discusses the story as an aesthetic fable of "the imagination striving to control and transform the corrosive elements of nature and to gain, through immortal beauty, the artist's triumph over death."[73]

Finally, we come to Poe's masterpiece, "The Fall of the House of Usher" (September 1839), a story that in many ways is the complete Poe paradigm because it pulls together so many of his basic themes and embodies so many of his innovative techniques. As usual, the major critical controversy concerning this story centers on the ontological nature of the events—either that Roderick is mad or the narrator is mad, although significant discussions of the story's allegorical embodiment of the ideas presented in *Eureka* have also been written.[74]

One important technique Poe uses in the story is to separate his central protagonist, the embodiment of obsession and desire, from his observing self, much the way he did by introducing a secondary narrator for the Dupin stories. The story begins with the entrance of the narrator into the world of Usher, which is the world of the story itself. The landscape he enters that surrounds the house—the "rank sedges," "the white trunks of decayed trees," the "singularly dreary tract of country"—is described in archetypal oneiric images which can be found in Browning's "Childe Roland to the Dark Tower Came," Turgenev's "Brezhin Meadow," and Conrad's *Heart of Darkness*.

But it is the house itself that causes the narrator, and the reader, the first difficulties: "I know not how it was—but, with the first glimpse of the building, a sense of insufferable gloom pervaded my spirit" (2:397). He then justifies the feeling as insufferable because it is not relieved by the poetic sentiment that usually allows one to accept the sternest natural images of the desolate and terrible. Furthermore, he says the house creates such a sense of "unredeemed dreariness of thought" that no "goading of the imagination could torture into aught of the sublime" (2:397). He himself poses the hermeneutical questions: "what was it that so unnerved me in the contemplation of the House of Usher? It was a mystery all insoluble" (2:397).

The narrator knows that some combinations of natural objects have the power of affecting one in such a way, but he also knows that the "analysis of this power lies among considerations beyond our depth" (2:398). He considers that maybe a "different arrangement of the particulars of the scene, of the details of the picture, would be sufficient to modify, or perhaps to annihilate its capacity for sorrowful impression" (2:398). Thus he tries the experiment of looking at the house from the perspective of its reflection in the tarn, but the inverted reflected image, much like a distorted image in one of Poe's own stories, gives him a shudder more thrilling than the house itself.

It is a wonderful opening, one of the most famous in all of literature, for the narrator simulates the process by which the reader enters into the patterned reality of the art work, obviously affected, but puzzled as to what could have created such an effect. Looking into the tarn deepens what the narrator calls his superstition, for when he lifts his eyes to the house itself, he seems to perceive: "that about the whole mansion and domain there hung an atmosphere peculiar to themselves and their immediate vicinity—an atmosphere that had no affinity with the air of heaven, but which had reeked up from the decayed trees, and the gray wall, and the silent tarn—a pestilent and mystic vapor, dull, sluggish, faintly discernible, and leaden-hued" (2:400). Indeed, what he has perceived is what short story writers such as Eudora Welty and Elizabeth Bowen have called the "atmosphere" of the story— something intangible, for which Poe reserves the term "mystic," given off like a "story glow," which Marlowe describes in "Heart of Darkness."[75]

Although the narrator tries to shake off this dreamlike sense and observe "the real aspect of the building," he notes a further fact about its construction that points to its reality as an aesthetic object. No portion of the masonry has fallen, but "there appeared to be a wild inconsistency between its still perfect adaptation of parts, and the crumbling condition of the individual stones" (2:400). The only other element of the building's "instability" is a fissure that runs from the roof to the base of the house in the tarn. Indeed, the instability of the house is like the instability of the art work itself, that gains life not because of its parts but because of its structure, but that in turn always carries within itself the means of its own deconstruction.

It is completely appropriate for this paradigmatic Poe story to feature a protagonist described in such a way that many have recognized him as Poe himself, and that the expression of his face is an arabesque one that the narrator cannot connect with any idea of "simple humanity." Indeed, Usher is not an embodiment of simple humanity, but rather is, as all Poe's protagonists are, what W. H. Auden calls a unitary state, an embodiment of desire. Like his house, there is also an "inconsistency" about Usher, an "incoherence," a sense that the parts do not fit together.

Like other Poe protagonists, Usher suffers from a disease characterized by an unusual attentiveness or focus, what the narrator calls "a morbid acuteness of the senses." For Usher, this acuteness means that he finds all but the most bland food intolerable, can wear garments of only certain textures, finds the odors of flowers oppressive, cannot bear anything but the faintest light, and cannot listen to anything but some peculiar sounds from stringed instruments. It is clear that Roderick is the artist who cannot tolerate any sensory input at all, has indeed cut himself from any stimulus from the external world, much as Prince Prospero wishes to do in "The Masque of the Red Death."

Usher's fear is of no particular thing, as indeed it could not be, for he embodies that fear of ultimate nothingness faced by the protagonist in "The Pit and the Pendulum." He says he dreads events of the future, not in themselves, but in their results in terror, and feels he must soon "abandon life and reason together, in some struggle with the grim phantasm, FEAR" (2:403). Usher's fear is not a plausible psychological fear, but a fear that can only be understood in aesthetic terms. His obsession centers on a family superstition about the relationship between the house and the self, in which the house affects his spirit— "an effect which the *physique* of the gray walls and turrets, and of the dim tarn into which they all looked down, had, at length, brought about upon the *morale* of his existence" (2:403). And this superstitious fear is complicated by the shadowy existence of Madeline, his sister, a figure the narrator regards with the same unspeakable dread with which he regarded the house, for both house and sister represent Roderick's own inherently flawed and detested physicality.

Although we know little about Roderick, we do know that he is an artist: he paints, he improvises on the guitar, and he writes poetry. His work is characterized by what the narrator calls a "highly distempered ideality" that throws a "sulphurous lustre over all." Of his paintings, the narrator says, "if ever mortal painted an idea, that mortal was Roderick Usher" (2:405). Concerned only with the purest of abstraction, with no relation to objects in the world, Roderick's paintings are hermetically sealed, like the one painting the narrator describes of a rectangular vault or tunnel under the earth with no outlet and no artificial light, yet which still is bathed in intense rays.

Usher's poem, which the narrator says has an "under or mystic current" of meaning, suggests the "tottering of his lofty reason upon her throne." And indeed the poem aesthetically mirrors the story itself because it identifies the haunted palace of art with the person of Usher himself, complete with images of eyes as windows and pearl and ruby as teeth and lips at the door. The poem reflects the underlying motivation of the story that so haunts Roderick: that of the "sentience of vegetable things," an obsession that Usher pushes to the extreme theory of the "kingdom of inorganization," that is, the sentience of the structure of nonliving things, specifically the house itself.

> The conditions of the sentience had been here, he imagined, fulfilled in the method of collocation of these stones—in the order of their arrangement, as well as in that of the many *fungi* which overspread them, and the decayed trees which stood around—above all in the long undisturbed endurance of this arrangement, and in its reduplication in the still waters of the tarn. Its evidence—the evidence of the sentience—was to be seen, he said (and I here started as he spoke), in the gradual yet certain condensation of an atmosphere of their own about the waters and the walls. (2:408).

A crucial statement about the aesthetic pattern being the source of sentience, the passage reminds us that as an artist, Roderick has cut himself off from any external sensory source for his art; thus all that he has left to feed on is himself. This is a story about the ultimate romantic artist who, like Kafka's hunger artist, devours himself.

After all this exposition and aesthetic motivation, the story moves rapidly toward its narrative portion and climax when Madeline is entombed and we discover that Roderick and Madeline are twins and that "sympathies of a scarcely intelligible nature had always existed between them" (2:410). Our suspicion that Madeline's "death" is metaphorically meaningful because she is Roderick's twin is intensified when the narrator notes that her disease has left "as usual in all maladies of a strictly cataleptical character, the mockery of a faint blush upon the bosom and the face, and that suspiciously lingering smile upon the lip which is so terrible in death" (2:410). The sympathy between Roderick and Madeline becomes the source of what the narrator suspects is an "oppressive secret" within Roderick that leads to an increasing tension that culminates in a storm of such whirlwind velocity that the previously mentioned atmosphere around the house enshrouds it with a luminous glow.

At this point in the story, when the narrator reads to Roderick a romance entitled the "Mad Trist," sounds described in the fiction are echoed in Roderick and the narrator's own fictional world. The shriek of the dragon in the "Mad Trist" is echoed by a shriek in "The Fall of the House of Usher," as is the terrible ringing sound of the romance hero's shield. This marks what Jean Ricardou has called the *mise en abyme* in the story—that point in which the story refers self-reflexively to its own structure: "It is by the microscopic revelation of the total narrative, therefore, that the mise en abyme challenges the preliminary order of the story. A prophecy, it disturbs the future by revealing it before its end, by anticipation."[76] It is an example of Poe's revealing the spatial nature of the story in the midst of its temporal unraveling, for in spite of the fact that it seems to be "continuing," it is already complete.

This interface between fiction and reality brings the story to its climax as Roderick shouts, *"Madman! I tell you that she now stands without the door!"* (2:416) and the utterance has the "potency of a spell"; the doors swing open and Madeline, with a moaning cry, falls inward upon Usher and, like falling cards, he falls to the floor, and the house falls into the tarn. The instability of the house, the fissure that splits it, widens, and the story deconstructs just as the house does, as everything collapses back into formulated precreation nothingness and the tale ends on the italicized words of its own title.

Conclusion

Although the short story has been called America's unique contribution to the world's literature, it has not been taken seriously as a genre until the last half dozen years. Thus, it is not surprising that Poe, the most important contributor to the development of the form, has been similarly neglected. Fortunately, the new interest in theoretical approaches to literature has recently encouraged critics to compensate for their previous oversight of an important literary genre and an influential literary figure. For those who have always admired the short story form and who have not been too embarrassed to say they love the works of Poe, this is good news. For although the vision embodied in the short story as a genre and the works of Poe in particular may be, as many critics have charged, narrow, it has to be admitted that it is primal and profound.

Moreover, the charge that both Poe and the short story form are characterized by their formalism and their emphasis on unity and technique may no longer be raised as an accusation but presented as a compliment. Now that the realistic fallacy has been exposed as such and fiction can be valued as a "world of words" rather than as a "mirror in the roadway," the short story may be seen as the highly self-conscious art form that Poe knew it could be. And Poe himself may be seen as a highly self-conscious artist whose aesthetic vision and knowledge of the nature of narrative made him, in spite of the condescension of his critics, the most influential American writer in the nineteenth century.

Notes to Part 1

1. Roman Jakobson, "The Dominant," in *Readings in Russian Poetics*, ed. Ladislav Matejka and Krystyna Pomorska (Boston: MIT Press, 1971), 85.

2. B. M. Éjxenbaum, *O. Henry and the Theory of the Short Story*, trans. I. R. Titunik (Ann Arbor: Michigan Slavic Contributions, 1968), 7.

3. My own ideas have been set forth in a number of places. See: "Introduction" to *Short Story Theories* (Athens: Ohio University Press, 1976), 1–12; "The Unique Effect of the Short Story," *Studies of Short Fiction* 13 (1976): 289–97; "The Nature of Knowledge in Short Fiction," *Studies in Short Fiction* 21 (1984): 327–38; "Metaphoric Motivation in Short Fiction," in *Short Story Theory at a Crossroads*, ed. Susan Lohafer and Jo Ellyn Clarey (Baton Rouge: Louisiana State University Press, 1989), 62–73; and "Artifice and Artificiality in the Short Story," *Short Story* 1 (1990): 72–82.

4. Francesco De Sanctis, "Boccaccio and the Human Comedy," trans. Lucio Bartolai, in *The Decameron*, ed. Mark Musa and Peter E. Bondanella (New York: W. W. Norton & Co., 1977), 217.

5. Charles C. Mish, "English Short Fiction in the Seventeenth Century," *Studies in Short Fiction* 6 (1969): 223–30.

6. Benjamin Boyce, "English Short Fiction in the Eighteenth Century: A Preliminary View," *Studies in Short Fiction* 5 (1968): 95–112.

7. Edward Wagenknecht, *Cavalcade of the English Novel* (New York: Henry Holt and Co., 1943), 32.

8. Horace Walpole, "Preface to the Second Edition," *The Castle of Otranto* (New York: Macmillan Publishing Co., 1963), 19.

9. Although Freud discusses displacement in numerous places, the discussion most relevant for this context appears in *The Interpretation of Dreams*, vol. 5 of *The Standard Edition of the Complete Works of Sigmund Freud*, ed. James Strachey (London: Hogarth Press, 1953), 655–56; Northrop Frye's most explicit definition of the term can be found in *Fables of Identity: Studies in Poetic Mythology* (New York: Harcourt, Brace & World, 1963), 36.

10. Friedrich Schlegel, *Nachrichten von den poetischen Werken des G. Boccaccio* (1801), cited in E. K. Bennett, *A History of the German Novelle*, 2d ed. (Cambridge: Cambridge University Press, 1965), 7.

11. Ludwig Tieck, *Gasammelte Werke*, vol. 11 (1829), cited in Bennett, *A History of the German Novelle*, 11.

12. Gerhard Hoffmann, "Edgar Allan Poe and German Literature," in

American-German Literary Interrelations in the Nineteenth Century, ed. Christoph Wecker (Munich: Wilhelm Fink Verlag, 1983), 52–104.

13. R. D. Gooder, "Edgar Allan Poe: The Meaning of Style," *Cambridge Quarterly* 16 (1987): 110–23.

14. For a complete discussion of Poe's development as a literary critic, see Robert D. Jacobs, *Poe: Journalist and Critic* (Baton Rouge: Louisiana University Press, 1969); Margaret Alterton, *Origins of Poe's Critical Theory* (Ames: University of Iowa Press, 1925); and Edd Winfield Parks, *Edgar Allan Poe as Literary Critic* (Athens: University of Georgia Press, 1964). For studies of specific sources of Poe's theories, see Floyd Stoval, "Poe's Debt to Coleridge," *University of Texas Studies in English* (1930): 70–82; and Albert J. Lubell, "Poe and A. W. Schlegel," *Journal of English and Germanic Philology* 52 (1953): 1–12.

15. Poe's reviews can be found in volumes 8–12 of *The Complete Works of Edgar Allan Poe,* ed. James A. Harrison (New York: Thomas Y. Crowell & Co., 1902).

16. For discussion of this distinction, see *Russian Formalist Criticism,* ed. Lee T. Lemon and Marion J. Reis (Lincoln, Nebr.: Bison Books, 1965).

17. R. W. Foust, "Aesthetician of Simultaneity: E. A. Poe and Modern Literary Theory," *South Atlantic Quarterly* 46 (1981): 24.

18. See J. Gerald Kennedy, *Poe, Death, and the Life of Writing* (New Haven: Yale University Press, 1987); Michael J. S. Williams, *A World of Words: Language and Displacement in the Fiction of Edgar Allan Poe* (Durham, N.C.: Duke University Press, 1988); and Joan Dayan, *Fables of Mind: An Inquiry into Poe's Fiction* (New York: Oxford University Press, 1987).

19. The best source for discussion of the Lacan/Derrida controversy is *The Purloined Poe: Lacan, Derrida, and Psychoanalytic Reading,* ed. John P. Muller and William J. Richardson (Baltimore: Johns Hopkins University Press, 1988). See also John T. Irwin, *American Hieroglyphics* (New Haven: Yale University Press, 1980); Joseph N. Riddel, "'The Crypt' of Edgar Poe," *Boundry 2* (1979): 117–44; and John Carlos Rowe, *Through the Custom-House: Nineteenth-Century American Fiction and Modern Theory* (Baltimore: Johns Hopkins University Press, 1982.

20. For a detailed discussion of this issue in "The Philosophy of Composition," see Michael Black, "Why It Is So and Not Otherwise," *New Literary History* 6 (1975): 477–89.

21. Robert D. Jacobs, *Poe: Journalist and Critic* (Baton Rouge: Louisiana State University Press, 1969), 163.

22. For further discussion of these issues, see Peter Brooks, *Reading for the Plot* (New York: Alfred A. Knopf, 1984) and Jonathan Culler, *The Pursuit of Signs* (Ithaca, N.Y.: Cornell University Press, 1981).

23. Thomas S. Kuhn, *The Structure of Scientific Revolutions,* 2d ed. (Chicago: University of Chicago Press, 1970).

24. G. R. Thompson, *Poe's Fiction: Romantic Irony in the Gothic Tales* (Madison: University of Wisconsin Press, 1973), 53.

25. Frank Kermode, *The Sense of an Ending* (London: Oxford University Press, 1967), 83.

26. All quotations from Poe's stories are from *Collected Works of Edgar Allan Poe*, ed. Thomas O. Mabbott (Cambridge: Harvard University Press, Belknap Press, 1978). Volume and page numbers will follow the quotation parenthetically in the text.

27. Tzvetan Todorov, *The Fantastic: A Structural Approach to a Literary Genre*, trans. Richard Howard (Ithaca, N. Y.: Cornell University Press, 1975), 25.

28. Daniel Hoffman, *Poe Poe Poe Poe Poe Poe Poe* (Garden City, N. Y.: Doubleday & Co., 1972), 146.

29. David Ketterer, *The Rationale of Deception in Poe* (Baton Rouge: Louisiana State University Press, 1979), 119.

30. Donald Barlow Stauffer, "The Two Styles of Poe's 'MS. Found in a Bottle,'" *Style* 1 (1967): 107.

31. David Halliburton, *Edgar Allan Poe: A Phenomenological View* (Princeton: Princeton University Press, 1973), 250.

32. Stauffer, "Two Styles," 110.

33. Halliburton, *Edgar Allan Poe*, 248.

34. Dennis W. Eddings, ed., *The Naiad Voice* (Port Washington, N.Y.: Associated Faculty Press, 1983).

35. Thompson, *Poe's Fiction*.

36. Stephen L. Mooney, "Comic Intent in Poe's Tales: Five Criteria," *Modern Language Notes* 76 (1961): 432–34; "The Comic in Poe's Fiction," *American Literature* 33 (1962): 433–41.

37. Constance Rourke, *American Humor* (1931; reprint, New York: Doubleday Anchor, n.d.), 31.

38. See Friedrich Schiller, *On the Aesthetic Education of Man*, trans. Ronald Snell (New York: Frederick Ungar Publishing Co., 1965).

39. For more discussion of these issues, see Johan Huizinga, *Homo Ludens: A Study of the Play Element in Culture* (Boston: Beacon Press, 1955); Jacques Ehrmann, ed., *Game, Play, Literature* (Boston: Beacon Press, 1971); and Peter Hutchinson, *Games Authors Play* (London: Methuen & Co., 1983).

40. Quotations from *Eureka* and Poe's other nonfiction prose are from *The Complete Works of Edgar Allan Poe*, ed. James A. Harrison (New York: Thomas Y. Crowell & Co., 1902. Volume and page numbers are given in parenthesis after the quotation in the text.

41. Quotations from Poe's letters are taken from *The Letters of Edgar Allan Poe*, ed. John Ward Ostrom (Cambridge: Harvard University Press, 1948). Volume and page numbers follow the quotation parenthetically in the text.

42. Gregory Bateson, "A Theory of Play and Fantasy," in *Play: Its Role*

in Development and Evolution, ed. Jerome S. Bruner, Alison Jolly, and Kathy Sylva (New York: Basic Books, 1976), 125.

43. Cited by P. Pendleton Cooke, "Edgar A. Poe," *Southern Literary Messenger,* Jan. 1848, in *The Recognition of Edgar Allan Poe*, ed. Eric W. Carlson (Ann Arbor: University of Michigan Press, 1966), 23.

44. Cooke, "Edgar A. Poe," 24.

45. Jonathan Auerbach, "Poe's Other Double," *Criticism* 24 (1982): 354.

46. Roland Barthes, "Textual Analysis of a Tale by Edgar Poe," trans. Donald G. Marshall, *Poe Studies* 10 (1977): 10.

47. Arthur Quinn, *Edgar Allan Poe: A Critical Biography* (New York: Appleton-Century Co., 1941), 401.

48. See Edward H. Davidson, *Poe: A Critical Study* (Cambridge: Harvard University Press, Belknap Press, 1957). The essays by Auden, Tate, and Wilbur can be found in *The Recognition of Edgar Allan Poe*, ed. Eric W. Carlson (Ann Arbor: University of Michigan Press, 1966); and *Poe: A Collection of Critical Essays*, ed. Robert Regan (Englewood Cliffs, N. J.: Prentice-Hall, 1967).

49. Richard Wilbur, "Poe and the Art of Suggestion," *University of Mississippi Studies in English* 3 (1982): 9.

50. Gregory Bateson, *Steps to an Ecology of Mind* (New York: Ballantine Books, 1972), 461.

51. Nina Baym, "The Function of Poe's Pictorialism," *South Atlantic Quarterly* 65 (1966): 47.

52. Taylor Stoehr, "'Unspeakable Horror' in Poe," *South Atlantic Quarterly* 78 (1979): 324.

53. Roy P. Basler, "The Interpretation of 'Ligeia,'" *College English* 5 (1944): 363–74; James Schroeter, "A Misreading of Poe's 'Ligeia,'" *PMLA* 76 (1961): 397–406.

54. For summaries of these various approaches, see Claudia C. Morrison, "Poe's 'Ligeia': An Analysis," *Studies in Short Fiction* 4 (1967): 234–44; and Joseph M. Garrison, Jr., "The Irony of 'Ligeia,'" *ESQ* 60 (1970): 13–17.

55. Jules Zanger, "Poe's 'Berenice': Philosophical Fantasy and Its Pitfalls," in *The Scope of the Fantastic*, ed. Robert A. Collins and Howard D. Pearce (Westport, Conn.: Greenwood Press, 1985), 139.

56. David Karnath, "Poe's Baroque Space and the Unity of Effect," *Studies in Short Fiction* 15 (1978): 267.

57. See Northrop Frye, *Fables of Identity* (New York: Harcourt, Brace & World, 1963), 28.

58. For a more complete discussion of the motifs of identity, time, and the eye/I, see the fine close reading by E. Arthur Robinson, "Poe's 'The Tell-Tale Heart,'" *Nineteenth-Century Fiction* 19 (1965): 369–78.

59. Many critics have noted the ironic structure of the story. See, for example, John Freehafer, "Poe's 'Cask of Amontillado': A Tale of Effect," *Jahrbuch Für Amerikastudien* 13 (1968): 136–42.

60. Ann Jefferson, *"Mise en abyme* and the Prophetic," *Style* 17 (1983): 196–208.

61. Maurice J. Bennett, "The Detective Fiction of Poe and Borges," *Comparative Literature* 35 (1983): 267–68; see also Michael Holquist, "Whodunit and Other Questions: Metaphysical Detective Stories in Post-War Fiction," *New Literary History* 3 (1971): 135–56; Peter Hühn, "The Detective as Reader: Narrativity and Reading Concepts in Detective Fiction," *Modern Fiction Studies* 33 (1987): 451–66; Timothy Steele, "The Structure of the Detective Story: Classical or Modern," *Modern Fiction Studies* 27 (1981–82): 555–70; Tzvetan Todorov, "The Typology of Detective Fiction," in *The Poetics of Prose,* trans. Richard Howard (Ithaca, N.Y.: Cornell University Press, 1977), 42–52; and Joseph J. Moldenhauer, "Murder as a Fine Art: Basic Connections between Poe's Aesthetics, Psychology, and Moral Vision," *PMLA* 83 (1968): 284–97.

62. Shawn Rosenheim, "The King of 'Secret Readers': Edgar Poe, Cryptography, and the Origins of the Detective Story," *ELH* 6 (1989): 382–83.

63. G. K. Chesterton, "Defence of Detective Stories," in *Detective Fiction: Crime and Compromise,* ed. Dick Allen and David Chacko (New York: Harcourt Brace Jovanovich, 1974), 384–86.

64. Jean Ricardou, "Gold in the Bug," trans. Frank Towne, *Poe Studies* 9 (1976): 36, Michael Williams, " 'The language of the cipher': Interpretation in 'The Gold-Bug,' " *American Literature* 53 (1982): 646–60.

65. Daniel Kempton, "The Gold/Goole/Ghoul Bug," *ESQ* 33 (1987): 7.

66. Most of the discussions that have clustered around the Lacan/Derrida debate are included in *The Purloined Poe,* ed. John P. Muller and William J. Richardson (Baltimore: Johns Hopkins University Press, 1988). See also John Irwin's contribution to the debate, "Mysteries We Reread, Mysteries of Rereading: Poe, Borges, and the Analytic Detective Story: Also Lacan, Derrida, and Johnson," *Modern Language Notes* 101 (1986): 1168–1215.

67. Harry Levin, *The Power of Blackness* (New York: Vintage Books, 1960), 152–54; David H. Hirsch, "The Pit and the Apocalypse," *Sewanee Review* 76 (1968): 632–52.

68. Donald Baylor Stauffer, "Style and Meaning in 'Ligeia' and 'William Wilson,' " *Studies in Short Fiction* 2 (1965): 326, 328.

69. Ruth Sullivan, "William Wilson's Double," *Studies in Romanticism* 15 (1976): 259.

70. See the discussion of this ironic reversal by Joseph Patrick Roppolo, "Meaning and 'The Masque of the Red Death,' " *Tulane Studies in English* 13 (1963): 59–69.

71. Levin, *Power of Blackness,* 149.

72. Halliburton, *Edgar Allan Poe,* 312.

73. Kermit Vanderbilt, "Art and Nature in 'The Masque of the Red Death,' " *Nineteenth-Century Fiction* 22 (1968): 379–89.

74. The most energetic debate over the matter of the reliability/unreliability of the narrator can be seen in the essays by Patrick F. Quinn and G. R. Thompson in *Ruined Eden of the Present*, ed. G. R. Thompson and Virgil L. Lokke (Lafayette, Ind.: Purdue University Press, 1981). For discussions of the *Eureka* connection, see Maurice Beebe, "The Universe of Roderick Usher," *Personalist* 37 (1956): 147–60; "Order and Sentience in 'The Fall of the House of Usher,'" *PMLA* 76 (1961): 68–81; and Thomas J. Rountree, "Poe's Universe: The House of Usher and the Narrator," *Tulane Studies in English* 20 (1972): 123–34.

75. For a discussion of these metaphors of short story atmosphere, see the essays by Bowen, Welty, and Nadine Gordimer in *Short Story Theories*, ed. Charles E. May (Athens: Ohio University Press, 1976).

76. Jean Ricardou, "The Story within the Story," trans. Joseph Kestner, *James Joyce Quarterly* 18 (1981): 323–38. The term "en abyme" was coined by André Gide to refer to such techniques as the play within the play in *Hamlet*, in which the whole play is reflected in the miniature play. More recently, it has been used by American deconstructionist critics such as J. Hillis Miller to designate that point in any art work at which the work's fictional or aesthetic nature is manifested and thus the illusion of the work is exposed as such.

Part 2

THE WRITER

Introduction

Poe probably contributed as much to the beginnings of literary criticism in America as he did to the beginnings of the short story. His insistence that critiques of individual works be founded on a unified literary theory and his untiring demand that the focus of criticism should be on the structure and technique of the work marked the first serious effort in American letters to make literary criticism a rigorous field of study rather than merely the generalized ruminations of the leisurely reader.

Poe's demand that inner coherence rather than external correspondence be the criteria by which to judge the artwork and his identification of "plot" with form played a significant role in the creation of his own fiction and the development of his thought. In fact, seldom has an artist's literary theory and practice been so bound up with his overall philosophy.

The following excerpts from Poe's reviews and essays trace the development of his theories most important to the short story, beginning with his awareness of the importance of the unity of interest or effect in his early reviews and concluding with his metaphysical ideas of unity in his prose poem *Eureka*. Of particular importance is Poe's definition of "plot" as an aesthetic pattern rather than as a series of temporal events and his insistence that an aesthetic pattern communicates a mystic undercurrent of meaning.

For a brief summary of the development of Poe's critical concepts, see the Critical Context chapter in part 1. These excerpts are from *Poe's Complete Works*, edited by James A. Harrison (New York: Thomas Y. Crowell & Co., 1902).

Totality of Interest

In poems of magnitude the mind of the reader is not, at all times, enabled to include in one comprehensive survey the proportions and proper adjustment of the whole. He is pleased—if at all—with particular passages; and the sum of his pleasure is compounded of the sums of the pleasurable sensations inspired by these individual passages during the progress of perusal. But in pieces of less extent—like the poems of Mrs. Sigourney—the pleasure is *unique*, in the proper acceptation of that term—the understanding is employed, without difficulty, in the contemplation of the picture *as a whole*—and thus its effect will depend, in a very great degree, upon the perfection of its finish, upon the nice adaptation of its constituent parts, and especially upon what is rightly termed by Schlegel, the *unity or totality of interest*.

From a review of *Zinzendorff, and Other Poems* by L. H. Sigourney, *Southern Literary Messenger*, January 1836. In *Complete Works*, 8:126.

The Brief Article

It is not every one who can put "a good thing" properly together, although, perhaps, when thus properly put together, every tenth person you meet may be capable of both conceiving and appreciating it. We cannot bring ourselves to believe that less actual ability is required in the composition of a really good "brief article," than in a fashionable novel of the usual dimensions. The novel certainly requires what is denominated a sustained effort—but this is a matter of mere perseverance, and has but a collateral relation to talent. On the other hand—unity of effect, a quality not easily appreciated or indeed comprehended by an ordinary mind, and a *desideratum* difficult of attainment, even by those who can conceive it—is indispensable in the "brief article," and not so in the common novel. The latter, if admired at all, is admired for its detached passages, without reference to the work as a whole—or without reference to any general design—which, if it even exist in some measure, will be found to have occupied but little of the writer's attention, and cannot, from the length of the narrative, be taken in at one view, by the reader.

From "Watkins Tottle and Other Sketches," *Southern Literary Messenger,* June 1836. In *Complete Works,* 9:45–46.

Unity of Plot

The word *plot,* as commonly accepted, conveys but an indefinite meaning. Most persons think of it as simple *complexity;* and into this error even so fine a critic as Augustus William Schlegel has obviously fallen, when he confounds its idea with that of the mere *intrigue* in which the Spanish dramas of Cervantes and Calderon abound. But the greatest involution of incident will not result in plot; which, properly defined, is *that which no part can be displaced without ruin to the whole.* It may be described as a building so dependently constructed, that to change the position of a single brick is to overthrow the entire fabric. In this definition and description, we of course refer only to that infinite perfection which the true artist bears ever in mind—that unattainable goal to which his eyes are always directed, but of the possibility of attaining which he still endeavors, if wise, to cheat himself into the belief. The reading world, however, is satisfied with a less rigid construction of the term. It is content to think that plot a good one, in which none of the *leading* incidents can be *removed* without *detriment* to the mass. . . .

Without excessive and fatiguing exertion, inconsistent with legitimate interest, the mind cannot comprehend at one time, and in one survey, the numerous individual items which go to establish the whole. Thus the high ideal sense of the *unique* is sure to be wanting:—for, however absolute in itself be the unity of the novel, it must inevitably fail of appreciation. We speak now of that species of unity which is alone worth the attention of the critic—the unity or totality *of effect.*

From a review of *Night and Morning: A Novel* by Edward Bulwer-Lytton, *Graham's Magazine*, April 1841. In *Complete Works*, 10:117, 10:122.

Mystery

We have given, as may well be supposed, but a very meagre outline of the story, and we have given it in the simple or natural sequence. That is to say, we have related the events, as nearly as might be, in the order of their occurrence. But this order would by no means have suited the purpose of the novelist, whose design has been to maintain the secret of the murder, and the consequent mystery which encircles Rudge, and the actions of his wife, until the catastrophe of his discovery by Haredale. The *thesis* of the novel may thus be regarded as based upon curiosity. Every point is so arranged as to perplex the reader, and whet his desire for elucidation. . . .

Now there can be no question that, by such means as these, many points which are comparatively insipid in the natural sequence of our digest, and which would have been comparatively insipid even if given in full detail in a natural sequence, are endued with the interest of mystery; but neither can it be denied that a vast many more points are at the same time deprived of all effect, and become null, through the impossibility of comprehending them without the key. . . . But the reader may easily satisfy himself of the validity of our objection. Let him *re-peruse Barnaby Rudge,* and, with a pre-comprehension of the mystery, these points of which we speak break out in all directions like stars, and throw quadruple brilliance over the narrative—a brilliance which a correct taste will at once declare unprofitably sacrificed at the shrine of the keenest interest of mere mystery.

From a review of *Barnaby Rudge* by Charles Dickens, *Graham's Magazine,* February 1842. In *Complete Works,* 11:49, 11:50.

The Mystic Undercurrent

This is an exceedingly meagre outline of the leading events of the story; which, although brief, is crowded with incident. Beneath all, there runs a mystic or under-current of meaning, of the simplest and most easily intelligible, yet of the most richly philosophical character. . . . We have no hesitation in saying that this portion of the design of the romance—the portion which conveys an undercurrent of meaning—does not afford the fairest field to the romanticist—does not appertain to the highest regions of ideality. Although, in this case, the plan is essentially distinct from Allegory, yet it has too close an affinity to that most indefensible species of writing—a species whose gross demerits we cannot now pause to examine.

From a review of *Undine: A Miniature Romance* by Baron de la Motte Fouqué, *Burton's Gentleman's Magazine*, September 1839. In *Complete Works*, 10:36–37.

Allegory

In defence of allegory, (however, or for whatever object, employed,) there is scarcely one respectable word to be said. Its best appeals are made to the fancy—that is to say, to our sense of adaptation, not of matters proper, but of matters improper for the purpose, of the real with the unreal, having never more of intelligible connection than has something with nothing, never half so much of effective affinity as has the substance for the shadow. The deepest emotion aroused within us by the happiest allegory, *as* allegory, is a very, very imperfectly satisfied sense of the writer's ingenuity in overcoming a difficulty we should have preferred his not having attempted to overcome. The fallacy of the idea that allegory, in any of its moods, can be made to enforce a truth—that metaphor, for example, may illustrate as well as embellish an argument—could be promptly demonstrated: the converse of the supposed fact might be shown, indeed, with very little trouble—but these are topics foreign to my present purpose. One thing is clear, that if allegory ever establishes a fact, it is by dint of over-turning a fiction. Where the suggested meaning runs through the obvious one in a *very* profound undercurrent, so as never to interfere with the upper one without our own volition, so as never to show itself unless *called* to the surface, there only, for the proper uses of fictitious narrative, is it available at all. Under the best circumstances, it must always interfere with that unity of effect which, to the artist, is worth all the allegory in the world. Its vital injury, however, is rendered to the most vitally important point in fiction—that of earnestness or verisimilitude.

From a review of *Twice-Told Tales* and *Mosses from an Old Manse* by Nathaniel Hawthorne, *Godey's Lady's Book*, November 1847. In *Complete Works*, 13:148.

The Prose Tale

But it is of his tales that we desire principally to speak. The tale proper, in our opinion, affords unquestionably the fairest field for the exercise of the loftiest talent, which can be afforded by the wide domains of mere prose. Were we bidden to say how the highest genius could be most advantageously employed for the best display of its own powers, we should answer, without hesitation—in the composition of a rhymed poem, not to exceed in length what might be perused in an hour. Within this limit alone can the highest order of true poetry exist. We need only here say, upon this topic, that, in almost all classes of composition, the unity of effect or impression is a point of the greatest importance. It is clear, moreover, that this unity cannot be thoroughly preserved in productions whose perusal cannot be completed at one sitting. We may continue the reading of a prose composition, from the very nature of prose itself, much longer than we can persevere, to any good purpose, in the perusal of a poem. This latter, if truly fulfilling the demands of the poetic sentiment, induces an exaltation of the soul which cannot be long sustained. All high excitements are necessarily transient. Thus a long poem is a paradox. And, without unity of impression, the deepest effects cannot be brought about. Epics were the offspring of an imperfect sense of Art, and their reign is no more. A poem *too* brief may produce a vivid, but never an intense or enduring impression. Without a certain continuity of effort—without a certain duration or repetition of purpose—the soul is never deeply moved. There must be the dropping of the water upon the rock. De Béranger has wrought brilliant things—pungent and spirit-stirring—but, like all immassive bodies, they lack *momentum*, and thus fail to satisfy the Poetic Sentiment. They sparkle and excite, but, from want of continuity, fail deeply to impress. Extreme brevity will degenerate into epigrammatism; but the sin of extreme length is even more unpardonable. *In medio tutissimus ibis.*

From a review of *Twice-Told Tales* by Nathaniel Hawthorne, *Graham's Magazine*, May 1842. In *Complete Works*, 11:106–9.

Were we called upon however to designate that class of composition which, next to such a poem as we have suggested, should best fulfil the demands of high genius—should offer it the most advantageous field of exertion—we should unhesitatingly speak of the prose tale, as Mr. Hawthorne has here exemplified it. We allude to the short prose narrative, requiring from a half-hour to one or two hours in its perusal. The ordinary novel is objectionable, from its length, for reasons already stated in substance. As it cannot be read at one sitting, it deprives itself, of course, of the immense force derivable from *totality*. Worldly interests intervening during the pauses of perusal, modify, annul, or counteract, in a greater or less degree, the impressions of the book. But simple cessation in reading would, of itself, be sufficient to destroy the true unity. In the brief tale, however, the author is enabled to carry out the fulness of his intention, be it what it may. During the hour of perusal the soul of the reader is at the writer's control. There are no external or extrinsic influences—resulting from weariness or interruption.

A skilful literary artist has constructed a tale. If wise, he has not fashioned his thoughts to accommodate his incidents; but having conceived, with deliberate care, a certain unique or single *effect* to be wrought out, he then invents such incidents—he then combines such events as may best aid him in establishing this preconceived effect. If his very initial sentence tend not to the outbringing of this effect, then he has failed in his first step. In the whole composition there should be no word written, of which the tendency, direct or indirect, is not to the one pre-established design. And by such means, with such care and skill, a picture is at length painted which leaves in the mind of him who contemplates it with a kindred art, a sense of the fullest satisfaction. The idea of the tale has been presented unblemished, because undisturbed; and this is an end unattainable by the novel. Undue brevity is just as exceptionable here as in the poem; but undue length is yet more to be avoided.

We have said that the tale has a point of superiority even over the poem. In fact, while the *rhythm* of this latter is an essential aid in the development of the poem's highest idea—the idea of the Beautiful— the artificialities of this rhythm are an inseparable bar to the development of all points of thought or expression which have their basis in *Truth*. But Truth is often, and in very great degree, the aim of the tale. Some of the finest tales are tales of ratiocination. Thus the field of this species of composition, if not in so elevated a region on the mountain of Mind, is a table-land of far vaster extent than the domain of the mere poem. Its products are never so rich, but infinitely more numerous, and more appreciable by the mass of mankind. The writer of the prose tale, in short, may bring to his theme a vast variety of modes or inflections of thought and expression—(the ratiocinative, for example, the sarcastic or the humorous) which are not only antagonistical to the nature of the poem, but absolutely forbidden by one of its most peculiar and indispensable adjuncts; we allude of course, to rhythm. It may be added, here, *par parenthèse,* that the author who aims at the purely beautiful in a prose tale is laboring at great disadvantage. For Beauty can be better treated in the poem. Not so with terror, or passion, or horror, or a multitude of such other points. And here it will be seen how full of prejudice are the usual animadversions against those *tales of effect* many fine examples of which were found in the earlier numbers of *Blackwood.* The impressions produced were wrought in a legitimate sphere of action, and constituted a legitimate although sometimes an exaggerated interest. They were relished by every man of genius: although there were found many men of genius who condemned them without just ground. The true critic will but demand that the design intended be accomplished, to the fullest extent, by the means most advantageously applicable.

The Philosophy of Composition

Charles Dickens, in a note now lying before me, alluding to an examination I once made of the mechanism of *Barnaby Rudge,* says—"By the way, are you aware that Godwin wrote his *Caleb Williams* backwards? He first involved his hero in a web of difficulties, forming the second volume, and then, for the first, cast about him for some mode of accounting for what had been done."

I cannot think this the *precise* mode of procedure on the part of Godwin—and indeed what he himself acknowledges, is not altogether in accordance with Mr. Dickens' idea—but the author of *Caleb Williams* was too good an artist not to perceive the advantage derivable from at least a somewhat similar process. Nothing is more clear than that every plot, worth the name, must be elaborated to its *dénouement* before any thing be attempted with the pen. It is only with the *dénouement* constantly in view that we can give a plot its indispensable air of consequence, or causation, by making the incidents, and especially the tone at all points, tend to the development of the intention.

There is a radical error, I think, in the usual mode of constructing a story. Either history affords a thesis—or one is suggested by an incident of the day—or, at best, the author sets himself to work in the combination of striking events to form merely the basis of his narrative—designing, generally, to fill in with description, dialogue, or autorial comment, whatever crevices of fact, or action, may, from page to page, render themselves apparent.

I prefer commencing with the consideration of an *effect*. Keeping originality *always* in view—for he is false to himself who ventures to dispense with so obvious and so easily attainable a source of interest—I say to myself, in the first place, "Of the innumerable effects, or impressions, of which the heart, the intellect, or (more generally) the soul is susceptible, what one shall I, on the present occasion, select?" Having chosen a novel, first, and secondly a vivid effect, I consider

From "The Philosophy of Composition," *Graham's Magazine,* April 1846. In *Complete Works,* 14:193–95.

whether it can best be wrought by incident or tone—whether by ordinary incidents and peculiar tone, or the converse, or by peculiarity both of incident and tone—afterward looking about me (or rather within) for such combinations of event, or tone, as shall best aid me in the construction of the effect.

I have often thought how interesting a magazine paper might be written by any author who would—that is to say, who could—detail, step by step, the processes by which any one of his compositions attained its ultimate point of completion. Why such a paper has never been given to the world, I am much at a loss to say—but, perhaps, the autorial vanity has had more to do with the omission than any one other cause. Most writers—poets in especial—prefer having it understood that they compose by a species of fine frenzy—an ecstatic intuition—and would positively shudder at letting the public take a peep behind the scenes, at the elaborate and vacillating crudities of thought—at the true purposes seized only at the last moment—at the innumerable glimpses of idea that arrived not at the maturity in full view—at the fully matured fancies discarded in despair as unmanageable—at the cautious selections and rejections—at the painful erasures and interpolations—in a word, at the wheels and pinions—the tackle for scene-shifting—the step-ladders and demon-traps—the cock's feathers, the red paint and the black patches, which, in ninety-nine cases out of the hundred, constitute the properties of the literary *histrio*.

I am aware, on the other hand, that the case is by no means common, in which an author is at all in condition to retrace the steps by which his conclusions have been attained. In general, suggestions, having arisen pell-mell, are pursued and forgotten in a similar manner.

For my own part, I have neither sympathy with the repugnance alluded to, nor, at any time, the least difficulty in recalling to mind the progressive steps of any of my compositions; and, since the interest of an analysis, or reconstruction, such as I have considered a *desideratum*, is quite independent of any real or fancied interest in the thing analyzed, it will not be regarded as a breach of decorum on my part to show the *modus operandi* by which some one of my own works was put together. I select "The Raven," as the most generally known. It is my design to render it manifest that no one point in its composition is referrible either to accident or intuition—that the work proceeded, step by step, to its completion with the precision and rigid consequence of a mathematical problem.

Let us dismiss, as irrelevant to the poem *per se*, the circumstance—or say the necessity—which, in the first place, gave rise to the intention of composing a poem that should suit at once the popular and the critical taste.

We commence, then, with this intention.

The initial consideration was that of extent. If any literary work is too long to be read at one sitting, we must be content to dispense with the immensely important effect derivable from unity of impression—for, if two sittings be required, the affairs of the world interfere, and every thing like totality is at once destroyed. But since, *ceteris paribus*, no poet can afford to dispense with *any thing* that may advance his design, it but remains to be seen whether there is, in extent, any advantage to counterbalance the loss of unity which attends it. Here I say no, at once. What we term a long poem is, in fact, merely a succession of brief ones—that is to say, of brief poetical effects. It is needless to demonstrate that a poem is such, only inasmuch as it intensely excites, by elevating, the soul; and all intense excitements are, through a psychal necessity, brief. For this reason, at least one half of the *Paradise Lost* is essentially prose—a succession of poetical excitements interspersed, *inevitably*, with corresponding depressions—the whole being deprived, through the extremeness of its length, of the vastly important artistic element, totality, or unity, of effect.

It appears evident, then, that there is a distinct limit, as regards length, to all works of literary art—the limit of a single sitting—and that, although in certain classes of prose composition, such as *Robinson Crusoe*, (demanding no unity,) this limit may be advantageously overpassed, it can never properly be overpassed in a poem. Within this limit, the extent of a poem may be made to bear mathematical relation to its merit—in other words, to the excitement or elevation—again in other words, to the degree of the true poetical effect which it is capable of inducing; for it is clear that the brevity must be in direct ratio of the intensity of the intended effect:—this, with one proviso—that a certain degree of duration is absolutely requisite for the production of any effect at all.

The Poetic Principle

In speaking of the Poetic Principle, I have no design to be either thorough or profound. While discussing, very much at random, the essentiality of what we call Poetry, my principal purpose will be to cite for consideration, some few of those minor English or American poems which best suit my own taste, or which, upon my own fancy, have left the most definite impression. By "minor poems" I mean, of course, poems of little length. And here, in the beginning, permit me to say a few words in regard to a somewhat peculiar principle, which, whether rightfully or wrongfully, has always had its influence in my own critical estimate of the poem. I hold that a long poem does not exist. I maintain that the phrase, "a long poem," is simply a flat contradiction in terms.

I need scarcely observe that a poem deserves its title only inasmuch as it excites, by elevating the soul. The value of the poem is in the ratio of this elevating excitement. But all excitements are, through a psychal necessity, transient. That degree of excitement which would entitle a poem to be so called at all, cannot be sustained throughout a composition of any great length. After the lapse of half an hour, at the very utmost, it flags—fails—a revulsion ensues—and then the poem is, in effect, and in fact, no longer such.

There are, no doubt, many who have found difficulty in reconciling the critical dictum that the *Paradise Lost* is to be devoutly admired throughout, with the absolute impossibility of maintaining for it, during perusal, the amount of enthusiasm which that critical dictum would demand. This great work, in fact, is to be regarded as poetical, only when, losing sight of that vital requisite in all works of Art, Unity, we view it merely as a series of minor poems. If, to preserve its Unity—its totality of effect or impression—we read it (as would be necessary) at a single sitting, the result is but a constant alternation of excitement and depression. After a passage of what we feel to be true poetry, there

From "The Poetic Principle," *Sartain's Union Magazine*, October 1850. In *Complete Works*, 14:266–72.

follows, inevitably, a passage of platitude which no critical pre-judgment can force us to admire; but if, upon completing the work, we read it again, omitting the first book—that is to say, commencing with the second—we shall be surprised at now finding that admirable which we before condemned—that damnable which we had previously so much admired. It follows from all this that the ultimate, aggregate, or absolute effect of even the best epic under the sun, is a nullity:—and this is precisely the fact. . . .

While the epic mania—while the idea that, to merit in poetry, prolixity is indispensable—has, for some years past, been gradually dying out of the public mind, by mere dint of its own absurdity—we find it succeeded by a heresy too palpably false to be long tolerated, but one which, in the brief period it has already endured, may be said to have accomplished more in the corruption of our Poetical Literature than all its other enemies combined. I allude to the heresy of *The Didactic.* It has been assumed, tacitly and avowedly, directly and indirectly, that the ultimate object of all Poetry is Truth. Every poem, it is said, should inculcate a moral; and by this moral is the poetical merit of the work to be adjudged. We Americans, especially, have patronised this happy idea; and we Bostonians, very especially, have developed it in full. We have taken it into our heads that to write a poem simply for the poem's sake, and to acknowledge such to have been our design, would be to confess ourselves radically wanting in the true Poetic dignity and force:—but the simple fact is, that, would we but permit ourselves to look into our own souls, we should immediately there discover that under the sun there neither exists nor *can* exist any work more thoroughly dignified—more supremely noble than this very poem—this poem *per se*—this poem which is a poem and nothing more—this poem written solely for the poem's sake.

Eureka

To the few who love me and whom I love—to those who feel rather than to those who think—to the dreamers and those who put faith in dreams as in the only realities—I offer this Book of Truths, not in its character of Truth-Teller, but for the Beauty that abounds in its Truth; constituting it true. To these I present the composition as an Art-product alone,—let us say as a Romance; or, if I be not urging too lofty a claim, as a Poem.

What I here propound is true:—therefore it cannot die:—or if by any means it be now trodden down so that it die, it will "rise again to the Life Everlasting."

Nevertheless, it is as a Poem only that I wish this work to be judged after I am dead.

E.A.P.

My general proposition, then, is this:—*In the Original Unity of the First Thing lies the Secondary Cause of All Things, with the Germ of their Inevitable Annihilation. . . .*

I now assert—that an intuition altogether irresistible, although inexpressible, forces me to the conclusion that what God originally created—that Matter which, by dint of his Volition he first made from his spirit, or from Nihility, could have been nothing but Matter in its utmost conceivable state of—what?—of *Simplicity?* . . .

Let us now endeavor to conceive what Matter must be when, or if, in its absolute extreme of *Simplicity*. Here the Reason flies at once to Imparticularity—to a particle—to *one* particle—a particle of *one* kind—of one character—of *one* nature—of *one* size—of *one* form—a particle therefore, "*without form and void*"—a particle positively a particle at all points—a particle absolutely unique, individual, undivided, and not

From *Eureka: An Essay on the Material and Spiritual Universe*, vol. 16 of the *Complete Works*. Quoted here is the preface and pp. 185–86, 206, 207, 211, 217–19, 292, 302, 306, 311.

indivisible only because He created it, by dint of his Will, can by an infinitely less energetic exercise of the same Will, as a matter of course, divide it.

Oneness, then, is all that I predicate of the originally created Matter; but I propose to show that this *Oneness is a principle abundantly sufficient to account for the constitution, the existing phenomena, and the plainly inevitable annihilation of at least the material Universe.* . . .

This constitution has been effected by *forcing* the originally and therefore normally *One* into the abnormal condition of *Many.* An action of this character implies reaction. A diffusion from Unity, under the conditions, involves a tendency to return into Unity—a tendency ineradicable until satisfied. . . .

Unless we are to conceive that the appetite for Unity among the atoms is doomed to be satisfied *never;*—unless we are to conceive that what had a beginning is to have no end—a conception which cannot *really* be entertained, however much we may talk or dream of entertaining it—we are forced to conclude that the repulsive influence imagined, will, finally—under pressure of the *Uni-tendency collectively* applied, but never and in no degree *until,* on fulfillment of the Divine purposes, such collective application shall be naturally made—yield to a force which, at that ultimate epoch, shall be the superior force precisely to the extent required and thus permit the universal subsidence into the inevitable, because original and therefore normal, *One.* . . .

Every atom, of every body, attracts every other atom, both of its own and of every other body, with a force which varies inversely as the squares of the distance between the attracting and attracted atom. . . . Does not so evident a brotherhood among the atoms point to a common parentage? Does not a sympathy so omniprevalent, so ineradicable, and so thoroughly irrespective, suggest a common paternity at its source? . . . In a word, is it not because the atoms were, at some remote epoch of time, even *more than together*—is it not because originally, and therefore normally, they were *One*—that one in all circumstances—at all points—in all directions—by all modes of approach—in all relations and through all conditions—they struggle *back* to this absolutely, this irrelatively, this unconditionally *one?* . . .

In Divine constructions the object is either design or object as we choose to regard it—and we may take at any time a cause for an effect, or the converse—so that we can never absolutely decide which is which. . . .

The pleasure which we derive from any display of human ingenuity is in the ratio of *the approach* to this series of reciprocity. In the construction of *plot*, for example, in fictitious literature, we should aim at so arranging the incidents that we shall not be able to determine, of any one of them, whether it depends from any one other or upholds it. In this sense, of course *perfection of plot* is really or practically unattainable—but only because it is a finite intelligence that constructs. The plots of God are perfect. The Universe is a plot of God. . . .

The sense of the symmetrical is an instinct which may be depended upon with an almost blindfold reliance. It is the poetical essence of the Universe—*of the Universe* which, in the supremeness of its symmetry, is but the most sublime of poems. Now symmetry and consistency are convertible terms:—thus Poetry and Truth are one. A thing is consistent in the ratio of its truth—true in the ratio of its consistency. *A perfect consistency, I repeat, can be nothing but an absolute truth.* We may take it for granted, then, that man cannot long or widely err if he suffer himself to be guided by his poetical, which I have maintained to be his truthful, in being his symmetrical, instinct. . . .

The cycles of the Universe are perpetual—the Universe has no conceivable end. Had an end been demonstrated, however, from so purely collateral a cause as an ether, Man's instinct of the Divine *capacity to adapt*, would have rebelled against the demonstration. We should have been forced to regard the Universe with some sense of dissatisfaction as we experience in contemplating an unnecessarily complex work of human art. Creation would have affected us as an imperfect *plot* in a romance, where the *dénoument* is awkwardly brought about by interposed incidents external and foreign to the main subject; instead of springing out of the bosom of the thesis—out of the heart of the ruling idea—instead of arising as a result of the primary proposition—as inseparable and inevitable part and parcel of the fundamental conception of the book. . . .

When on fulfillment of its purposes, then, Matter shall have returned into its original condition of *One*— . . . it will then (to speak paradoxically for the moment) be Matter without Attraction and without Repulsion—in other words, Matter without Matter—in other words again, *Matter no more*. In sinking into Unity, it will sink at once into that Nothingness which, to all Finite Perception, Unity must be—into that Material Nihility from which alone we can conceive it to have been evoked—to have been *created* by the Volition of God. . . .

Guiding our imaginations by that omniprevalent law of laws the law of periodicity, are we not, indeed, more than justified in entertaining a belief—let us say, rather, in indulging a hope—that the process we have here ventured to contemplate will be renewed forever, and forever, and forever; a novel Universe swelling into existence, and then subsiding into nothingness, at every throb of the Heart Divine?

And now—this Heart Divine—what is it? *It is our own.*

Part 3

THE CRITICS

Introduction

Literary critics and academic scholars have often ignored Poe because of the sensational gothic surface of his work—a neglect encouraged by the famous accusation of Henry James and T. S. Eliot that an appreciation of Poe was the mark of an adolescent mind. It is only fitting after being dismissed by other writers that the first revival in Poe studies began in the 1950s with the provocative remarks of such respected artists as Richard Wilbur and W. H. Auden.

The comments of Wilbur and Auden, as well as the studies by influential New Critics such as Allen Tate and Edward Davidson, caused a new interest in Poe as a religious and philosophic thinker. Nonetheless, his true stature as an artist was not recognized until the introduction into American criticism of structuralist, poststructuralist, and reader-response theories in the 1960s.

The three essays in this section represent the most influential critical approaches to literature in the last 25 years. Kermit Vanderbilt's study of "The Masque of the Red Death" is in the best tradition of formalist close reading and reveals Poe's thematization of his aesthetic concerns. Michael Williams's structuralist-influenced analysis of "The Gold Bug" is a stimulating study of Poe's tactic of embedding interpretative strategies within his stories and his philosophic concern with the power of language. Ronald Bieganowski's analysis approaches Poe's two best-known stories from the perspective of reader-response theory and reveals the importance of the narrator in his fiction.

Kermit Vanderbilt

The intended effect and meaning of "The Masque of the Red Death" have challenged and eluded Poe critics over the years. Readings of the tale have advanced Poe studies by offering valuable glimpses into Poe's fictional world; but none has achieved a satisfactory account of the story in all of its significant parts.[1] An approach to Poe's meaning overlooked up to now has been a study of "The Masque" in the immediate context of Poe's esthetic ideas in 1842. Interpreted in the light of Poe's developing esthetic theory in this crucial year, the story, which appeared in the May issue of *Graham's Magazine*, becomes somewhat more than a tale of horror on the coming of Death. The hero Prospero, who bears an interesting resemblance to his namesake in Shakespeare's *The Tempest*, appears to be not a fear-crazed ruler but instead an exact portrait of Poe's artist-hero, and "The Masque of the Red Death" becomes a fable of nature and art. Placed in a larger context, the tale allowed Poe to dramatize the tensions of the "Romantic" artist in America, and helped him to discover the way which led through "The Domain of Arnheim" into the cosmic regions of *Eureka*.

I

The month before "The Masque of the Red Death" appeared, Poe explored the contention between the artist and the limits imposed by mortality. The occasion was a review of Longfellow's recent poetry.[2] In this essay, which later would be enlarged as "The Poetic Principle," Poe defined the poet or creator of Beauty as a man of "taste" rather than of "pure intellect" or "moral sense." He concerns himself not with temporal duty or earthly truth but with supernal beauty. He is thereby superior to the rest of mankind. They delight in the "manifold forms and colors and sounds" of things-as-they-are, and in the conventional record of nature fashioned by the imitative craftsman. But the true artist strives to create rather than imitate, and his vision therefore transcends mere nature. His "burning thirst" for supernal beauty, a passion approaching even to madness, is related to "the *immortal* es-

From "Art and Nature in 'The Masque of the Red Death,'" *Nineteenth-Century Fiction*, March 1968, 379–89.

sence of man's nature." In making this "wild effort to reach the beauty above," the artist rearranges and transforms material reality: "Inspired with a prescient ecstasy of the beauty beyond the grave, [the imagination] struggles by multiform novelty of combination among the things and thoughts of Time, to anticipate a portion of that loveliness whose very elements, perhaps, appertain solely to Eternity."

The next month in "The Masque of the Red Death" Prince Prospero will exactly match this description of the artist-hero. When he isolates himself and one thousand knights and ladies of his court during the pestilence, the Prince is not following the dictates of a judicious "intellect" or a dutiful "moral sense." The Prince, as Poe notes, is a man of "taste." Though his courtiers conceive the adventure to be a well-planned escape from the Red Death itself, the Prince has motives of another order. Objective nature outside having been ravaged by the plague, Poe's hero will employ his taste and imagination to create a symbolic equivalent of nature's elements—a combination which can transform earthly reality into the artist's liberating vision of immortal beauty.

The colors of the Prince's bizarre suite, together with their ordering from east to west, establish the leading clues to Prospero's subjective world. Poe does not seem, at first, to insist that the colors are meaningful. He sketches the seven rooms with fairly rapid strokes, seemingly to illustrate that the Prince is "gaudy," "bizarre," "wanton," and "fantastic" in his artistic predilections:

> That at the eastern extremity was hung, for example, in blue—and vividly blue were its windows. The second chamber was purple in its ornaments and tapestries, and here the panes were purple. The third was green throughout, and so were the casements. The fourth was furnished and litten with orange—the fifth with white—the sixth with violet. The seventh apartment was closely shrouded in black velvet tapestries. . . . The panes here were scarlet—a deep blood color.

Prospero's suite, arranged from east to west, with the first apartment blue and the seventh black, connotes generally the daily cycle of nature and Shakespeare's seven ages of man, as more than one critic has remarked. No one, however, has taken Poe's art seriously enough here to confirm that the pattern is deliberate and precise. Yet Poe in the same issue of *Graham's* had reviewed Hawthorne's *Twice-Told Tales* and set down his requirement that in the tale "there should be no word written, of which the tendency, direct or indirect, is not to the one pre-established design."[3]

A meaningful symmetry does develop precisely in Prospero's seven-room suite. The middle or fourth room, for example, is orange, the warmest color in Poe's spectrum, and analogous to midday. Returning to the cold, blue eastern room, one recognizes the image of dawning human life. It is succeeded by the purple room—an infusion of blue with the warmer tone of red—suggesting perhaps the quickening of life. The third room of green connotes growth, aspiration, youth; and the orange room, corresponding to the high noon of existence, becomes the harvest or fulfillment of human labor and ambition. The next room is white, at once all-color and no-color, a sudden and chill contrast which evokes decline, old age, decomposition, and approaching death. Or as Poe put it in "Tamerlane": "Let life, then, as the day-flower, fall / With the noon-day beauty—which is all." After the white apartment comes the next-to-last room of violet, a bluish blue-red colder than the corresponding purple of the second room, and pre-figuring imminent death in the seventh room. In this western room, the blood-colored panes depict, of course, the dread effects of the plague, and the black tapestries represent death itself. And most prominently stands the massive ebony clock against the western wall. Its "dull, heavy monotonous clang" pervades the entire suite and further marks the ravages of time in each of the seven stages of earthly mortality.[4]

If Prospero's suite is a metaphor of nature and mortality, one naturally asks why the Prince, apparently bent on escape from death, should have patterned his suite after the very reminders of mutability, decay, and the Red Death. The previous essay on Longfellow has suggested the answer. Poe is writing a fable of the imagination striving to control and transform the corrosive elements of nature and to gain, through immortal beauty, the artist's triumph over death. Prospero has designed an imperial suite to embody, first of all, the cycle of natural life, including what Poe had termed in the Longfellow review "the things and thoughts of Time." Next, he has created the "multiform novelty of combinations" which will permit him to move through and beyond the confinements of nature, time, and finite reality. The suite, with its windings, its stained-glass windows, closed outer corridors, artificial illumination, and bizarre embellishments—its "multitude of gaudy and fantastic appearances"—represents Prospero's imaginative re-ordering of actuality. He has created a setting which can evoke the magic and unearthly visions of the liberated sensibility. These enclosed apartments, both singly and together, define the magic circle which Poe earlier had termed "the circumscribed Eden" of the poet's dreams.

Prospero's elaborate masque provides the main drama of Poe's tale. As in Shakespeare's *The Tempest,* the masque also climaxes the struggle between the hero's art and nature's opposing forces of darkness. In fact, the illuminating parallels between the two works, while they may not prove that Poe consciously used Shakespeare's play as a source, do suggest at least a way to read Poe's climactic action in the tale.[5] Shakespeare's Prospero, it will be remembered, succeeds in controlling a savage island and turning it into a land suffused with idyllic greenness and ethereal music. To achieve this triumph of his art over barbaric nature, Prospero frees Ariel from a cloven pine where he had been imprisoned by the "earthly and abhorred commands" of the witch-hag Sycorax (I, ii, 273). So liberated from the destructive element of earth, the delicate Ariel becomes the spiritual quality of nature which unites with the powers of Prospero's art to create a landscape of paradisal beauty. Ariel helps to preserve Prospero's island dominion, though he reminds his master that this magic service will presently end.

Prospero's island rule, then, is precarious, and made more so by his chief enemy Caliban, the bestial offspring of Sycorax. Caliban embodies the withering threat of destructive nature of the artist's imagination. Shakespeare brilliantly condenses this antagonism toward Prospero's higher powers by giving Caliban's curse on his master: "the red plague rid you, / For learning me your language" (I, ii, 364–365).

The climax of Prospero's reign occurs in the masque which he conjures in the fourth act. During the dance of nymphs and reapers which follows Ceres' song of harvest abundance, Prospero grows distracted and petulant. He breaks off the masque. His imagination has failed him, his worldly fears of Caliban's "foul conspiracy" have returned, and as a result of both, he gives in to a despairing vision of cosmic dissolution. In this decline of imagination, Shakespeare's artist-hero confronts utter reality and admits, in effect, that man's creative art cannot transcend the life-threatening forces of hostile nature. In particular, he concedes his failure either to elevate or to vanquish Caliban: "This thing of darkness I / Acknowledge mine" (V, i, 275–276). At the end,

he owns that his liberation from darkness, death, and the limits of earth
must arrive from a power greater than his own:

> Now I want
> Spirits to enforce, art to enchant
> And my ending is despair,
> Unless I be reliev'd by prayer,
> Which pierces so that it assaults
> Mercy itself and frees all faults.
> (Epilogue, 13–18)[6]

Poe's Prospero also meets the ultimate challenge to his art as he
stages his bizarre masque "while the pestilence raged most furiously
abroad." The Prince's "guiding taste," once again, dictates the colors
and effects. Like Shakespeare's hero, also, Poe's Prospero gives character to the masqueraders themselves. And their character is such stuff
as dreams are made of. They are no longer people, but have become,
instead, "a multitude of dreams": "And these—the dreams—writhed
in and about, taking hue from the rooms, and causing the wild music
of the orchestra to seem as the echo of their steps." Prospero has combined light and color, arabesque sculpture, wild music, and the
rhythms of the dance to create his dreamland, out of space, out of time.
Only the measured, hourly chiming of the ebony clock threatens to
dissipate the fantasy; but this brief, contrapuntal note of reality also
emphasizes, by contrast, the prevailing "glare and glitter and piquancy
and phantasm" of Prospero's conjured assembly of spirits: "The
dreams are stiff-frozen as they stand. But the echoes of the chime die
away—they have endured but an instant— . . . And now again the
music swells, and the dreams live, and writhe to and fro more merrily
than ever, taking hue from the many-tinted windows through which
stream the rays from the tripods." Like Shakespeare's hero, Prospero
has controlled the movements of his visitors, transcended the limita-
tions of nature, and approached the threshold of supernal beauty. But
at the midnight hour, the figure of the Red Death—the counterpart of
Caliban—appears at the masque.

Prospero's failure is first signaled not by the imminent threat of
death, but by his troubled reaction to its appearance. His convulsion
and anger indicate the failure of imagination even before he waves his
hand to end the masque. His fearful command to his courtiers, "'Un-
case the varlet that we may know whom we have to hang to-morrow at

sunrise from the battlements,'" is both impotent and utterly mundane, the conventional reflex of a petulant, earthly ruler. The world, in short, is finally too much with him. The mummer of Death strides majestically past him and through the seven apartments (Poe once more underscores the exact sequence of the polychromatic décor) in symbolic triumph over each stage of earthly life and over Prospero's art and aspiring imagination. As in *The Tempest*, Ariel has taken leave and Prospero alone must confront his mortality and ultimate defeat. While the courtiers shrink from the grim figure, Prospero acknowledges this thing of darkness to be his own. In a self-destructive charge, he pursues the spectre of death westward into the seventh apartment. And predictably, death gains his midnight victory in the western room where the dread clock and macabre appointments had been the artist's ultimate challenge to his powers of imagination.

Prospero's defeat becomes inevitable within the precise logic which supports Poe's esthetic fable. And it suggests one last parallel to *The Tempest*. Anticipating the return of Caliban, Shakespeare's Prospero can no longer prolong his masque. Instead, he entertains a vision of cosmic dissolution and offers the dispiriting prophecy that

> the great globe itself
> Yea, all which it inherit, shall dissolve
> And, like this insubstantial pageant faded,
> Leave not a rack behind.
> (IV, i, 153–156)

Poe repeats this cataclysmic vision of destructive nature and triumphant death. The outer and inner worlds of his defeated hero fade, and the final curtain lowers to the measured and fateful cadence of Poe's closing rhetoric: "And the life of the ebony clock went out with that of the last of the gay. And the flames of the tripods expired. And Darkness and Decay and the Red Death held illimitable dominion over all."[7]

II

In "The Masque of the Red Death," Poe gave fictional expression to the esthetic ideas he had been formulating in the previous months. "The Masque" gains further esthetic meaning when one enlarges the context of the tale to embrace Poe's writing in the months immediately afterward. In his essay on Longfellow in April, Poe had described the poetic spirit of the various arts, but made no mention of landscape gardening. The next month in "The Masque," Prospero for obvious reasons does not cultivate a landscape garden. He does, however, try (and fail) to create an earthly paradise, the artist's heightened transfiguration of nature which will transcend the limits imposed by mere nature and the Red Death. Either during the composition of the tale or immediately thereafter, Poe began to develop an articulate notion of the landscape garden as the supreme expression of human art. Within weeks, he had elaborated this extension of his esthetic theory in "The Landscape Garden" (*Ladies' Companion*, October, 1842).[8] In this short fiction, Prospero reappears as Ellison and proclaims that in the art of landscape gardening one discovers "the fairest field for the display of invention, or imagination, in the endless combining of forms of novel Beauty." Ellison prefers the creative "artificial" landscape garden to the "natural" style which merely imitates the proportion and congruity of nature. To Ellison, such imitation recalls the negative merit of Addison's esthetic and is "better suited to the grovelling apprehension of the herd." But the artificial style calls forth the true poetic sentiment ("the fervid dreams of the man of genius"). Working as precisely as the rational-scientific intellect, the artist's superior taste then re-orders matter and form to create "special wonders or miracles" in the landscape garden. Ellison cannot prescribe the rules which the landscape-gardener as poet must follow to achieve this higher order of beauty—"it is in vain that we are told *how* to conceive a 'Tempest' "— but given sufficient wealth (and Ellison has an annual inheritance which exceeds thirteen million dollars), the landscape-artist might "so imbue his designs at once with extent and novelty of Beauty" that "the sophists of the *negative* school" could only stand amazed at the result. Here at last might human art envision "a Nature which is not God, nor an emanation of God, but which still is Nature, in the sense that it is the handiwork of the angels that hover between man and God."

Poe expanded "The Landscape Garden," though how soon afterward is hard to determine. Revised and lengthened, it appeared several years later as "The Domain of Arnheim." Ellison's man-made pastoral paradise now has progressed from theory to actuality. On the river-journey into Arnheim one discovers at once a continuity with the symbolic landscape of "The Masque of the Red Death." The boat leaves early in the morning, travelling westward. During the journey, the magic landscape resembles the windings of Prospero's apartments: "The stream took a thousand turns, so that at no moment could its gleaming surface be seen for a greater distance than a furlong. At every instant the vessel seemed imprisoned within an enchanted circle. . . ." Ellison has shaped and transformed nature so that it exhibits "a weird symmetry, a thrilling uniformity, a wizard propriety in these her works." The river maintains a Walden-like purity as it mirrors an inverted heaven. The landscape suggests "dreams of a new race of fairies" while music emanates from an "unseen origin." (Again, as in "The Masque," one thinks of parallels with *The Tempest*.) Sailing toward the red sunset beside chiselled precipices draped in lush foliage and limbs of black walnut, the traveller seems to approach an enormous western gate which will bar him from the promised glimpse of paradise (shades here of Caliban and the Red Death). But the gate is illusory and the boat passes through to enter Ellison's transcendent kingdom of supernal beauty. The traveller is overwhelmed by ethereal music, exotic trees, perfumed flowers, and a bizarre assemblage of architecture which seems "the phantom handiwork, conjointly, of the Sylphs, of the Fairies, of the Genii, and of the Gnomes." Through his landscape artistry, Ellison has happily achieved the divine marriage of nature and art which Prospero earlier had attempted and then lost to the forces of darkness, death, and dissolution.

In "The Masque of the Red Death," then, Poe not only gave dramatic formulation to his esthetic creed but also was tracing the shadowy outlines of a more grandiose theory of art and nature for "The Landscape Garden" and beyond. Prospero's symbolic chambers, together with his artful masque of the red death, became a transitional moment in Poe's estheticism in 1842. When the Longfellow essay later became "The Poetic Principle," Poe would repeat that the poetic sentiment can be satisfied in the various fine arts; but he would climax the statement this time by adding that this sense of beauty gains expression "very peculiarly, and with a wide field, in the composition of the Landscape Garden." The artist creatively re-ordering the natural landscape for his earthly paradise had become the intermediary between man and God, had moved ever closer to the role of divine Creator. And in the final stage, Poe's esthetic would extend into the cosmic reaches set forth in *Eureka*.

Equally important, "The Masque of the Red Death" reveals a conflict at the heart of Poe's esthetic in 1842 which throws light also on his response to America in the mid-nineteenth century. With Hawthorne, Emerson, Thoreau, Melville, and Whitman, Poe shared basic esthetic and moral concerns over the advance of scientific rationalism, technology, and urbanism, though Poe's response appears to have been the most ambivalent. On one hand, he nurtured in "The Masque of the Red Death" a defiant estheticism (though precisely formulated) and expanded it in the landscape tales and *Eureka;* and in these same years, he continued to write his tales of ratiocination, though his detective hero relied heavily on intuition. In his "Romantic" effort to harmonize the rational and intuitive forces contending in his esthetic and within himself, Poe met his contemporaries on common ground. Emerson, Thoreau, and Whitman, standing with feet on the earth and head bathed in the blithe air, labored to unite the lower intellect and higher intuition. Melville's heroes pursued the linked analogies between nature and mind, and Hawthorne's poet continued the quest in the woods at Blithedale. Through his artist-heroes Prospero and Ellison, Poe joined his effort to reconcile the higher claims of ideal beauty and truth with the lower demands of utility, to render nature the willing servant of man's earthly desire and his heaven-soaring intuition. With Prospero's failure to achieve this mastery, Poe was writing Romantic tragedy to corroborate the vision of Hawthorne and Melville; but in the triumph of Ellison, Poe also confirmed the American optimism of Emerson and his disciples.[9] In the conflict and the wedding of nature and art which he explored in "The Masque of the Red Death" and elaborated in the landscape sequels, Poe too had suggested for his audience, in 1842 and after, the highly creative, and some of the self-destructive, energies set loose by Romantic individualism in America.

Notes

1. For a selected survey of these diverse readings, ranging from clinical diagnosis to mystic impressionism, see Joseph P. Roppolo, "Meaning and 'The Masque of the Red Death.'" *Tulane Studies in English*, XIII (1963), 59–64.

2. "Ballads and Other Poems," *Graham's Magazine*, XX (April, 1842), 248–251.

3. *Graham's Magazine*, XX (May, 1842), 299. Walter Blair first remarked that Prospero's suite suggests, in a loose way, a metaphor of nature's cycle and man's mortality. See "Poe's Conception of Incident and Tone in the Tale," *Modern Philology*, XLI (May, 1944), 239. But Mr. Blair's suggestion was quickly challenged by a critic who favored a more impressionistic reading of Poe's fictional craft. The effort to assign objective and detailed meaning to Prospero's suite would limit rather than enlarge the reader's experience: "We must accept the story as we accept a piece of music: in spite of program notes which would

limit the meaning of what we hear, we generally let ourselves go and create our own meaning." (Bryllion Fagin, *The Histrionic Mr. Poe* [Baltimore, 1949], p. 216.)

4. Wilson O. Clough, "The Use of Color Words by Edgar Allan Poe," *PMLA*, XLV (June, 1930), 598–613, corroborates much of the color association I have indicated. In his tabulation, Mr. Clough reveals that Poe used greens almost exclusively for vegetation and landscape settings. While yellow often connoted sickliness and decay, orange did not. Whites, blacks and reds in the tales of horror were usually associated with death. Since blue and purple had no predictable meaning among the tales, and violet was used only for the next-to-last apartment in "The Masque," one must rely here on the context. Finally, Poe applied variegated colors "most often to nature" (p. 612).

Did Poe borrow a leaf directly from *As You Like It?* One balks at the precise linking of Poe's progressive coloration and Shakespeare's seven ages of man, but the Shakespearean analogy is astonishingly close: the infant (blue), school-boy (purple), lover (green), soldier (orange), judge (white), the piping school-boy again (violet), and finally the dotard "*sans* everything" (black).

5. Poe, of course, knew his Shakespeare and admired Prospero and *The Tempest* in particular. He regarded *The Tempest* and its hero to be the quintessence of the poetic spirit. See *Southern Literary Messenger*, II (July, 1836), 501–503, a slight expansion of Poe's "Letter to B——," the preface to the New York edition of his *Poems* (1831). "B" was probably Elam Bliss, publisher of this second edition.

6. *The Tempest* has been interpreted as a fable of art before. Most recent is Leo Marx's highly suggestive reading of the play as an anticipation of American pastoral themes. See *The Machine in the Garden: Technology and the Pastoral Ideal in America* (New York, 1964), pp. 34–72.

7. Roppolo, "Meaning and 'The Masque of the Red Death,'" cites Poe's later *Eureka* as evidence that Poe meant to suggest in this ending not annihilation of Prospero and his world but merely the end of one cosmic cycle in an "eternal process of contraction and expansion" (p. 68). One can more safely trace the continuity of Poe's imagination here by bringing forward his "Colloquy of Monos and Una" which appeared in *Graham's* several months before. Anticipating the esthetic credo of the Longfellow review and "The Masque," Monos, speaking from beyond the grave, ascribes his death to a general decline of taste, "that faculty which holding a middle position between the pure intellect and the moral sense . . . could have led us gently back to Beauty, to Nature, and to Life." And near the end he recalls his "chamber of Death" at midnight when the impressions of "Darkness" and "Decay" were to merge into a liberation out of time and into eternity.

8. This piece was already completed in July, submitted to *The Democratic Review*, and rejected. For a discussion of the landscape vogue in America in 1842, an excitement to which Poe clearly had begun to respond, see Robert

D. Jacobs, "Poe's Earthly Paradise," *American Quarterly*, XII (Fall, 1960), 405–406.

9. Suggested here is the continuing need in Poe studies to relate Poe's imagination to the currents of American life in his time. Leo Marx has recently argued that *The Tempest* is Shakespeare's "American fable," that it "anticipates the moral geography of the American imagination" by suggesting the pastoral tensions among scientism, nature, and art (*The Machine in the Garden*, p. 72). For the mid-nineteenth century, Marx stresses the conflict between nature and technology in the major writers other than Poe. As I have intimated, one discovers *Tempest* themes updated in Poe also. Briefly to amplify one pastoral configuration: In "Monos and Una" (1841), the hero bemoans that in his lifetime "huge smoking cities" had destroyed the natural landscape as "green leaves shrank before the hot breath of furnaces." This man-made pestilence, in which "the fair face of Nature was deformed as with the ravages of some loathesome disease," may well have suggested to Poe the crisis for Prospero and his art several months later. After Prospero's aborted effort to create his insular paradise comes the renewed attempt by his successor Ellison. As Poe's landscape artist, Ellison achieves the pastoral harmony of the "middle landscape" (Marx, p. 71) which reconciles the contrary impulses of primitivism and modern urbanism. For the site of his landscape garden, Ellison rejects a primitive island ("I am not Timon") in favor of "a spot not far from a populous city."

Michael Williams

In the doubled text of "The Gold-Bug" a bewildered narrator recounts, first, a series of events the full significance of which escapes him, and then, in recursion, the events as explained to him by the ingenious central figure, Legrand, on whose intelligence the disclosure of meaning depends. The protagonist's rational powers are manifested most obviously in his role as cryptographer—he decodes a cipher which points to the ultimate discovery of treasure long since concealed by Captain Kidd. Legrand's arrogance about his skills, along with Poe's own assumption of the persona of master-cryptographer in the columns

From "'*The* language *of the cipher': Interpretation in 'The Gold-Bug,'*" *American Literature* 53, no. 4 (January 1982): 646–60. © 1982 by Duke University Press.

of *Graham's Magazine* and *Alexander's Weekly Messenger,* has fueled literalistic complaints about flaws in the tale's cryptographic methodology.[1] The conception of literature underlying such evaluations is made explicit by J. Woodrow Hassell, Jr., who assumes that "while a narrative based upon the solution of a cipher need not be completely realistic in every particular, it must at the very least be credible as a record of fact. The author of such a tale must be most careful to fulfill the demands of verisimilitude."[2] Hassell's criteria for detecting "violations of realism" derive from a philosophy of language in which writing is regarded as a "transcription of the real" and the relationship between signifier and signified is believed to be secure.[3] But "The Gold-Bug," like many other tales by Poe, subjects this very security to critical scrutiny and explores the uncertainties of referential language. In a commentary that recognizes this aspect of Poe's work, Alan C. Golding shows that *Eureka* exposes fundamental misunderstandings that can arise from a strictly referential view of language which fails to acknowledge that "words are approximations on which we cannot afford to place ultimate dependence"; at best, words "stand only as functional approximations of meaning." Consequently, Golding argues, one strategy in *Eureka* moves "toward a denotatively precise language of expository discourse which seeks accurate statements about the apprehensible universe" while confronting language's limited ability to make such statements.[4]

Although a version of this strategy can be seen in the progressive demystification of event and cipher in "The Gold-Bug," in fact the tale opens a considerably deeper perspective on the semantics of referential language than Golding's formulation suggests. At its center, as in *Eureka,* lies Poe's recognition of the instability of the arbitrary relationship between word and referent and, as a consequence, the contingency of meaning upon conventions of use and context. In a commentary that stresses how "the text requires and defines the kind of reading which can decipher its workmanship," Jean Ricardou provides a useful starting point for an examination of this tale's exploration of referential language: "It is by their way of reading [that is, of interpreting signs, linguistic and otherwise] that the nature of each of the three characters is determined. Only Legrand is capable of decoding. Jupiter and the narrator, for their part, are on bad terms with language."[5] As the following will demonstrate, Jupiter and the narrator are entrapped in opposed but equally inadequate language strategies; in contrast, Legrand is an exemplary interpreter by whose practice the reader can gauge the shortcomings of his companions. He is aware that the relationship between word and referent is ultimately arbitrary, and alert to the consequent semantic implications of changing contexts. Legrand's interpretive strategy depends on a sensitivity to the possibilities of intention which allows him to restore words to those contexts in which they convey significant meaning, contexts in which an essential consistency can be perceived.[6] Because his approach to context remains flexible, he eventually reconstitutes the "links of a great chain" leading to the treasure[7]—the tale's dramatic validation of his stance toward referential language.

I

Throughout the tale, the contingent nature of the sign is repeatedly implied. The narrative's shifting terminology for its central image, the gold-bug, emphatically illustrates the arbitrariness of the relationship between word and referent. Legrand introduces the insect by its genus, "*scarabaeus*," but he and the other characters soon fall back on the even more inclusive term "bug" (p. 808). The physical absence of the bug and the lack of a specific classification make general description necessary, but words prove inadequate to capture the attributes of this nameless insect: of the quality of the color, the mysteriously "brilliant metallic lustre," the narrator "cannot judge till to-morrow," when he will be able to see it (p. 809). Meanwhile, a sketch must suffice to give him some idea of its shape. When the narrator eventually sees the bug for himself, he refers to it indiscriminately as "*scarabaeus*," "bug," "beetle," and "insect" (pp. 815–16). The synonyms circumscribe a still-unnamed center; the connection of names to that referent is obviously arbitrary and unstable. In most cases, the narrator's terms merely point to the bug as a physical object rather than describe or classify it in a stable context.

The drawing of the shape of the bug bears a "remarkable similarity of outline" to the representation of the death's-head on the back of the parchment (p. 829). Although this similarity of form creates the possibility of confusion, the drawings have distinctive meanings, discernible, however, only by "reading" them in their intended frames of reference. The drawings are thus analogous to homophones, which also must be taken in context to be understood. A parallel instance of homophonic confusion occurs, in fact, at a crucial point in the narrative.

Jupiter, out of sight in the tulip tree, signals a discovery after following Legrand's instructions to crawl out along the seventh branch:

> "—o-o-o-o-oh! Lor-gol-a-marcy! What *is* dis here pon de tree?"
> "Well!" cried Legrand, highly delighted, "what it is?"
> "Why taint noffin but a skull—somebody bin lef him head up de tree, and de crows done gobble ebery bit ob de meat off."
>
> (pp. 820–21)

Jupiter's comments (punning on absent-mindedness) establish one meaning of the word "left." When Legrand tells Jupiter to "find the left eye of the skull," Jupiter is unable to shift his usage of "left" to the new context, replying "Hum? hoo! dat's good! why dar aint no eye lef' at all." Struggling to impose his own context on Jupiter so that the servant can drop the bug through the appropriate eye-socket of the skull, Legrand relates the abstraction to a practical function, that of chopping wood: "To be sure! you are left-handed; and your left eye is on the same side as your left hand. Now, I suppose, you can find the left eye of the skull, or the place where the left eye has been. Have you found it?" (p. 821). The process of instruction is beset with ambiguities of reference: "Is de lef eye of de skull pon de same side as de lef hand of de skull, too?—cause de skull aint got not a bit ob a hand at all—nebber mind! I got de lef eye now. . . ." But, we learn later, he has not. What he believes to be his left eye is actually his right: "'Oh, my golly, Massa Will! ain't dis here my lef eye for sartain?' roared the terrified Jupiter, placing his hand upon his *right* organ of vision. . . ." (p. 824). Comically displaying the absence of necessary relationship between word and referent, the tale again stresses that meaning is created by conventions of use and context, which alone stabilize the interpretation of signs.

The text similarly dramatizes the obstacles to communication which arise when words are considered to be naively referential, as if word and thing were indissolubly linked. Such extreme referentiality characterizes Jupiter's use of an elemental vocabulary; he fixes on a single referent in the speech of others, recognizing familiar sounds rather than understanding meaning in context. For example, when he hears Legrand refer to the gold-bug's "*antennae*," he interrupts: "Dey ain't *no* tin in him, Massa Will, I keep a tellin on you . . . de bug is a goole bug, solid, ebery bit of him" (pp. 808–09). Jupiter believes that the middle syllable has only one referent—the metal, tin.[8] Similarly, when the narrator asks "what cause have you?" for thinking Legrand has been bitten by the bug, Jupiter replies, "Claws enuff, massa, and mouff too" (p. 812). His lexical economy admits only one name for each object in his world: when he is asked, "Did you bring any message from Mr. Legrand?" he replies, "No, massa, I bring dis here pissel" (p. 813). Legrand has given him a name for what he carries and, because his language use precludes synonyms, he does not recognize "message" as an alternate signifier.

Such a linguistic practice also inhibits abstraction, as illustrated by Jupiter's struggles with the concepts of left and right. Discovering a scythe and three spades in the bottom of the boat bound from Charleston to Sullivan's Island, the narrator asks, "What is the meaning of all this, Jup?"; "Him syfe, massa, and spade," Jupiter replies (p. 814). He can go no further than the meaning contained in naming. Thus, when the narrator ponderously asks, "to what fortunate circumstance am I to attribute the honor of a visit from you today?" Jupiter, bewildered, replies, "What de matter, massa?" (p. 813); the formulaic words, without reference to any object that Jupiter can identify, do, in one sense, lack "matter" for him.

By contrast, the narrator illustrates the dangers of language dependent upon a single, inflexible framework for controlling the relationship of word and referent. Because the narrator's language strategies are linked to a fairly broadly defined perspective and cognitive style, it is necessary to consider his character in some detail. In a tale that demonstrates the value of heightened intellectual powers, the narrator's laziness of mind is marked. His conversation with Legrand, in which he learns of the discovery of the "totally new" *scarabaeus*, is characteristic. In response to Legrand's regret that he could not show him the bug that evening, the narrator thinks only of the chill from which he suffers and wishes "the whole tribe of *scarabaei* at the devil" (p. 808). The same intellectual torpor underlies his approach to language (typical of what Poe calls in *Eureka* "the common understanding of words"), and gives rise to contextual confusion:

Legrand: "Stay here tonight, and I will send Jup down for it at sunrise. It is the loveliest thing in creation!"

Narrator: "What?—sunrise?"

Legrand: "Nonsense! no!—the bug."

(p. 808)

Significantly, the narrator misidentifies the referent of "it," the understanding of which demands, of course, that distant syntactic elements be held in mind in order to be linked correctly.[9] We discover as the tale progresses that the narrator's lapse is emblematic: he is irremediably obtuse to the possibilities of fixing words in displaced or alternate contexts.

Unlike Legrand, the narrator's thoughtless acceptance of the conventions of his class limits both his own use of language and his understanding of others. He recognizes only one context in which to place words, the societal, and when words and behavior violate the expectations it establishes, he is simply bewildered. The first sentence neatly establishes his manner with words: "Many years ago, *I contracted an intimacy* with a Mr. William Legrand. He was *of an ancient Huguenot family,* and had once been wealthy; but a series of misfortunes had *reduced him to want.* To *avoid the mortification consequent upon his disasters,* he left New Orleans, the *city of his forefathers,* and *took up his residence* at Sullivan's Island, near Charleston, South Carolina" (p. 806; emphasis mine). The narrator's discourse is little more than a series of clichés and formulaic expressions that keep harsh realities at a comfortable distance. The "residence" so formally taken up is, we soon learn, a hut, and the effete nature of merely social "mortification" is exposed later in the tale by a confrontation with the results of literal mortification—the skull and the skeletons. Even his admiration of Legrand is tempered with the condescension of a socially secure urbanite for a displaced peer, as seen in his measured evaluation that "there was much in the recluse to excite interest and esteem" (p. 807). This condescension is made explicit in his immediate reaction to Legrand's note demanding his company: "What 'business of the highest importance' could *he* possibly have to transact?" (p. 814).

The world of socially defined value sharply delimits the narrator's reactions to the unpredictable. The first part of the narrative shows his inability to comprehend events that violate his expectations as other than symptomatic of the "otherness" of insanity—a convenient catchall for the mysterious or the ostensibly irrational. He interprets Legrand's "moods of alternate enthusiasm and melancholy" accordingly, speculating that his relatives have contrived Jupiter's guardianship of a man "somewhat unsettled in intellect" (p. 807). The narrator can only describe Legrand's enthusiasms as "fits." Unlike Jupiter, he clearly has a vocabulary to generate alternate names for the behavior, and by the very question, "how else shall I term them?" he, or rather the text, lays open the possibility of other interpretations (p. 808). He actually reacts, however, by withdrawing into the security of "prudent" silence; subsequently, he withdraws physically, having "deemed it proper to take leave" for his own world of Charleston. His incomprehensions, at the outset innocent enough, foreshadow his later settled conviction of Legrand's lunacy.

The narrator's growing persuasion of his friend's "aberration of mind" (p. 817) springs from the assumption that a man who has fallen from wealth and social prominence to unrelieved poverty and obscurity is likely to go mad: "I dreaded lest the continued pressure of misfortune had, at length, fairly unsettled the reason of my friend" (p. 814). His criterion for "madness" is whether behavior is readily comprehensible in the context of social convention. If it is not, then such behavior can be appropriated to that context only by being named as "mad"; once so labeled, it cannot threaten or force the readjustment of the narrator's point of view. The arbitrary nature of this defensive strategy is implied by the narrator's reaction to the proposed nocturnal expedition—"The man is surely mad!"—a conventional expression of astonishment which can be translated as "I do not understand you" (p. 816). For the narrator, then, words have become mere signals of social approval or disapproval. Such a use of language allows him to reserve for himself the stance of sane judgment and reaffirms the adequacy of his settled perspective in the face of experience which it cannot accommodate. Such an approach is, of course, as limited in the face of complexity as Jupiter's obsessively referential use of language, for it imposes rather than discovers meaning, the possibilities of which are severely constrained by premature closure.[10] Legrand offers an eclectic and flexible alternative.

II

Legrand's task is doubly difficult; he has not only to cope with the unreliability of language but also to discover meaning in a text which human ingenuity has deliberately rendered obscure. That meaning, which in this instance can be validated by empirical investigation, lies beneath a series of obfuscating layers: on the underside of the sketch of the bug is a text concealed by its invisibility; once the text is made visible, its words are concealed by its being in code; once the code has been broken and the words made manifest, their meaning is obscured by their use of pirate conventions and by their distance from their referents. Under such conditions, the interpreter (like the cosmologer in *Eureka*) must proceed largely on faith in the existence of some final order to which the apparently arbitrary can be reconciled.

Legrand's belief in that process of discovery by which nature appears to conform to man's need for order is clear. Having found "an unknown bivalve, forming a new genus" (p. 808), Legrand displays his awareness of how conventional taxonomy establishes likenesses, makes connections, and thus finds meaning in the natural world. Having "hunted down and secured . . . a *scarabaeus* which he believed to be totally new," he recognizes that taxonomy must also be flexible. He can make the accommodations that new circumstances require, an ability that is tested to the full by the cipher. In confronting the concealed text, he follows a process of reification, recognizing displacements and concealments in order to reach through them to original meaning. Just as he is able to reify the form of the boat at the seashore, he is able to reconstitute the text and its purposes in order to discover its meaning. The true form of each is hidden: one has suffered disintegration by the forces of nature so that "the resemblance to boat timbers could scarcely be traced" (p. 830), while the other has been disguised by the agency of man. Legrand is successful in each instance.

That his successful strategy for reading a disguised text derives from a particular way of looking at the world is implied by a crucial juxtaposition in Legrand's account of his capture of the gold-bug and his coincident discovery of the parchment with the concealed text: "Upon my taking hold of it, it gave me a sharp bite, which caused me to let it drop. Jupiter, with his accustomed caution, before seizing the insect, which had flown towards him, looked about him for a *leaf*, or something *of that nature*, by which to take hold of it. It was at this moment that his eyes, and mine also, fell upon the scrap of *parchment*, which I then supposed to be paper" (p. 830; emphasis mine). "Leaf" is here a middle term with a double reference, both to leaves of the natural world and to leaves of paper or parchment. This possibility is kept in view as Legrand details his pursuit of the "*rationale*" of the cipher and refers to "the natural alphabet" and "the natural division intended by the cryptographist" (pp. 837, 840).

Legrand believes in an order that lies beneath the surface of apparent coincidence; he describes the struggle of the mind to discover a "connexion—a sequence of cause and effect" (p. 829) which establishes the one significant context among the many possibilities. When this attempt meets resistance, his mind lapses into a "species of temporary paralysis." Yet even then, faced with the sudden mysterious appearance of the image of the skull, "there seemed to glimmer, faintly, within the most remote and secret chambers of [Legrand's] intellect, a glow-worm-like conception of that truth which last night's adventure brought to so magnificent a demonstration." His methodical examination of the circumstances in which he found the document leads him to establish a connection between "two links of a great chain," for the boat and the parchment are conjoined by the death's-head, "the well-known emblem of the pirate" (p. 831). He reasserts his belief in the existence of such a chain when he claims, "My steps were sure, and could afford but a single result." His steps are governed by thoughtful common sense, intuition, and an insistence that the meaning of words and signs is contingent on a multiplicity of possible contexts.

The sequence in which the elements of the message emerge from the parchment reflects a hierarchy of increasing complexity and privacy of language requiring radical shifts of perspective on the part of the interpreter. When the narrator perceives the shape on the paper as that of "a skull, or a death's-head" (p. 809), he proves himself blind to the possibility of other meanings: "'it is a very *excellent* skull, according to the vulgar notions about such specimens of physiology. . . .' The whole *did* bear a very close resemblance to the ordinary cuts of a death's-head" (p. 810). Beyond the social labels "vulgar" and "ordinary," the narrator contemplates no other frame of reference in which to interpret the sketch. Legrand, however, immediately tests for other possibilities: "There was a boat lying on a sea-coast, and not far from the boat was a parchment—*not a paper*—with a skull depicted on it. You will, of course, ask 'where is the connection?' I reply that the skull, or death's-head, is the well-known emblem of the pirate" (p. 831). The next element to emerge, "diagonally opposite" the skull, appears to be the figure of a goat; a "closer scrutiny," however, suggests to Legrand "that it was intended for a kid" (pp. 832–33). To the narrator, goats and kids are "pretty much the same thing," and in labored humor he asserts that "pirates, you know, have nothing to do with goats; they appertain to the farming interest" (p. 833). Legrand, however, recognizes that a sign's significance changes according to the context in which it is read, and his sensitivity to the intentions of the design enables him to place the "kid" in the appropriate one. Thus he perceives, first, that the figure is a hieroglyph and, second, that it is a "punning . . . signature" of the pirate, Captain Kidd.[11] The death's-head and the kid on the opposite corners of the sheet are no longer for Legrand merely figures; their positioning follows the conventions of letter-writing: they are "stamp" and "signature," suggesting that additional texts might emerge from the space between them. After a narrative delay, detailing Legrand's procedural difficulties, the last and most obscure elements emerge on the parchment: "figures arranged in lines" (p. 834). The narrator is lost, "as much in the dark as ever," and immediately admits his own inability to solve "this enigma." While he sees merely numbers, Legrand recognizes that they "form a cipher—that is to say, they convey a meaning" (p. 835).

Even after Legrand successfully decodes the numbers so that English words are distinguishable, the narrator cannot imagine how to "extort a meaning from all this jargon about 'devil's seats,' 'death's-heads,' and 'bishop's hotels.'" He remains "in the dark" (p. 840), for the language that emerges from the cryptograph is in another kind of code in which the meanings of some words are established by convention and those of others by reference to a particular landscape. To interpret the first group, Legrand must place them in the context of the specialized jargon of sailors, reading, for example, "good glass" as "nothing but a telescope" (p. 841). The second group of meanings is more difficult to discover for, while the features of the landscape might remain stable, the words naming them drift away from their referents, as the search for the "bishop's hostel" illustrates. The phrase modulates: "hostel," a recognizable archaism, changes to "hotel" (the narrator has already made this shift but not, like Legrand, consciously, with an awareness of the implications); Legrand changes "Bishop's" to "Bessop's," making it conform with the locality to which he hopes the message refers. The phrase when finally linked to the landscape becomes "*Bessop's Castle*," which only remotely resembles the original "bishop's hostel," and which, moreover, refers not to a castle at all but to "an irregular assemblage of cliffs and rocks—one of the latter being quite remarkable for its height as well as for its insulated and artificial appearance" (pp. 840–41).

Legrand's final superimposition of the decoded text upon the landscape presupposes, in his terms, a "definite point of view, *admitting no variation*," by which meaning can be discovered (p. 841). The conditions of the realm of the referent, at this last stage, impose "but one interpretation" upon the text (p. 842). Separate, landscape and text would remain indeterminate—the first, a wilderness "excessively wild and desolate" (p. 817), the second, obscure—and this apparent inde-

159

terminacy opens them to misreading. Without the limits provided by the landscape, the deciphered text remains a series of floating signifiers which, like the single word "blood" that Arthur G. Pym reads in the hold of the *Grampus,* can be variously and subjectively interpreted. Furthermore, without the significance conveyed to it by the text, the landscape is merely "infinitely . . . dreary" and sternly solemn (p. 817). But as text and topography are superimposed, it becomes clear, despite the fact that "no trace of a human footstep was to be seen," that the landscape is not simply unencoded wilderness; it, as well as the text, has been previously structured by Kidd so that the conformity between them will yield the meaning that is, finally, the discovery of the treasure. Landscape and text give meaning, each to the other. Legrand is able to discover the determinate relation of the two by virtue of his sensitivity both to the multiple conventions that govern the formation of the text and to the relationship between the conventions and the referential world. To a great extent, this sensitivity results from his ability to intuit Kidd's intentions. When he claims that "it may well be doubted whether human ingenuity can construct an enigma of the kind which human ingenuity may not, by proper application, resolve" (p. 835), the phrasing emphasizes the identity of the activities of construction and resolution.[12] This identification enables Legrand, once he has consciously resisted the inherent instability of language by clarifying the various contingencies affecting text and referent, to establish an ultimate determining context within which the words may be read.

III

Legrand's final explanations direct attention once more to the three interdependent factors in his method of interpretation—the identification of context, of authorial intention, and of appropriate reference—no one of which is adequate independently. The narrator, after Legrand has clarified the system of pirate signs for him, suggests that Kidd used the skull as a marker on the tree because of his desire for "poetical consistency" (p. 843). Legrand accepts this interpretation as possible but incomplete. Displacing a symbolic reading with one that takes into account the conditions of the surrounding landscape, he feels that "common-sense had quite as much to do with the matter," for "to be visible from the Devil's seat, it was necessary that the object, if small, should be *white;* and there is nothing like your human skull for retaining and even increasing its whiteness under exposure to all vicissitudes of weather." Legrand's resolutely prosaic demystification of the symbolic possibilities of the skull evidently derives from his suspicion that in attributing poetical significance to objects the interpreter runs the risk of merely creating his own subjective constructs. The risks inherent in symbolic reading are exemplified in the narrator's misinterpretation of one particular system of signs—Legrand's "grandiloquence . . . conduct in swinging the beetle . . . [and insistence] on letting fall the bug, instead of a bullet, from the skull" (pp. 843–44). As has been indicated, the narrator's unquestioning acceptance of social codes leads him to categorize this behavior as symptomatic of insanity. Such an interpretive procedure, which relies only on the internal consistency of a codification arbitrarily applied, ignores the vital consideration of intention. Here, the intention is to deceive. As Ricardou has noted (p. 39), Legrand has been fulfilling a double office, that of encoder of his own text as well as decoder of Kidd's. Having recognized the nature of the narrator's reading of events—that he, Legrand, is insane—he creates a set of signs that reinforce that interpretation, thus dramatizing its arbitrary nature and, implicitly, the arbitrary nature of all interpretations which cannot be grounded in clear evidence of intentions and frames of reference.

Legrand's confession of his authorial role encourages speculation, in turn, about the interpretation of Poe's text. The gold-bug, its most obtrusive sign and thus that element most subject to symbolic readings, serves as a test case. Throughout the tale, the narrator invests the bug with poetical significance; it, to paraphrase Ricardou, consumes his interest just as it consumed the corner of the parchment. Yet Legrand insists that it bears only a tenuous relation to the meaning of the cipher and his own actions, and that he has kept it in view only as part of his "sober mystification" (p. 844). It is not merely the narrator, however, who has been distracted by a sign that proved to be empty. Poe swings the gold-bug before the eyes of the reader right from the point of entry into the story—the title—and symbolic interpretation of the bug places the reader in the narrator's dilemma: is Poe, like Legrand, offering us a "sober mystification" which provides only a deceptive opportunity for such a reading? If we attempt to establish the validity of a symbolic reading, we are faced with that problem of intention illustrated by the narrator's interpretation of Kidd's motives for using the skull. As Legrand has shown, symbolic readings depend on subjective constructs of authorial intentions, and the reader, like the narrator, has no way to test them.

Such considerations suggest a way to account for those violations of verisimilitude that have disturbed readers such as Hassell, who points out that Legrand's explanations, while pretending to comprehensiveness, actually contain notable inconsistencies and elementary mistakes in, for example, his specification of the ink used for the cipher, his listing of letter frequencies in cryptography, and his calculations determining the location of the treasure.[13] Given Poe's generally meticulous approach to detail, it is surely inadequate to write such errors off as mere carelessness. Poe is most careful to provide that information by which the reader can judge him careless—as, for example, in the case of the muddled triangulation. These "violations" subvert every attempt to authorize Poe's fiction solely by reference to conditions outside itself. As Ricardou has shown, the text establishes a logic of its own, one aspect of which is the subversion of the priority of an "*extratextual subject*" (p. 33). Just as it is Poe, not "Fortune," who has set up the "series of accidents and coincidences . . . so *very* extraordinary" by which Legrand becomes aware of the existence of the death's-head (p. 833), so it is Poe who wills the solutions posited by Legrand, despite any lapses in verisimilitude. Even if the reader shares Legrand's faith in an ultimate order to which the text may be reduced, in "The Gold-Bug" he is faced, as Poe's disruptive "errors" remind us, with a text lacking an external "landscape" against which to measure it: the implied realm of the referent is whatever Poe wills it to be, and our access to his intentions, as noted above, is limited to the models we can construct but cannot test.

"The Gold-Bug," then, addresses the problem of its own interpretation under those conditions of semantic indeterminacy which are shared by every text. Though it subverts the illusion that representation is the "transcription of the real," it also offers us as consolation a limiting paradigm of the reading process. A text can be recovered by clarifying definition, establishing a determining context, and recognizing authorial intention. Some texts resist such recuperation more than others—an utterly fictional text can be as empty of reference to the empirical world as the sign of the gold-bug itself—but if we approach any text without an active awareness of the requirements of the interpretive act, we are, like the narrator of "The Gold-Bug," constantly "in the dark," moving from one bewilderment to the next.

Notes

1. Cortell Holsapple, "Poe and Conradus," *American Literature*, 4 (1932), 62–65; Alfred Allen Kern, "News for Bibliophiles," *Nation*, 97 (22 Oct. 1913), 381–82; W. K. Wimsatt, Jr., "What Poe Knew about Cryptography," *PMLA*, 58 (1943), 778–79. See "A Few Words on Secret Writing," in *The Complete Works of Edgar Allan Poe*, ed. James A. Harrison (1902; rpt. New York: AMS Press, 1965), XIV, 114–49.

2. "The Problem of Realism in 'The Gold Bug,'" *American Literature*, 25 (1953), 171.

3. Rosalind Coward and John Ellis, *Language and Materialism: Developments in Semiology and the Theory of the Subject* (London: Routledge, 1977), p. 47.

4. "Reductive and Expansive Language: Semantic Strategies in *Eureka*," *Poe Studies*, 11 (1978), 1–2. See also John Carlos Rowe, "Writing and Truth in Poe's *The Narrative of Arthur Gordon Pym*," *Glyph: Johns Hopkins Textual Studies*, 2 (1977), 102–21.

5. "Gold in the Bug," trans. Frank Towne, *Poe Studies*, 9 (1976), 36. Another valuable analysis of the tale is Barton Levi St. Armand's more traditional study, "Poe's Sober Mystification: The Uses of Alchemy in 'The Gold-Bug,'" *Poe Studies*, 4 (1971), 1–7.

6. On the relationship between consistency and truth, see *Eureka*, in *Complete Works*, XVI, 196.

7. Thomas Ollive Mabbott, ed., *Collected Works of Edgar Allan Poe* (Cambridge, Mass.: Harvard Univ. Press, 1978), III, 831. Further references will be to this edition, cited in the text by page number.

8. Mabbott points out that the Southern pronunciation of "antennae" would have been "Ann-tinny" (p. 845, n. 9).

9. See Emile Benveniste, *Problems in General Linguistics*, trans. Mary Elizabeth Meek (Coral Gables: Univ. of Miami Press, 1971), p. 219.

10. The narrator is in this way similar to the Prefect in "The Purloined Letter"; see Sergio L. P. Bellei, "'The Purloined Letter': A Theory of Perception," *Poe Studies*, 9 (1976), 40–42.

11. John T. Irwin, "The Symbol of the Hieroglyphics in the American Renaissance," *American Quarterly*, 26 (1974), 103–26. In his discussion of Champollion's deciphering of the hieroglyphs of the Rosetta Stone, Irwin notes that the symbols could operate on one of three levels of increasing complexity—I. figurative: in which the hieroglyph stood for the thing it represented; 2. symbolic: in which it represented simple ideas associated with the objects represented; 3. phonetic: in which the hieroglyph represented sounds (pp. 106–07). The narrator of "The Gold-Bug" can make only the most elementary associations and does not recognize that the hieroglyph is phonetic. In his recent book, *American Hieroglyphics: The Symbol of the Egyptian Hieroglyph-*

ics in the American Renaissance (New Haven: Yale Univ. Press, 1980), Irwin notes Poe's emphasis of the distinction between ideogram and phonetic hieroglyph in this tale.

12. "The Gold-Bug" here echoes Poe's July, 1841, article in *Graham's Magazine;* see *Complete Works,* XIV, 116.

13. Hassell, *passim.*

Ronald Bieganowski

I

In his analysis of the dialectical dimensions to literature, Stanley Fish argues for a transfer of attention from the content of art (that it reflects, contains, or expresses Truth) to its effects: "from what is happening on the page to what is happening in the reader. A self-consuming artifact signifies most successfully when it fails, when it points *away* from itself to something its forms cannot capture."[1] This proposal has led to fresh and stimulating readings of a number of texts. It can also, I believe, help clarify some very elusive tales of Edgar Allan Poe: Poe appears to have created self-consuming narrators in "Ligeia" and "The Fall of the House of Usher." These narrators focus attention less on what they would seem to point to (Beauty, Truth) and more on what happens in them as they attempt to express the ineffable.[2] These works represent two of Poe's most read and talked about stories, perhaps two of the best known stories in American literature.[3] Though not presuming to have discovered a final interpretation, I do have a sense that Poe is much more obvious in these stories than has been commonly recognized and that, in a relatively simple structure, Poe's "The Imp of the Perverse" helpfully reveals his self-consuming narrator at work.

In "The Imp of the Perverse," Poe shows the power language has on the narrator as well as on the reader. The impact of the story on the reader follows the impact of a "rough voice" resounding in the narrator's ears. The story's second part, where the narrator tells of his suc-

From "*The Self-Consuming Narrator in Poe's 'Ligeia' and 'Usher,'*" *American Literature* 60, no. 2 (May 1988): 175–87. © 1988 by the Duke University Press.

cessfully undetected murder of a friend and his subsequent confession, clearly illustrates the general description of "perverseness" given in the first part. Poe then concludes a general analysis of the soul's faculties and impulses:

> We stand upon the brink of a precipice. We peer into the abyss— we grow sick and dizzy. . . . By slow degrees our sickness, and dizziness, and horror, become merged in a cloud of unnameable feeling. By gradations, still more imperceptible, this cloud assumes shape, as did the vapor from the bottle out of which arose the genius in the Arabian Nights. But out of this *our* cloud upon the precipice's edge, there grows into palpability, a shape, far more terrible than any genius, or any demon of a tale, and yet it is but a thought, although a fearful one, and one which chills the very marrow of our bones with the fierceness of the delight of its horror. It is merely the idea of what would be our sensations during the sweeping precipitancy of a fall from such a height.[4]

The sequence outlined here—"cloud of unnameable feeling" to "shape" to "palpability"—describes the dynamic growth of "merely the idea of what would be our sensations" into a creature more powerful ("terrible") than "any demon of a tale." According to the story's analysis of the soul's faculties, the human imagination creates a tangible, readily perceptible being. In part two, the narrator's story shows him as victim of his own imagining when he consciously rejects making an "open confession" to the murder. "No sooner had I spoken these words, than I felt an icy chill creep to my heart." The thought, words, chill assume a shape: "some invisible fiend, I thought, struck me with his broad palm upon the back. The long imprisoned secret burst forth from my soul."

The imagining, then verbal expression, create the fiend that overtakes the narrator's reason; it touches his soul in one of its hidden, inarticulate impulses. His language, not attempting to express or contain Truth, represents his own experience, experience that he would not have if it were not for his own words. His experience follows, flows from, his language. Language here creates experience. Even the murder plot comes from "reading some French Memoirs" where, as the narrator says, "The idea [of a poisoned candle] struck my fancy at once."

For the reader of "The Imp of the Perverse," experience necessarily follows upon the word as it does for all readers. As the reader moves line by line further into Poe's text, the mere thought or idea of perverseness begins to take a shape, almost a palpable one when the frame of reference shifts from a consideration of the soul's forces to the reader's implied question. Shortly after using the example of the brink of a precipice, Poe replaces the "we" of that section with a narrative "I" addressing the reading audience's "you." "I have said thus much, that in some measure I may answer your question, that I may explain to you why I am here, that I may assign to you something that shall have at least the faint aspect of a cause for my wearing these fetters, and for my tenanting this cell of the condemned." For us readers, the discourse has turned from what appeared to be exposition to direct address by a narrator assuming a particular shape because of the question presumed to be within the reader. I certainly did not know that I had a question; I had no thought of the narrator being anywhere in particular. As the text turns on me the reader, giving me ideas, there begins to take shape a genius much like the vapor in the *Arabian Nights*, much like the imp of the perverse. Language in this fictive mode creates an almost palpable character out of the narrator right before our eyes.[5] Though describing the spirit of perversity, Poe also suggests the spirit of fiction. "We might, indeed, deem this perverseness a direct instigation of the archfiend, were it not occasionally known to operate in the furtherance of good" (p. 829). The good: every time we read a story, especially one of Poe's.

The event that this story is begins to unfold, then, in the description of what happens to the reader in the process of following the text. What happens to the reader reveals what happens to the narrator. And what happens to the narrator suggests the process the reader undergoes in the reading of Poe's story: a circle, to be sure, but rippling concentrically from the words of Poe's text. Just as the reader becomes an active mediator containing the psychological effects of the story's utterance, so the narrator's imagination records a series of psychological effects that constitute the action of Poe's text. To an important extent, some of Poe's most memorable stories record in vivid fashion the sequence of responses experienced by the narrator.[6] The stories describe what happens to the narrators as each responds to an utterance, to the words "I am safe . . . if I be not fool," to "that sweet word alone," Ligeia, or to a letter, a MS. "that admitted of no other than a personal reply." Poe's narrators exemplify the kind of reader the stories require because the narrators themselves are engaged by the power of language.[7] Among Poe's stories, "Ligeia" offers a clear, important instance of this strategy and becomes, in turn, particularly suggestive of a way of reading "Usher."

II

"Ligeia" begins with the narrator trying to overcome his faint memory with the incantation of his beloved's name: "Ligeia! Ligeia! Buried in studies of a nature more than all else adapted to deaden impressions of the outward world, it is by that sweet word alone—by Ligeia—that I bring mine eyes in fancy the image of her who is no more. And now, while I write, a recollection flashes upon me . . ." (P. 262). To a large extent, these lines summarize the basic action of the story: the narrator in uttering "Ligeia" brings before imagination's eye the image of Ligeia. It is, of course, the dynamic process of literary art. In a text containing a narrator particularly self-conscious of narrating, the story becomes an illustration of what verbal utterance does to its narrator as well as to its reader.

Following the surface events, the story can be divided into two parts, the speaker's recollections first of Ligeia and then his recollections of Rowena. In the first part, the narrator recalls Ligeia's beauty, learning, passion as well as his own intense feelings for her. What Ligeia stands for has certainly been much discussed.[8] What has not been widely noticed is that the narrator, in straining to remember, relies on such linguistic metaphors as the power of language, of text and utterance, to restore, if only for a moment, his lost Ligeia. From the very outset of the story, he has declared the power of the sweet word, Ligeia. He dismisses "expression" of her eyes as "word of no meaning" (p. 264). Among the circle of analogies expressive of Ligeia's eyes that aroused a sentiment comparable to gazing into her eyes, he was reminded of that sentiment "not unfrequently by passages from books" (p. 265). The text from Joseph Glanvill stands out in particular. For all the notice given to the Glanvill statements about will power, a clearly significant force, it seems to me of first importance that the quotation is a text expressive of Ligeia, words particularly affecting the narrator. There is "some remote connection between this passage in the English moralist and a portion of the character of Ligeia." Not only the expansion of her eyes and melody of her voice, but "the fierce energy . . . of the wild words which she habitually uttered" demonstrated her passion (p. 266). As his maternal instructor, his muse, she made language vibrant and bright. At her decline, language loses its vibrance: "wanting the radiant lustre of her eyes, letters, lambent and golden, grew duller than Saturnian lead" (p. 267). The description of Ligeia's last moments appears to be a record of his response to her utterances, a record of the power of her language to move him with feeling. The verses she composed not only describe "a play of hopes and fears," "the tragedy, 'Man,'" but also become a means of recalling her genius—a verbal form capable of repetition and so of recall.

Part one shows the narrator, in search of Ligeia among his memories, particularly dependent on utterance as the resource for bringing her image before his fancy. To neglect what the narrator does here (to recall Ligeia from his memory through particular recourse to verbal forms) for the sake of investigating the motives for such persistence or identifying what Ligeia stands for, though substantive issues, is to miss the story on an important level. Part two becomes an illustration in relatively concrete circumstances of what is outlined as the narrator's process in part one.

The memories connected with the English abbey are identified with the narrator's feelings of loss. In parallel with part one, he probes his memory: "I minutely remember the details of the chamber." The presence of Rowena drives his memory back to Ligeia. He "revelled in recollections" of her: "Now, then, did my spirit fully and freely burn with more than all the fires of her own. . . . I would call upon her name, during the silence of the night, or among the sheltered recesses of the glens, as if . . . I could restore her to the pathway she had abandoned . . . upon earth." In calling her name, the narrator, repeating what he did in part one, relies on the power of the word as if he could restore her—and he does restore her with the fictive power of language. The force of fiction relies precisely on such a sense of the imagined world as if it were the world of experience.

In detailing the process of his deathbed watch, he describes a process starting with his intense longing, with the thought of Legeia; he notes sounds ("inarticulate breathings" of the wind), passes "some palpable although invisible object," hears a "gentle foot-fall," and imagines seeing "three or four large drops of a brilliant and ruby colored fluid"; finally the thought appears to take shape, becomes palpable, reaching full presence in the utterance of her name—the last word of the text, the word that is the story—"Ligeia." The story ends where it began: with the sweet word, bringing before the narrator's fancy the image of her who is no more.

This narrator shares the experience of the speaker in "Imp." A cloud of unnameable feeling, a thought, an idea assumes form, growing to palpability, a shape comparable to the genius of the *Arabian Nights*, to any demon of a tale. The flow of the story begins with the single word, which action stirs all memories of what Ligeia has come to represent for the narrator. The feelings, memories, thoughts surrounding the name coalesce into the image represented by the name, the story, the word "Ligeia."

This kind of experience shown in the story of the narrator's imagining Ligeia suggests what Poe's text does to its readers. In creating a story-teller as especially self-conscious of telling the tale, the text calls attention to itself as narration, as an action going on in the present time of its being read. Such an observation can be so true that it becomes transparent in its obviousness and thus the full effect—the reader's experience of the narrator's self-consuming as well as the reader's own—is missed.

The story opens with the calling of Ligeia's name followed immediately by the narrator's self-conscious statement, "While I write, a recollection flashes upon me. . . ." In the midst of the story, he calls attention to his act of narrating. Regarding Ligeia's wild longing for life, he says, "I have no power to portray—no utterance capable of expressing" (p. 268). Concerning the English abbey, he decides, "I must not pause to detail." Other memories of that place are "not now visibly before me." But he reminds the reader, "I have said that I minutely remember the details of the chamber" (p. 270). The third to last paragraph emphatically calls attention to the act of narrating going on before the reader's eyes. The paragraph opens: "And again I sunk into visions of Ligeia—and again, (what marvel that I shudder as I write) *again* there reached my ears. . . ." The paragraph ends: "Let me hurry to a conclusion."[9]

This self-conscious narration suggests the nature of the reader's experience: the resurrection of Ligeia is a linguistic event, an event re-enacted through the recall of fiction. The writing or telling or reading brings Ligeia to life again. As the reader's experience parallels that of the narrator's shudder and horror, so what happens to the narrator, what the text does to the narrator, becomes the point of the story: it brings before the reader's fancy the image of Ligeia. The reader, engaged by Poe's words and perhaps even straining for some verifiable truth, is led by the text to actively experiencing the creation of the imagined Ligeia, and that experience becomes Poe's fiction—Ligeia.

III

Recognizing Poe's texts as utterances that affect the narrator as well as the reader can help reveal "The Fall of the House of Usher" as a subtle variation on the patterns established in "Imp" and "Ligeia." This story contains a spirit of perverseness in at least the burial of Madeline; Roderick totters, much like the narrator in "Imp," on the brink of the irrational; his poem, "The Haunted Palace," describes the overthrow of the "monarch Thought's domain." More important, the narrator, from the inciting incident on, has been led through the story's events by Roderick's imaginative creations: his letter, music, painting, poetry, his "fantastic yet impressive superstitions." When we trace what happens to the narrator, the story appears to be a series of utterances taking on palpable shape for the narrator, ultimately becoming the very House of Usher and its fall.[10]

In the middle of the final stormy night, the narrator tries to pass the dark hours with Roderick by reading from the "Mad Trist." Each of the readings from the text is followed by sounds and actions from within the house that duplicate what have been described in the "Mad Trist." After the second reading, the narrator is amazed by the sounds he hears from the distant parts of the house—"the exact counterpart of what my fancy had already conjured up for the dragon's unnatural shriek as described by the romancer." Canning's text creates the narrator's experience. The other quoted text in the story, Roderick's "The Haunted Palace," predicts what the narrator describes as the tottering of Usher's "lofty reason upon her throne." Earlier in the story, Roderick's speaking of his sister seems to evoke a vision of Madeline: "While he spoke, the lady Madeline (for so was she called) passed slowly through a remote portion of the apartment . . ." (p. 323). The speaking calls her forth. The inciting incident of the story's action arises from the singular summons of Roderick's letter to the narrator, a letter "which, in its wildly importunate nature, had admitted of no other than a personal reply." Because of "the apparent *heart* that went with his request," the narrator cannot hesitate in answering Roderick's letter. The story's final action, the dank tarn silently closing over the fragments of the "*House of Usher*" (Poe's emphasis for the story's last words), follows "a long tumultuous shouting sound like the voice of a thousand waters." As the tarn's waters become silent, the House of Usher (family, mansion, and fiction) as utterance is no more.

Appropriately the story ends in silent waters, an archetypal source for the story itself.[11] While Roderick's written word starts the narrator on his journey through a "soundless day," it is the reflected image of the house in the tarn that represents the narrator's destination. Twice in the opening pages, the narrator contemplates the house's reflection in the surface of the water. Instead of the incantation in "Ligeia," these repeated sightings produce the house. He distinguishes the reflected image from the house's "real aspect," the dreary sensation of its appearance in "everyday life." To relieve the insufferable gloom he attempts to goad his imagination into something of the sublime. To counter the effect of "the hideous dropping off of the veil" that facing natural objects requires, the narrator rearranges the particulars of the scene, so veiling nature with poetic sentiment.

> I reined my horse to the precipitous brink of a black and lurid tarn that lay in unruffled lustre by the dwelling and gazed down—but with a shudder even more thrilling than before—upon the remodeled and inverted images of the gray sedge, and the ghastly tree-stems, and the vacant and eye-like windows.
>
> Nevertheless, in this mansion of gloom I now proposed to myself a sojourn of some weeks.

His second description of the house before entering it ends with his eye following the "barely perceptible fissure" until "it became lost in the sullen waters of the tarn." Beginning with the mere idea of teasing the physical appearance of the mansion into "aught of the sublime," the narrator childishly, as the text suggests, (impishly?) gazes at the reflected, watery appearance of the house. Hovering at the "precipitous brink" of the tarn, the cloud of feeling assumes a form, a palpable shape, so much so that the narrator can announce that "in this mansion," into the image mirrored in the water, will he travel through fancy. In what today could be likened to a cinematic effect, Poe shows the narrator, at the beginning of the story's action, staring into the waters with the reader, as it were, looking over the narrator's shoulder. With more intense scrutiny of the reflected image, the narrative tightens its focus on the specific details shimmering in the water, and the action appears to begin but is really a continuation of what began with the story's first sentence. Only at the end does the narrative focus lengthen to reveal that for the duration of the story the narrator, still standing at the tarn's edge, has been contemplating the image of the house reflected in the water.

After recalling the "childish experiment" of looking into the tarn and later shaking off "what *must* have been a dream," the speaker crosses over in imagination to the Gothic archway of the hall. He then proceeds to enter the House of Usher: "A valet, of stealthy step, thence conducted me, in silence, through many dark and intricate passages in my progress to the *studio* of his master. Much that I encountered on the way contributed, I know not how, to heighten the vague sentiments of which I have already spoken." This valet to a family with a "passionate devotion to the intricacies . . . of musical science" silently conducts the narrator through intricate passages to Roderick's study, a wild composition representing his imaginative state. Without musical score or baton, the valet conducts the narrator through Usher's creation, appearing as self-consuming narrator to the teller of the story. The narrator in turn, of course, leads the reader into the fictive house.

The story has been a journey into the realm of the narrator's disembodied imagination where imps, Ligeia, and Ushers become palpable for the duration of the text. The narrator, as obviously the reader, has been led by the imagination's power to create images more thrilling than the physical world. What idea, word, or utterance does to the narrator becomes the first point of Poe's stories. For the narrator, this text records the fall of the House of Usher, Madeline's toppling Roderick, while for us readers it records the arousal of these images. "Usher" has become a dialectic within our imaginations of us/her created by Poe's words. As the valet conducts the narrator further into the imagined world stirred by the reflection in the tarn so Poe's narrator leads (ushers) readers to actively engaging their interior worlds of fancy. And the readers have been staring at their own images of Poe's fiction much as the narrator has been transfixed by the reflections in the tarn.

IV

Seeing Poe's readers as actively mediating presences suggests a new perspective to the stories: as a set of responses by the narrator to the creative, imaginative, poetic word. The reader represents Poe's ideal narrator, and Poe's narrator represents his ideal reader. These stories portray a thoroughly imagined world, "the spirit's outer world," as Poe describes it in one of his "Marginalia." And the valuable result here is the refusal to settle for an identification of what constitutes Poe's spiritual world as the entire substance of his fiction. Rather, the exciting experience is to recognize as essential to Poe's fiction the process of discovering that spiritual realm, and this self-consuming process becomes the structure and substance of these stories.

"Ligeia" and "Usher" show us narrators intensely pre-occupied with images reflecting their sense of the beautiful, which pre-occupation displaces all else including themselves in the stories. As the narrators become fixed on their experience of the imagination's power, specifically the power of language, their narrations take on a life of their own, thus engaging the reader with the power of Poe's words. In the context of these stories, the narrators become self-consuming precisely in the action of trying to tell of their experience which necessarily calls attention to each attempt to express the ideal. Poe's narrators appear to mediate between the mundane and the sublime, present dreariness and recollected excitement (Poe's terror), the unpoetical and poetical, the text and the reader. Richard Wilbur, in his analysis of Poe's stories as journeys toward the inner, spiritual self, concludes that "Usher" is "a triumphant report by the narrator that it *is* possible for the poetic soul to shake off this temporal, rational, physical world and escape, if only for a moment, to a realm of unfettered vision."[12] These stories record the narrators pursuing glimpses of Beauty in the momentary intimations suggested through language, with the reader experiencing the poetic vision.

In his description of the artist's attempt to recollect Beauty, Poe provides an apt description of these narrators and so of his readers. For Poe, a Platonic sense of the Beautiful abides in the human imagination as a recollection of existence prior to the soul's birth as well as a prescience of eternity. For such an artist and narrator, the beauty of nature and of one's beloved become delightful because they offer some particular, partial manifestation of the ideal. Reflected images double the intensity of such beauty. Poetic language also duplicates such manifestations: "as the lily is repeated in the lake, or the eyes of Amaryllis in the mirror, so is the mere oral or written repetition of these forms, and sounds, and colours, and odours, and sentiments, a duplicate source of delight."[13] And the reader's imagination redoubles these reflections, further intensifying the delight. These perceptions of beauty become "a class of fancies, of exquisite delicacy" that offer "a glimpse of the soul's outer world."[14] Such fancies occur at the "very brink of sleep," between the waking world and the world of dreams. These fancies hold the artist's entire attention because they point toward the ideal.

And so, significant for the artist and narrator is the power of words. In his dialogue, "The Power of Words," Poe has Agathos speak of "the *physical power of words*."[15] Poe himself declared, "so entire is my faith in the *power of words*, that at times, I have believed it possible to embody even the evanescence of fancies such as I have attempted to describe."[16] These stories show Poe's narrators seeking to embody in words—Ligeia, Usher—their evanescent fancies of beauty and finally failing because they cannot capture the ideal. But these narrators signify most successfully precisely because they so fail and self-consume.

Notes

1. *Self-Consuming Artifacts* (Berkeley: Univ. of California Press, 1972), p. 4.

2. G. R. Thompson and Patrick F. Quinn, in their debate over Poe's narrators especially in "Usher," make many thoughtful, suggestive observations concerning the stories and Poe's fiction. Their disagreement, however, rests to an important extent upon their concern with the narrator's reporting details verifiable according to norms outside the story's action, according to some objective or rational criteria. My suggestion here is that the narrator reports the effects on him of images created through language or the tarn's mirror surface. See G. R. Thompson, *Poe's Fiction: Romantic Irony in the Gothic Tales* (Madison: Univ. of Wisconsin Press, 1973) and his "Poe and the Paradox of Terror: Structures of Heightened Consciousness in 'The Fall of the House of Usher'" as well as Patrick F. Quinn, "A Misreading of Poe's 'The Fall of the House of Usher,'" and his "Usher Again: Trust the Teller" in *Ruined Eden of the Past: Hawthorne, Melville, and Poe*, ed. G. R. Thompson and Virgil I. Lokke (West Lafayette: Purdue Univ. Press, 1981).

3. *Edgar Allan Poe: Modern Critical Views*, ed. Harold Bloom (New York: Chelsea House, 1985); *Critics on Poe*, ed. David B. Kesterson (Coral Gables: Univ. of Miami Press, 1973); Robert L. Marrs, "'The Fall of the House of Usher': A Checklist of Criticism sine 1960," *Poe Studies*, 5 (1972), 23–24; *Twentieth Century Interpretations of Poe's Tales: A Collection of Critical Essays*, ed. William L. Howarth (Englewood Cliffs, N.J.: Prentice-Hall, 1971); *Twentieth Century Interpretations of "The Fall of the House of Usher": A Collection of Critical Essays*, ed. Thomas Woodson (Englewood Cliffs, N.J.: Prentice-Hall, 1969); *Poe: A Collection of Critical Essays*, ed. Robert Regan (Englewood Cliffs, N.J.: Prentice-Hall, 1967).

4. "The Imp of the Perverse," *Edgar Allan Poe: Poetry and Tales*, ed. Patrick F. Quinn (New York: Library of America, 1984), p. 829. All subsequent references to fiction are from this volume.

5. In "The Power of Words," Poe has his two speakers discuss the "*physical power of words*" (Poe's emphasis), p. 825.

6. Charles Feidelson, Jr., recognizes "The wonder and the horror of the images that assail the narrator and preoccupy Roderick" in "Poe as Symbolist," *Twentieth Century Interpretations*, ed. Woodson, p. 77. Also see James W. Gargano, "The Question of Poe's Narrators" in *Poe*, ed. Regan, pp. 164–71. Also, of course, the Thompson-Quinn debate.

7. James M. Cox suggests that the stories embody a kind of self-consciousness when he describes them as "wrecking the forms [gothic and romantic] upon which they prey." "Edgar Poe: Style as Pose," *Twentieth Century Interpretations*, ed. Woodson, p. 114.

8. Maurice J. Bennett, "'The Madness of Art': Poe's 'Ligeia' as Metafiction," *Poe Studies*, 14 (1981), 1–6; Joseph M. Garrison, Jr., "The Irony of 'Ligeia,'" *Emerson Society Quarterly*, 60 (1970) Supplement, 13–17; Claudia C. Morrison, "Poe's 'Ligeia': An Analysis," *Studies in Short Fiction*, 4 (1967), 234–44; John Lauber, "'Ligeia' and Its Critics: A Plea for Literalism," *Studies in Short Fiction*, 4 (1966), 28–32; Roy P. Basler, *Sex, Symbolism, and Psychology in Literature* (New York: Octagon, 1967), pp. 143–59; Paul John Eakin, "Poe's Sense of an Ending," *American Literature*, 45 (1973), 1–22; James Schroeter, "A Misreading of Poe's 'Ligeia,'" *PMLA*, 76 (1961), 397–406.

9. Poe revised "Ligeia" several times, the most extensively for New York *New World*, 15 February 1845, according to Thomas Ollive Mabbott, *Collected Works of Edgar Allan Poe, II: Tales and Sketches, 1831–1842* (Cambridge: Harvard Univ. Press, 1978), p. 309. In that particular revision, Poe adds the repetitive, second Ligeia in the story's first paragraph as well as a few phrases calling explicit attention to utterances of Ligeia and to self-conscious expressions of the narrator. Earlier revisions eliminated several instances of the proper name, replacing it with the pronoun. The overall effect of Poe's revising would seem to be a heightening both of deliberate use of the proper name and of the narrator's self-consciousness. Mabbott concluded: "The story was revised with greatest care. It must be regarded as a thoroughly conscious and complete work of art" (p. 306).

10. Charles Feidelson, Jr., identifies the subject of "Usher" to be aesthetic sensibility in "Poe as Symbolist."

11. Georges Poulet sees the House of Usher as existing "only in the dense vapor issued from the ground. It has, so to speak, created its own space"; "When sinking into its own pool, the House of Usher disappears into itself." "The Metamorphoses of the Circle," *Twentieth Century Interpretations*, ed. Woodson. See also Thompson, *Poe's Fiction*, p. 90.

12. "The House of Poe," in *Poe*, ed. Regan, p. 110, also p. 108.

13. "The Poetic Principle," p. 77.

14. "Marginalia," March 1846, *Edgar Allan Poe: Essays and Reviews*, ed. G. R. Thompson (New York: Library of America, 1984), p. 1383.

15. "The Power of Words," p. 825.

16. "Marginalia," p. 1384.

Chronology

1809 Edgar Allan Poe born in Boston 19 January, the second of three children, to David Poe, an actor, and Elizabeth Poe, an actress.

1811 After his mother's death, is taken in by Mr. and Mrs. John Allan of Richmond, Virginia.

1815 Goes to England with the Allans where he attends school.

1820 Returns to Richmond with the Allans.

1826 Enters the University of Richmond; becomes engaged to Sarah Elmira Royster.

1827 Engagement is broken; enlists in the army in Boston; publishes *Tamerlane and Other Poems.*

1829 Leaves the army; Mrs. John Allan dies; publishes *Al Aaraaf* and *Tamerlane and Minor Poems.*

1830 Enters West Point.

1831 Gets himself discharged from West Point; moves to New York and then to Baltimore, where he lives with the Clemms; publishes *Poems.*

1832 Publishes "Metzengerstein."

1833 Wins a prize for "MS Found in a Bottle."

1834 John Allan dies, leaving Poe nothing in his will.

1835 Becomes editor of *Southern Literary Messenger;* publishes "Berenice," "Morella," "Hans Pfaal," and "King Pest."

1836 Marries his cousin, Virginia Clemm.

1837 Leaves *Southern Literary Messenger* to go to New York.

1838 Moves to Philadelphia; publishes "Ligeia" and *The Narrative of Arthur Gordon Pym.*

1839 Joins the staff of *Burton's Gentleman's Magazine;* publishes "William Wilson" and "The Fall of the House of Usher."

1840   Leaves *Burton's* to try to establish his own magazine; publishes "The Man of the Crowd" and *Tales of the Grotesque and Arabesque*.

1841   Joins *Graham's Magazine;* publishes "The Murders in the Rue Morgue" and "A Descent into the Maelstrom."

1842   Leaves *Graham's Magazine;* publishes review of Hawthorne's *Twice-Told Tales*, "The Masque of the Red Death," "The Mystery of Marie Roget," and "The Oval Portrait."

1843   Wins a contest with "The Gold-Bug"; publishes "The Black Cat" and "The Tell-Tale Heart."

1844   Moves to New York; joins the *New York Mirror;* publishes "The Balloon-Hoax," "The Premature Burial," "A Tale of the Ragged Mountains," and "The Purloined Letter."

1845   Publishes "The Raven," which earns him great popular success; becomes editor of the *Broadway Journal;* publishes "The Imp of the Perverse," *Tales*, and *The Raven and Other Poems*.

1846   Moves to a cottage in Fordham; publishes "The Cask of Amontillado" and "The Philosophy of Composition."

1847   Virginia Poe dies; publishes "The Domain of Arnheim."

1848   Publishes "The Rationale of Verse" and *Eureka;* delivers "The Poetic Principle" lecture.

1849   Publishes "Hop-Frog" and "Von Kempelen and His Discovery"; dies 7 October in Baltimore.

Selected Bibliography

Primary Works

Editions

The Collected Works of Edgar Allan Poe. Edited by Thomas O. Mabbott. 3 vols. Cambridge: Harvard University Press, Belknap Press, 1978.

The Complete Tales of Edgar Allan Poe. New York: Modern Library, 1938.

The Complete Works of Edgar Allan Poe. Edited by James A. Harrison. 17 vols. New York: Thomas Y. Crowell & Co., 1902.

The Letters of Edgar Allan Poe. Edited by John Ward Ostrom. 2 vols. Cambridge: Harvard University Press, 1948.

Literary Criticism of Edgar Allan Poe. Edited by Robert L. Hough. Lincoln: University of Nebraska Press, 1965.

The Short Fiction of Edgar Allan Poe. Edited by Stuart Levine and Susan Levine. Indianapolis: Bobbs-Merrill Co., 1976.

The Unabridged Edgar Allan Poe. Philadelphia: Running Press, 1983.

Secondary Works

Bibliographies

Dameron, J. Lasley, and Irby B. Cauthen, Jr. *Edgar Allan Poe: A Bibliography of Criticism: 1827–1967.* Charlottesville: University Press of Virginia, 1974.

Hyneman, Esther. *Edgar Allan Poe: An Annotated Bibliography of Books and Articles in English: 1827–1973.* Boston: G. K. Hall & Co., 1974.

Biographies

Allen, Hervey. *Israfel: The Life and Times of Edgar Allan Poe.* New York: George H. Doran Co., 1926.

Bittner, W. R. *Poe: A Biography.* Boston: Little, Brown & Co., 1962.

Braddy, Haldeen. *Glorious Incense: The Fulfillment of Edgar Allan Poe.* Washington, N.Y.: Kennikat Press, 1968.

Krutch, Joseph. *Edgar Allan Poe: A Study in Genius.* New York: Russell and Russell, 1965.
Lindsay, Philip. *The Haunted Man: A Portrait of Edgar Allan Poe.* New York: Philosophical Library, 1954.
Mankowitz, Wolf. *The Extraordinary Mr. Poe: A Biography.* London: Wiedenfeld and Nicolson, 1978.
Moskowitz, Samuel, comp. *The Man Who Called Himself Poe.* New York: Doubleday, 1969.
Porges, Irwin. *Edgar Allan Poe.* Philadelphia: Chilton Books, 1963.
Quinn, A. H. *Edgar Allan Poe: A Critical Biography.* Carbondale: University of Southern Illinois Press, 1957.
Symons, Julian. *The Tell-Tale Heart: The Life and Works of Edgar Allan Poe.* London: Faber & Faber, 1978.
Thomas, Dwight, and David J. Jackson. *The Poe Log: A Documentary Life of Edgar Allan Poe, 1809–1849.* Boston: G. K. Hall & Co., 1987.
Woodberry, George E. *The Life of Edgar Allan Poe.* New York: Houghton, Mifflin Co., 1909.

Criticism: Books

Alexander, Jean, ed. *Affidavits of Genius: Edgar Allan Poe and the French Critics, 1947–1924.* Port Washington, N.Y.: Kennikat Press, 1971.
Allen, Michael. *Poe and the British Magazine Tradition.* New York: Oxford University Press, 1969.
Alterton, Margaret. *Origins of Poe's Critical Theory.* (1925). New York: Russell & Russell, 1965.
Anderson, Carl L. *Poe in Northlight: The Scandinavian Response to His Life and Work.* Durham, N.C.: Duke University Press, 1973.
Asselineau, Roger. *Edgar Allan Poe.* Minneapolis: University of Minnesota Press, 1970.
Baudelaire, Charles P. *Baudelaire on Poe.* Translated and edited by Lois Hyslop and Francis E. Hyslop, Jr. State College, Penn.: Bald Eagle Press, 1952.
Bloom, Clive. *Reading Poe/Reading Freud: The Romantic Imagination in Crisis.* New York: St. Martin's Press, 1988.
Bloom, Harold, ed. *Edgar Allan Poe: Modern Critical Views.* New York: Chelsea House, 1985.
Bonaparte, Marie. *The Life and Works of Edgar Allan Poe: A Psychoanalytic Interpretation.* Translated by John Rodker. London: Hogarth Press, 1949.
Broussard, Louis. *The Measure of Poe.* Norman: University of Oklahoma Press, 1969.
Buranelli, Vincent. *Edgar Allan Poe.* 2d ed. Boston: Twayne, 1977.
Campbell, Killis. *The Mind of Poe and Other Studies.* Cambridge: Harvard University Press, 1933.

Carlson, Eric W., ed. *Critical Essays on Edgar Allan Poe.* Boston: G. K. Hall & Co., 1987.

Chiari, Joseph. *Symbolism from Poe to Mallarme: The Growth of a Myth.* London: Rockliff, 1956.

Davidson, E. H. *Poe: A Critical Study.* Cambridge: Harvard University Press, Belknap Press, 1964.

Day, Leroy T. *Narrative Transgression and the Foregrounding of Language in Selected Prose Works of Poe, Valéry, and Hofmannsthal.* New York: Garland Publishing, 1988.

Dyan, Joan. *Fables of Mind: An Inquiry into Poe's Fiction.* New York: Oxford University Press, 1987.

Eddings, Dennis W., ed. *The Naiad Voice: Essays on Poe's Satiric Hoaxing.* Port Washington, N.Y.: Associated Faculty Press, 1983.

Fletcher, Richard M. *The Stylistic Development of Edgar Allan Poe.* The Hague, Netherlands: 1973.

Halliburton, David. *Edgar Allan Poe: A Phenomenological View.* Princeton: Princeton University Press, 1973.

Hammond, John R. *An Edgar Allan Poe Companion.* London: Macmillan, 1981.

Hoffman, Daniel. *Poe Poe Poe Poe Poe Poe Poe.* Garden City, N.Y.: Doubleday, 1972.

Howarth, William L., comp. *Twentieth Century Interpretations of Poe's Tales.* Englewood Cliffs, N.J.: Prentice-Hall, 1971.

Ingram, John H. *Edgar Allan Poe: His Life, Letters, and Opinions.* New York: AMS Press, 1965.

Jacobs, Robert D. *Poe: Journalist and Critic.* Baton Rouge: Louisiana State University Press, 1969.

Kennedy, J. Gerald. *Poe, Death, and the Life of Writing.* New Haven: Yale University Press, 1987.

Kesterson, David B., ed. *Critics on Poe.* Coral Gables, Fla.: University of Miami Press, 1973.

Knapp, Bettina L. *Edgar Allan Poe.* New York: Frederick Ungar Publishing Co., 1984.

Lee, A. Robert, ed. *Edgar Allan Poe: The Design of Order.* Totowa, N.J.: Barnes & Noble, 1987.

Levin, Harry. *The Power of Blackness.* New York: Alfred A. Knopf, 1964.

Levine, Stuart. *Edgar Poe: Seer and Craftsman.* Deland, Fla.: Everett/Edwards, 1972.

Moss, Sidney. *Poe's Literary Battles.* Durham, N.C.: Duke University Press, 1963.

———. *Poe's Major Crisis.* Durham, N.C.: Duke University Press, 1970.

Muller, John P., and William J. Richardson, eds. *The Purloined Poe: Lacan, Derrida, and Psychoanalytic Reading.* Baltimore: Johns Hopkins University Press, 1988.

Parks, Edd Winfield. *Edgar Allan Poe as Literary Critic.* Athens: University of Georgia Press, 1964.

Phillips, Elizabeth. *Edgar Allan Poe: An American Imagination.* Port Washington, N.Y.: Kennikat Press, 1979.

Pollin, Burton. *Discoveries in Poe.* Notre Dame, Ind.: University of Notre Dame, 1970.

Ransome, Arthur. *Edgar Allan Poe: A Critical Study.* New York: M. Kennerley, 1910.

Regan, Robert, ed. *Poe: A Collection of Critical Essays.* Englewood Cliffs, N.J.: Prentice-Hall, 1967.

Rein, David M. *Edgar A. Poe: The Inner Pattern.* New York: Philosophical Library, 1960.

Thompson, G. R. *Poe's Fiction: Romantic Irony in the Gothic Tales.* Madison: University of Wisconsin Press, 1973.

University of Mississippi Studies in English 3 (1982). Special Issue on Poe.

Wagenknecht, Edward C. *Edgar Allan Poe: The Man behind the Legend.* New York: Oxford University Press, 1966.

Walker, I. M., ed. *Edgar Allan Poe: The Critical Heritage.* New York: Routledge & Kegan Paul, 1986.

Walsh, John E. *Poe the Detective.* New Brunswick, N.J.: Rutgers University Press, 1968.

Whitman, Sarah. *Edgar Poe and His Critics.* New York: AMS Press, 1966.

Williams, Michael J. S. *A World of Words: Language and Displacement in the Fiction of Edgar Allan Poe.* Durham, N.C.: Duke University Press, 1988.

Criticism: Articles and Parts of Books

Abel, Darrel. "A Key to the House of Usher." *University of Toronto Quarterly* 18 (January 1949): 176–85.

Andriano, Joseph. "Archetypal Projection in 'Ligeia': A Post-Jungian Reading." *Poe Studies* (19 December 1986): 27–31.

Baldwin, Summerfield. "The Aesthetic Theory of Edgar Poe." *Sewanee Review* 27 (1918): 210–21.

Basler, Roy P. "The Interpretation of 'Ligeia.'" *College English* 5 (1944): 363–72.

Baym, Nina. "Function of Poe's Pictorialism." *South Atlantic Quarterly* 65 (1966): 46–54.

Bennett, Maurice J. "The Detective Fiction of Poe and Borges." *Comparative Literature* 35 (Summer 1983): 262–75.

Benton, Richard P. "Is Poe's 'The Assignation' a Hoax?" *Nineteenth-Century Fiction* 19 (1963): 193–97.

Berces, Francis. "Poe and the Imagination: An Aesthetic for Short Story Form." *Journal of the Short Story in English* 2 (January 1984): 105–13.

Bieganowski, Ronald. "The Self-Consuming Narrator in Poe's 'Ligeia' and 'Usher.'" *American Literature* 60 (May 1988): 175–87.

Black, Michael. "Why It Is So, and Not Otherwise." *New Literary History* 6 (1975): 477–89.

Blair, Walter. "Poe's Conception of Incident and Tone in the Tale." *Modern Philology* 41 (1944): 228–40.

Blanch, Robert J. "Poe's Imagery: An Undercurrent of Childhood Fears." *Furman Studies* 14 (May 1967): 19–25.

Bloch, Robert. "Poe and Lovecraft." In *H. P. Lovecraft: Four Decades of Criticism*, edited by S. T. Joshi, 158–60. Athens: Ohio University Press, 1980.

Bronzwaer, W. "Deixis as a Structuring Device in Narrative Discourse: An Analysis of Poe's 'The Murders in the Rue Morgue.'" *English Studies* 56 (August 1975): 345–59.

Brophy, Brigid. "Detective Fiction: A Modern Myth of Violence." *Hudson Review* 18 (1965): 11–30.

Byer, Robert H. "Mysteries of the City: A Reading of Poe's 'The Man of the Crowd.'" In *Ideology and Classic American Literature*, edited by Sacvan Bercovitch and Myra Jehlen, 221–46. Cambridge: Cambridge University Press, 1986.

Cecil, L. Moffitt. "Poe's 'Arabesque.'" *Comparative Literature* 18 (1960): 55–70.

Chambers, Ross. "Narratorial Authority and 'The Purloined Letter.'" In *Story and Situation: Narrative Seduction and the Power of Fiction*, 50–72. Minneapolis: University of Minnesota Press, 1984.

Coad, Oral Sumner. "The Gothic Element in American Literature before 1835." *Journal of English and Germanic Philology* 24 (1925): 72–93.

Cobb, Palmer. "Edgar Allan Poe and Friedrich Spielhagen: Their Theory of the Short Story." *Modern Language Notes* 25 (1910): 3–7.

Conger, Syndy M. "Another Secret of the Rue Morgue: Poe's Transformation of the *Geisterseher* Motif." *Studies in Short Fiction* 24 (Winter 1987): 9–14.

Cox, James R. "Edgar Poe: Style as Pose." *Virginia Quarterly Review* 44 (Winter 1968): 67–89.

Crossley, Robert. "Poe's Closet Monologues." *Genre* 10 (1977): 215–32.

Current-Garcia, Eugene. "Poe's Short Fiction." In *The American Short Story before 1850*, 59–83. Boston: Twayne, 1985.

Danner, Richard. "The Poe-Matthews Theory of the American Short Story." *Ball State University Forum* 8 (Winter 1967): 45–50.

Defalco, Joseph M. "The Source of Terror in Poe's 'Shadow—A Parable.'" *Studies in Short Fiction* 6 (Fall 1969): 643–48.

Donahue, Patricia. "Misreading Students' Texts." *Reader*, no. 17 (1987): 1–13.

Eakin, Paul J. "Poe's Sense of an Ending." *American Literature* 45 (1973): 1–22.

Egan, Kenneth V., Jr. "Descent to an Ascent: Poe's Use of Perspective in 'A

Descent into the Maelstrom.'" *Studies in Short Fiction* 19 (Spring 1982): 157–62.

Fetterley, Judith. "Reading about Reading: 'A Jury of Her Peers,' 'The Murders in the Rue Morgue,' and 'The Yellow Wallpaper.'" In *Gender and Reading: Essays on Readers, Texts, and Contexts*, edited by Elizabeth A. Flynn and Patrocinio P. Schweickart, 147–64. Baltimore: Johns Hopkins University Press, 1986.

Finholt, Richard D. "Poe's Cosmology." In *American Visionary Fiction*, 83–97. Port Washington, N.Y.: Kennikat Press, 1978.

———. "The Vision at the Brink of the Abyss: 'A Descent into the Maelstrom' in Light of Poe's Cosmology." *Georgia Review* 27 (Fall 1973): 356–66.

Fisher, Benjamin F. "Poe's 'Metzengerstein': Not a Hoax." *American Literature* 42 (1971): 487–94.

———. "Poe's 'Tarr and Fether': Hoaxing in the *Blackwood* Mode." *Topic* 31 (1977): 29–40.

Flory, Wendy Stallard. "Usher's Fear and the Flaw in Poe's Theories of the Metamorphosis of the Senses." *Poe Studies* 7 (June 1974): 17–19.

Foust, R. E. "Aestheticism of Simultaneity: E. A. Poe and Modern Literary Theory." *South Atlantic Review* 46 (1981): 17–25.

Frank, Frederick S. "The Aqua-Gothic Voyage of 'A Descent into the Maelstrom.'" *American Transcendental Quarterly* 29 (Winter 1976): 85–93.

Freundlieb, Dieter. "Understanding Poe's Tales: A Schema-Theoretic View." *Poetics* 11 (1982): 25–44.

Fukuchi, Curtis. "Repression and Guilt in Poe's 'Morella.'" *Studies in Short Fiction* 24 (Spring 1987): 149–54.

Gargano, James W. "Art and Irony in 'William Wilson.'" *Emerson Society Quarterly* 40 (1970): 18–22.

———. "'The Black Cat.': Perverseness Reconsidered." *Texas Studies in Literature and Language* 2 (Summer 1960): 172–78.

———. "Poe's 'Ligeia': Dream and Destruction." *College English* 23 (February 1962): 335–42.

Garrison, Joseph M., Jr. "The Function of Terror in the Work of Edgar Allan Poe." *American Quarterly* 18 (1960): 136–50.

Gerber, Gerald. "Poe's Odd Angel." *Nineteenth-Century Fiction* 23 (1968): 88–93.

Girgus, Sam B. "Poe and R. D. Laing: The Transcendent Self." *Studies in Short Fiction* 13 (1976): 299–309.

Goldhurst, William. "Self-Reflexive Fiction by Poe: Three Tales." *Modern Language Studies* 16 (1986): 4–14.

Gooder, R. D. "Edgar Allan Poe: The Meaning of Style." *Cambridge Quarterly* 16 (1987): 110–23.

Gregory, Horace. "The Gothic Imagination of Edgar Allan Poe." In *Spirit of Time and Place*, 52–61. New York: W. W. Norton & Co., 1973.

Griffith, Clark. "Poe's 'Ligeia' and the English Romantics." *University of Toronto Quarterly* 24 (1954): 8–25.

Gross, Seymour. "Poe's Revision of 'The Oval Portrait.'" *Modern Language Notes* 74 (January 1959): 16–20.

Grossvogel, David I. "'The Purloined Letter': The Mystery of the Text." In *Mystery and Its Fictions*, 93–107. Baltimore: Johns Hopkins University Press, 1979.

Gruener, Gustav. "Notes on the Influence of E. T. A. Hoffmann upon Edgar Allan Poe." *PMLA* 19 (1904): 1–25.

———. "Poe's Knowledge of German." *Modern Philology* 2 (1904): 125–40.

Herrmann, Claudine, and Nicholas Kostis. "'The Fall of the House of Usher' or the Art of Duplication." *Sub-stance* 26 (1980): 36–42.

Hess, Jeffrey. "Sources and Aesthetics of Poe's Landscape Fiction." *American Quarterly* 22 (1970): 177–89.

Hirsch, David H. "The Pit and the Apocalypse." *Sewanee Review* 76 (1968): 632–52.

Hoffman, Gerhard. "Edgar Allan Poe and German Literature." In *American-German Interrelations in the Nineteenth Century*, edited by Christy Wecker, 52–104. Munich: Wilhelm Fink, 1983.

Hoffman, Michael J. "The House of Usher and Negative Romanticism." *Studies in Romanticism* 4 (1965): 158–68.

Hoffman, Steven K. "Sailing into the Self: Jung, Poe, and 'MS Found in a Bottle.'" *Tennessee Studies in Literature* 26 (1981): 66–74.

Hofrichter, Laura. "From Poe to Kafka." *University of Toronto Quarterly* 29 (July 1960): 405–19.

Howard, Leon. "Artificial Sensitivity and Artful Rationality: Basic Elements in the Creative Imagination of Edgar Allan Poe." *Poe Studies* 20 (June 1987): 1–9.

Jannaccone, Pasquale. "The Aesthetics of Edgar Poe." Translated by Peter Miltilineos. *Poe Studies* 7 (June 1974): 1–13.

Jefferson, Ann. "*Mise en abyme* and the Prophetic in Narrative." *Style* 17 (Spring 1983): 196–208.

Jones, Daryl E. "Poe's Siren: Character and Meaning in 'Ligeia.'" *Studies in Short Fiction* 20 (Winter 1983): 33–37.

Kanjo, Eugene R. "'The Imp of the Perverse': Poe's Dark Comedy of Art and Death." *Poe Newsletter* 2 (October 1969): 41–44.

Keller, Mark. "Dupin in the 'Rue Morgue': Another Form of Madness." *Arizona Quarterly* 33 (Autumn 1977): 249–55.

Kelly, George. "Poe's Theory of Beauty." *American Literature* 27 (1956): 521–36.

Kempton, Daniel. "The Gold/Goole/Ghoul Bug." *ESQ* 33 (1987): 1–19.

Kennedy, J. Gerald. "The Limits of Reason: Poe's Deluded Detectives." *American Literature* 48 (May 1975): 184–96.

————. "Phantasms of Death in Poe's Fiction." In *The Haunted Dusk: American Supernatural Fiction, 1820–1920*, edited by Howard Kerr, John Crowley, and Charles Crow, 39–65. Athens: University of Georgia Press, 1983.

Ketterer, David. "Poe's Use of the Hoax and the Unity of 'Hans Pfaal.'" *Criticism* 13 (1971): 377–85.

Kock, Christian. "The Irony of Oxygen in Poe's 'Eiros and Charmion.'" *Studies in Short Fiction* 22 (Summer 1985): 317–21.

Laser, Marvin. "The Growth and Structure of Poe's Concept of Beauty." *Journal of English Literary History* 15 (1948): 69–84.

Lauber, John. "'Ligeia' and Its Critics: A Plea for Literalism." *Studies in Short Fiction* 4 (Fall 1966): 28–32.

Lemay, J. L. Leo. "The Psychology of 'The Murders in the Rue Morgue.'" *American Literature* 54 (May 1983): 165–88.

Lévy, Maurice. "Poe and the Gothic Tradition." *ESQ* 18 (1970): 19–29.

Liebman, Sheldon W. "Poe's Tales and His Theory of the Poetic Experience." *Studies in Short Fiction* 7 (Fall 1970): 582–96.

Lind, S. E. "Poe and Mesmerism." *PMLA* 42 (1947): 1077–94.

Ljungquist, Kent. "Poe and the Sublime: His Two Short Sea Tales in the Context of an Aesthetic Tradition." *Criticism* 17 (Spring 1975): 131–51.

————. "Poe's 'The Island of the Fay': The Passing of Fairyland." *Studies in Short Fiction* 14 (Summer 1977): 265–71.

Lubell, Albert J. "Poe and Schlegel." *Journal of English and Germanic Philology* 52 (1953): 1–12.

Lundquist, James. "The Moral of Averted Descent: The Failure of Sanity in 'The Pit and the Pendulum.'" *Poe Newsletter* 2 (April 1969): 25–26.

Lyons, Nathan. "Kafka and Poe—and Hope." *Minnesota Review* 5 (May–July 1965): 158–68.

Mabbott, Thomas O. "On Poe's Tales of the Folio Club." *Sewanee Review* 36 (1928): 171–76.

McElroy, John H. "The Kindred Artist; or, The Case of the Black Cat." *Studies in American Humor* 3 (1976): 103–17.

McLuhan, Herbert Marshall. "Edgar Poe's Tradition." *Sewanee Review* 52 (1944): 24–33.

Mainville, Stephen. "Language and the Void: Gothic Landscapes in the Frontiers of Edgar Allan Poe." *Genre* (1981): 347–62.

Martin, Bruce K. "Poe's 'Hop-Frog' and the Retreat from Comedy." *Studies in Short Fiction* 10 (Summer 1973): 288–90.

Martindale, Colin. "A Quantitative Analysis of Diachronic Patterns in Some Narratives of Poe." *Semiotica* 22 (1978): 287–308.

————. "Transformation and Transfusion of Vitality in the Narratives of Poe." *Semiotica* 8 (1973): 46–59.

Matthiessen, F. O. "Poe." *Sewanee Review* 54 (1946): 175–205.

Mengeling, Marvin, and Frances Mengeling. "From Fancy to Failure: A Study of the Narrators in the Tales of Edgar Allan Poe." *University Review* 33 (1967): 293–98; 34 (1967): 31–36.

Miller, Karl. "The Adventures of Peregrine Poe." In *Doubles: Studies in Literary History*, 154–66. New York: Oxford University Press, 1985.

Miller, Linda. "The Writer in the Crowd: Poe's Urban Vision." *American Transcendental Quarterly* 44 (1979): 325–39.

Moldenhauer, Joseph. "Murder as Fine Art: Basic Connections between Poe's Aesthetics, Psychology, and Moral Vision." *PMLA* 83 (May 1968): 284–97.

Mooney, Stephen L. "Comic Intent in Poe's Tales: Five Criteria." *Modern Language Notes* 76 (May 1961): 432–34.

———. "The Comic in Poe's Fiction." *American Literature* 33 (January 1962): 433–41.

Oliver, Lawrence J., Jr. "Kinesthetic Imagery and Helplessness in Three Poe Tales." *Studies in Short Fiction* 20 (Spring–Summer 1983): 73–77.

Pahl, Dennis. "Poe/Script: The Death of the Author in *The Narrative of Arthur Gordon Pym*." *New Orleans Review* 14 (Fall 1987): 51–60.

Pochmann, Henry August. "Germanic Materials and Motifs in the Short Story: E. A. Poe." In *German Culture in America*, 388–409. Madison: University of Wisconsin Press, 1957.

Pollin, Burton R. "Poe's 'Murders in the Rue Morgue': The Ingenious Web Unravelled." *Studies in the American Renaissance*, edited by Joel Meyerson, 235–59. Boston: G. K. Hall & Co., 1977.

Reeder, Roberta. "'The Black Cat' as a Study in Repression." *Poe Studies* 7 (June 1974): 20–21.

Ricardou, Jean. "The Story within the Story." *James Joyce Quarterly* 18 (Spring 1981): 323–38.

Richards, Sylvie L. F. "The Eye and the Portrait: The Fantastic in Poe, Hawthorne, and Gogol." *Studies in Short Fiction* 20 (Fall 1983): 307–15.

Ringe, Donald A. "Edgar Allan Poe." In *American Gothic*, 128–205. Lexington: University of Kentucky, 1982.

Robinson, Douglas. "Poe's Mini-Apocalypse: 'The Conversation of Eiros and Charmion.'" *Studies in Short Fiction* 19 (Fall 1982): 329–37.

———. "Trapped in the Text: 'The Pit and the Pendulum.'" *Journal of the Short Story in English* 7 (Autumn 1986): 63–75.

Rosenheim, Shawn. "'The King of Secret Readers': Edgar Poe, Cryptography, and the Origins of the Detective Story." *ELH* 6 (Summer 1989): 375–400.

Rosenzweig, Paul. "'Dust within the Rock': The Phantasm of Meaning in *The Narrative of Arthur Gordon Pym*." *Studies in the Novel* 14 (1982): 137–51.

Rubin, Louis D. "Edgar Allan Poe: A Study in Heroism." In *The Curious Death of the Novel*, 47–66. Baton Rouge: Louisiana State University Press, 1967.

Samuels, Charles Thomas. "Usher's Fall; Poe's Rise." *Georgia Review* (1964): 208–16.

Sanford, Charles. "Edgar Allan Poe: A Blight upon the Landscape." *American Quarterly* 20 (1967): 54–66.

Saxena, M. C. "Edgar Allan Poe and His Theory of the Short Story." *Triveni* 45 (1967): 61–69.

Scharnhorst, Gary. "Another Night-Sea Journey: Poe's 'MS. Found in a Bottle.'" *Studies in Short Fiction* 22 (Spring 1985): 203–8.

Schroeter, James. "A Misreading of Poe's 'Ligeia.'" *PMLA* 76 (September 1961): 397–406.

Schwaber, Paul. "On Reading Poe." *Literature and Psychology* 21 (1971): 81–99.

Schulman, Robert. "Poe and the Powers of the Mind." *ELH* 37 (June 1970): 245–62.

Skaggs, Merrill Maguire. "Poe's Longing for a Bicameral Mind." *Southern Quarterly* 19 (Winter 1981): 54–64.

Smith, Grace. "Poe's 'Metzengerstein.'" *Modern Language Notes* 48 (1933): 357–59.

Smith, H. E. "Poe's Extension of His Theory of the Tale." *Modern Philology* 16 (August 1918): 27–35.

Spanier, Sandra Whipple. "'Nests of Boxes': Form, Sense, and Style in Poe's 'The Imp of the Perverse.'" *Studies in Short Fiction* 17 (Summer 1980): 307–16.

Stauffer, Donald. "The Two Styles of Poe's 'MS. Found in a Bottle.'" *Style* 1 (1967): 107–20.

Stepp, Walter. "The Ironic Double in Poe's 'The Cask of Amontillado.'" *Studies in Short Fiction* 13 (Fall 1976): 447–53.

Stoehr, Taylor. "'Unspeakable Horror' in Poe." *South Atlantic Quarterly* 78 (1979): 317–32.

Stoval, Floyd. "The Conscious Art of Edgar Allan Poe." *College English* 24 (March 1963): 417–21.

———. "Poe's Debt to Coleridge." *University of Texas Studies in English* 10 (July 1930): 70–127.

Strandberg, Victor. "Poe's Hollow Men." *University Review* 35 (Spring 1969): 203–12.

Sullivan, Ruth. "William Wilson's Double." *Studies in Romanticism* 15 (Spring 1976): 253–63.

Sweeney, Gerard M. "Beauty and Truth: Poe's 'A Descent into the Maelstrom.'" *Poe Studies* 6 (June 1973): 22–25.

Tate, Allen. "The Angelic Imagination: Poe and the Power of Words." *Kenyon Review* 14 (1952): 455–75.

Thompson, G. R. "Dramatic Irony in 'The Oval Portrait': A Reconsideration of Poe's Revision." *English Language Notes* 6 (December 1968): 107–14.

————. "Poe's 'Flawed' Gothic: Absurdist Techniques in 'Metzengerstein' and the *Courier* Satires." *Emerson Society Quarterly* 60 (1970): 38–56.

Twitchell, James. "Poe's 'The Oval Portrait' and the Vampire Motif." *Studies in Short Fiction* 14 (Fall 1977): 387–93.

Unrue, Darlene. "Poe and Subjective Reality." *Ariel* 7 (July 1976): 68–76.

Varnado, S. L. "Poe and the Initiation into the Sacred." In *Haunted Presence: The Numinous in Gothic Fiction*, 60–77. Tuscaloosa: University of Alabama Press, 1987.

Voloshin, Beverly. "Explanation in 'The Fall of the House of Usher.'" *Studies in Short Fiction* 23 (Fall 1986): 419–28.

Von der Lippe, George B. "The Figure of E. T. A. Hoffmann as *Doppelganger* to Poe's Roderick Usher." *Modern Language Notes* 92 (April 1977): 525–34.

Whipple, William. "Poe's Political Satire." *University of Texas Studies in English* 35 (1956): 81–95.

Williams, Michael. "'The Language of the Cipher': Interpretation in 'The Gold Bug.'" *American Literature* 53 (January 1982): 646–60.

Winters, Yvor. "Edgar Allan Poe: A Crisis in the History of American Obscurantism." *American Literature* 8 (1937): 319–40.

Yonce, Margaret J. "The Spiritual Descent into the Maelstrom: A Debt to 'The Rime of the Ancient Mariner.'" *Poe Newsletter* 2 (April 1969): 26–29.

Zanger, Jules. "Poe's 'Berenice': Philosophical Fantasy and Its Pitfalls." In *The Scope of the Fantastic—Theory, Technique, Major Authors*, edited by Robert A. Collins and Howard D. Pearce, 135–42. Westport, Conn.: Greenwood Press, 1985.

————. "Poe and the Theme of Forbidden Knowledge." *American Literature* 49 (January 1978): 533–43.

Index

Index

Index

The Author

Charles E. May received his Ph.D. in literature from Ohio University in 1966 and is currently a professor of English at California State University, Long Beach. He is the editor of *Short Story Theories* (1977) and *Twentieth-Century European Short Story: An Annotated Bibliography* (1989). He is the author of over a hundred essays, most of which are on short fiction, in various books and journals, including *Modern Fiction Studies, Studies in Short Fiction, Genre, College English,* and *Criticism.* He is a consulting editor for the journal *Short Story.*

The Editor

Gordon Weaver earned his Ph.D. in English and creative writing at the University of Denver, and is currently professor of English at Oklahoma State University. He is the author of several novels, including *Count a Lonely Cadence, Give Him a Stone, Circling Byzantium*, and most recently *The Eight Corners of the World*. His short stories are collected in *The Entombed Man of Thule, Such Waltzing Was Not Easy, Getting Serious, Mortality Play*, and *A World Quite Round*. Recognition of his fiction includes the St. Lawrence Award for Fiction (1973), two National Endowment for the Arts fellowships (1974 and 1989), and the O. Henry First Prize (1979). He edited *The American Short Story, 1945–1980: A Critical History* and is currently editor of the *Cimarron Review*. Married and the father of three daughters, he lives in Stillwater, Oklahoma.